FROM SLAVERY

TO CITIZENSHIP

FROM SLAVERY
TO CITIZENSHIP

Richard Ennals

John Wiley & Sons, Ltd

Other Wiley Editorial Offices

John Wiley & Sons Inc., 111 River Street, Hoboken, NJ 07030, USA

Jossey-Bass, 989 Market Street, San Francisco, CA 94103-1741, USA

Wiley-VCH Verlag GmbH, Boschstr. 12, D-69469 Weinheim, Germany

John Wiley & Sons Australia Ltd, 42 McDougall Street, Milton, Queensland 4064,
Australia

John Wiley & Sons (Asia) Pte Ltd, 2 Clementi Loop #02-01, Jin Xing Distripark,
Singapore 129809

John Wiley & Sons Canada Ltd, 6045 Freemont Blvd, Mississauga, ONT, L5R 4J3,
Canada

Wiley also publishes its books in a variety of electronic formats. Some content that appears
in print may not be available in electronic books.

Library of Congress Cataloging-in-Publication Data

Ennals, J. R. (John Richard), 1951–
        From slavery to citizenship / Richard Ennals.
            p. cm.
        Includes bibliographical references and index.
        ISBN-13: 978-0-470-02832-2 (cloth : alk. paper)
    1. Slavery—History.   2. Slaves—Emancipation—History.   3. Human rights—
History.   4. Civil rights—History.   5. Political participation—History.
6. Citizenship—History.   I. Title.
        HT861.E56 2007
        306.3′6209—dc22   2006036077

British Library Cataloguing in Publication Data
A catalogue record for this book is available from the British Library

ISBN 13 978-0-470-02832-2 (HB)

Typeset in 11.5/15pt Bembo by SNP Best-set Typesetter Ltd., Hong Kong
Printed and bound in Great Britain by TJ International Ltd, Padstow, Cornwall, UK

This book is printed on acid-free paper responsibly manufactured from sustainable forestry
in which at least two trees are planted for each one used for paper production.

CONTENTS

PREFACE

The agenda and timetable for this book have been set by external events, both in 1807 and 2007. The United Nations Educational, Scientific and Cultural Organisation (UNESCO) have addressed the challenge of the global impact of the Transatlantic Slave Trade. The UK and USA were absent from UNESCO from 1985, and have been slow to participate in international dialogues where they might be expected to apologise for past events. Reflection is needed.

Whereas education was formerly based on curricula set by national governments, the situation is now more complex. Classrooms are increasingly multicultural, and the Internet provides access to alternative information sources from across the world. It may no longer be appropriate to deliver courses which give a narrowly national emphasis, in coverage of periods such as the Transatlantic Slave Trade and British Empire. This does not mean that the topics should be omitted. New thinking is required. Unsustainable accounts need to be repaired, in a form of educational reparation.

This book appears in a business and management series. Managers are in part the products of their education, and their approaches to business are coloured by their views of the past and present. Slavery is a short-term business strategy, which involves an extreme case of the denial of autonomy and control to the individual worker, who is unable to participate in decision making. Slavery is not inherently based on racial difference, and has been part of the history of many cultures. We consider diverse perspectives, with particular focus on issues of control and participation.

1807 was a momentous year. Not only did the British Parliament vote to abolish the Transatlantic Slave Trade, but John Wiley and Sons publishers were founded. Over the subsequent two hundred years Wiley have published books and journals in the diverse disciplines which come together in "From Slavery to Citizenship". Here Wiley is partnering the Council for Education in World Citizenship. The joint Citizenship project is based on Dialogue, with the objective of launching a process of healing.

After two centuries during which silences have been maintained, there are gaps in available knowledge. Some of the gaps will be filled during the period between this book being completed and the date of publication. The book cannot claim to be complete. Rather, it is part of the Dialogue process, during which we can share our questions and answers. The core text is complemented by "impulse texts" from external contributors. The debate needs to continue if we are not to be the slaves of our past, but citizens with an active role in determining our own futures. Readers will be equipped to continue asking questions about work, and to consider modern forms of slavery, including hazardous child labour. This has concerned the International Labour Organisation and the World Health Organisation, as well as the International Commission on Occupational Health. The ongoing campaign for emancipation from slavery has benefited from the commitment of Non Governmental Organisations such as Anti Slavery International.

The book project was originally proposed by Stephen Smith, Senior Vice President for International Development at Wiley, with the support of Francesca Warren, Commissioning Editor for

Business and Management. The Wiley team have been active partners, across the disciplines and across the Atlantic. The project could not have been possible without the team at the Council for Education in World Citizenship (CEWC), working in association with Kingston University School of Education and Rendezvous of Victory.

CEWC co-ordinates the UNESCO Associated Schools Project Network in the UK, building a network of 100 schools in the UK to work with 8000 schools in 175 countries around the world. CEWC's mission since 1939 has been education for international understanding. "From Slavery to Citizenship" is an example of taking a global perspective to a controversial problem which has often been considered in national terms. The Transatlantic Slave Trade launched a process of globalisation and African Diaspora which continues today.

The book is intended for a general audience, including in education and business. It is designed to provide the basis for Forum Theatre, and an Appendix introduces Model United Nations activities, addressing the themes of slavery and child labour.

Richard Ennals

Professor, Kingston University
Chairman, Council for Education in World Citizenship

Hampton
July 2006

INTRODUCTION

Toussaint L'Ouverture summarised the events in Santo Domingo, which he led from slavery to independence. The rebellion of 1791 culminated in the Republic of Haiti in 1804.

> The colony of Santo Domingo, of which I was commander, enjoyed the greatest tranquillity; agriculture and commerce flourished there. The island had attained a degree of splendor which it had never before seen . . .
>
> Having driven from the colony the enemies of the Republic, calmed the factions and united all parties; perceiving, after I had taken possession of Santo Domingo, that the Government made no laws for the colony, and feeling the necessity of police regulations for the security and tranquility of the people, I called an assembly of wise and learned men, composed of deputies from all the communities, to conduct this business . . .
>
> At the time of the evacuation of the English, there was not a penny in the public treasury; money had to be borrowed to pay the troops and the officers of the Republic . . .

The island was invaded by the enemies of the Republic; I had then but a thousand men, armed with pikes. I sent them back to labor in the field, and organized several regiments . . . The Spanish portion had joined the English to make war upon the French . . . I drove out the English . . . I also conquered the Spanish . . . I received upon different occasions seventeen wounds.

. . . As a reward for all these services, I have been arbitrarily arrested at Santo Domingo, bound, and put on board ship like a criminal . . . My liberty is taken away from me.

Tyson, G., Jr (ed.) (1973) *Toussaint L'Ouverture*. New York: Prentice Hall, pp. 27–45.

PREPARATION

English language histories of the Abolition of the Transatlantic Slave Trade rarely begin with an account of the triumph of slave rebellions in the West Indies. The preference has been to see abolition, and the later emancipation of the slaves, as a consequence of enlightened British policy. Britain, we are told, led the world in the abolition of the slave trade and of slavery. Having freed the slaves, so the story goes, Britain helped African nations achieve independence and democracy. It is rarely noted that the French abolished slavery in 1794.

After such an extended period of denial and silence on the subject of the Transatlantic Slave Trade and slavery, there is a need to prepare the way for a new debate, informed by the results of international research and scholarship. In a Shakespearian manner, we can introduce the story through the leading actors, whose names may be familiar, but whose roles and inter-relationships may be surprising.

History has been a means of socialising new generations, and laying the foundations for business activities. Where systemic silences have distorted the debate, the results may include traumatic adjustments of perceptions. We cannot move directly to a new single linear narrative. The next step is dialogue across communities. Our engagement in current dialogue may offer insights into the past, and vice versa.

Bicentenaries

The following could be said about 1807 or 2007:

- A new century started, with fears of institutional collapse. The old century had ended in uncertainty and change, as the old order collapsed. The UK claimed stability and continuity, while régimes fell around the world.
- The great powers sought to preserve their dominant positions, prepared to fight wars all around the world if necessary. Arguments on human rights could be deployed for political purposes. The UK claimed the moral high ground, and gave particular emphasis to Africa.
- What priority should be given to emancipation, to making poverty history? Why should those in power jeopardise their own positions? What changes are required in order to build a sustainable economy and society?

The choices have been remarkably similar over the centuries: "Moral Sentiment" or "The Wealth of Nations". Adam Smith located the latter, written in 1776, in the context of the former, written in 1759. Those who describe themselves as followers of Adam Smith emphasise market forces and a laissez faire approach for government. The framework of moral relationships has dropped out of consideration. For the dominant power, empire has its attractions, including the opportunity to set the rules which others must follow. The present government of the USA are taking a similar approach to Empire, with their Project for the New American Century.

In 2007 we celebrate the bicentenary of the Abolition of the Transatlantic Slave Trade by the British Parliament. There will be many detailed accounts, praising the achievement of William Wilberforce MP and the British Abolitionists, who changed the law in one country, and succeeded in creating what became the convenient myth that the British led the world in the abolition of slavery. The truth is much more complicated: for example, the abolition of the Transatlantic Slave Trade did not in itself mean the emancipation of slaves. We consider what is to be celebrated, and we point to areas where there is continued silence, which is best broken through informed dialogue.

Participative Democracy

To participate in the debate, whether in 1807 or 2007, requires education, confidence and access to the arena where issues are discussed. Not all can be present in person. Those who attend must, in some sense, represent the others. This will be more or less democratic. Perhaps whole groups will be systematically excluded, with dangerous consequences. We hope to engage the readers in the debate.

Discussions have to move from debate to decisions. This requires rules, procedures and institutions. Once established, institutions tend to seek to maintain their existence. Citizens need to understand how the system works.

The official myth is that decisions are made on a rational basis, with access to full information. The reality will be that decisions are made for particular reasons, and then rationalised in subsequent reports and public communications. In a diverse context, with dominant and lesser groups, there will be competing rationalities and sets of reasons. The art of ruling, especially where Empires are concerned, is to bridge the gaps through the imposition of power which is accepted by consent. Underlying explanations and reasons will be complex.

PERSONAL CONTEXT

It is important to recognise that there will be no one agreed history of a set of events and relationships which continue to be sensitive. Each writer must reflect on their own background, and recognise that we are all engaged in the issues of Slavery and Citizenship. There are no spectators. To the extent that we seek understanding and reconciliation, we are engaged in action research. If our predisposition is to favour the case of the poor and dispossessed, we could term this Emancipatory Action Research.

Africa since Childhood

A different perspective is now possible, in a more globalised world. As a child, my first words were probably in an African language, such as Ashanti or Kikuyu, as my family always had African students as lodgers. On their return home to Africa after their studies, the students took on leading roles in their newly independent countries, and remained in contact.

America and Slavery

As a student at school in the UK, I studied slavery in the context of American history. There seemed to be a confusing clash between the rhetoric of liberty, and the practical reality of slavery. The role of the British in the Transatlantic Slave Trade was not highlighted. The curriculum appeared to be constructed so as to avoid awkward topics.

Taking my studies of slavery further in the USA, I found that the focus of the syllabus was the American Supreme Court, and its handling of a series of constitutional cases. To my surprise, the constitutional amendments on the abolition of slavery, emancipation and civil rights were interpreted by the Supreme Court in terms of due process applied to property rights.

As a student of history at Cambridge University, I pursued American history further, with less emphasis on law. From outside the USA it was possible to take a more detached view. I also studied modern world history.

East Africa

As a student at London University Institute of Education, I specialised in education in developing countries, writing a dissertation about education in Kenya. The history brought a number of further surprises, as I encountered several cultures, much older than the European culture from which I had come.

Archaeologists and anthropologists have investigated the origins of man in Kenya and Tanzania, with a series of finds in Olduvai. The Rift Valley has hosted civilisation for millennia. We in Europe had a much shorter history.

The perspective from East Africa, before the days of Empire, was complex. There had been Arab traders for thousands of years: their voyages by sea complemented overland trade. East Africa was a meeting point, and linked to trade routes to the East, while Europe lived in relative ignorance.

From a European perspective, East and Southern Africa had been part of the Dark Continent, explored by the British and others who started from the coast. Discoveries were seen in terms of what they offered to the visitors, who imported their own language, institutions and values. The interior was explored from the coast, and with confused ideas of geography.

Kenya had a particular appeal to the British, as the climate was congenial, and colonial settlers took over the most fertile farms. It could feel like home. The British imposed their rule, aided by Indian administrators and small businessmen. As the credibility of Empire declined after the Second World War, the strength of nationalist feeling, particularly among the dominant Kikuyu tribe, expressed itself in violent form, through Mau Mau, which was suppressed. The story had largely been told from a British colonial perspective, in terms of keeping order. The African side of the story was less often told.

A turning point for me came with the African Writers Series, published in English, providing rich pictures of African society and culture. Perhaps the most illuminating were accounts, such as Chinua Achebe's "Things Fall Apart", of the encounter between Africans and Europeans, and the complex changes at the end of Empire. There is a wealth of excellent writing, in English, from both East and West Africa.

Nigeria

Having trained as a teacher, I taught modern world history in the UK and Nigeria. In order to teach African and contemporary history in Nigeria, it was apparent that I had a great deal to learn. African history turned out to be rich and varied, with complex states and societies across the interior of the continent, which was largely unknown to the European sailors who had progressively explored the coast.

Teaching the history of slavery, to West African Islamic students, as part of a course which ended with Parliamentary Democracy, was very different. We were based in the ancient trading city of Kano, with camel caravans crossing the Sahara for over a thousand years. The Hausa people are proud of their tradition. The Saharan caravans included slaves, meeting the needs of numerous clients. Slavery, and the slave trade, were integral parts of African life and history. Trading conquered peoples as slaves across Africa was long established. The Sahara was the central arena. The coasts were neglected.

At the coasts, the story was of failure to communicate and understand. Europeans and Africans knew little about each other, and there was little attempt to mix and learn. Europeans talked of discovery. Africans knew they were there. They saw traders as representing a new market, adding to existing routes and supply chains.

In Kano, the history was primarily African and Arab. The area had been part of the British Empire, but it could be seen as a marriage of convenience. The British colonial Governor Lugard captured this in his system of indirect rule, whereby a skeleton crew of colonial residents were notionally rulers of a vast and complex area, reporting back official data to London. In fact, the local political power remained with the traditional ruler, the Emir.

For slave traders and slave owners, it was not seen as necessary to know about Africa or Africans, beyond the pragmatic advisability of separating slaves from the same community, in order to ease control. Ignorance has continued, at least on the part of British and Europeans about Africa and Africans. It has been assumed that British and European civilisation was somehow inherently superior. The British social class system was imported, taking precedence over Indian mediators, who were themselves distinct from native Africans.

The British were welcome in Northern Nigeria in the 1970s, because they had come to be seen as neutral in terms of local tensions between the major tribal groups across federal Nigeria. The British could be bought on the illusory promise of a luxurious expatriate life style. Their services were seen as preferable to Yoruba or Ibo teachers from the South, who had been westernised during Empire, and now represented rival groups.

A number of my colleagues at Kano State Polytechnic admitted that they would have liked to work in Nigeria in the age of Empire. They liked what they had heard about the expatriate lifestyle, which in reality had been stronger in Kenya. In the 1970s, just over a decade after independence, they found themselves in relatively modest accommodation, with low salaries and status by comparison with expatriate businessmen. It was hard for them to understand their circumstances.

Citizenship Project

2007 is the bicentenary of the foundation of John Wiley & Sons Ltd, international publishers based in Chichester. Publishers, by their work, feed and free the minds of men, which, as UNESCO has declared, is where conflicts and wars begin. Wiley has contributed to enlightenment in each of the sectors covered by UNESCO: education, natural sciences, human and social sciences, culture and communication. This book has implications for each of those sectors, and it is significant that each UNESCO sector, in a distinctive manner, is contributing to efforts concerning the bicentenary of the abolition of the Transatlantic Slave Trade.

"From Slavery to Citizenship" is a joint project of Wiley and the Council for Education in World Citizenship. Recognising that in today's globalised world we are becoming increasingly aware of our interdependence, the project seeks to encourage international citizens to read, to think, to exchange ideas, and to explore alternative ways forward together. There are more questions than answers. If the project encourages more people to ask more questions, and to listen to the diverse answers, it will have succeeded. The process of emancipation is not complete.

The project is not a campaign. It does not argue for a partisan position. However, building on shared values, and exploring the nature of human rights at work, it reflects a belief in the importance of mature citizenship, and an optimistic view that change for the better is possible. This involves dialogue, sometimes arriving at consensus, but on occasion exposing fundamental differences, from which we can learn. There can be differences between various established national histories and traditions. There is a continuing central role for international publishing, in different media, enabling dialogue to be informed.

The Book

The book comprises a core text which is complemented by short "impulse texts" from external contributors around the world, which are intended to stimulate thought and discussion, in particular around themes of control and participation, and human rights.

To take account of 2007, there is a growing wave of new publications, based on detailed historical research, filling in particular gaps, often casting fresh doubt on old comfortable orthodoxies. This can be destabilising, as some of our heroes are shown to have had feet of clay, to have been fallible human beings, as indeed we are. Our opportunities for understanding of the historical past are increasing, although the focus of the published research is often relatively narrow. We still encounter numerous silences, dating from the time of the slave trade. It is time to try to break those silences, to reflect on the past, to understand ourselves and our relations with others, and to change our policies and practices for the future. This requires a process of dialogue.

This book considers Slavery and Citizenship today, as well as in the past. It reaches conclusions with implications for workplaces, democratic society and citizenship education all around the world. Although the Transatlantic Slave Trade was organized on racial lines, with whites enslaving blacks, over the centuries slavery has been more widespread and more complex. We consider the experience of several Empires, and the legacies of the African Diaspora.

WORK

Work Organisation

This book is concerned with the present world of work, and forms of work organisation, as well as the past. Even if we were to accept that there is a single pattern of development of forms of work organisation over time, in a globalised world we encounter many organisational stages at the same time. We start by considering slavery as a form of work organisation, in which the slave is regarded as an instrument of production, engaged in mechanical activity.

We consider *Slavery* as an extreme case of the lack of *Control* by individuals over their own work. By contrast, *Citizenship* involves individual autonomy in the workplace, and the means of *Participation* in decision-making, which is denied to slaves.

In the case of chattel slavery, where people are treated as pro-perty, this means a lack of *Control*, not just over work, but over their lives as a whole, combined with an absence of opportunity for *Participation* in decision-making in society. *Slavery* is a total institution. The issue of "work life balance" does not arise. Slaves are excluded from *Citizenship*. They are seen as lacking human rights.

The chattel slave was not seen as requiring education, and would thus not be appropriate for tasks where education is required. Decisions were to be made by the master or overseer. The slave was not considered as having explicit, implicit or tacit knowledge.

Developing new plantations in the Americas required man-power for hard physical work in often difficult climatic conditions. Few Europeans were interested in engaging in such work. Native Americans proved vulnerable to European diseases. Thus forced labour was seen as necessary, using a supply of slaves from West Africa. Thanks to the slave trade, slaves could be bought readily and cheaply.

Enslavement meant a transformation for Africans, who had been accustomed to living and working as subsistence farmers, members of local communities, and engaging in joint activities, including seasonal work. Communities would work together at seedtime and harvest. African slaves, where the opportunity for freedom arose, sought to fulfil their ambitions of returning to subsistence farming. After long experience of chattel slavery, they did not want to become industrial employees, denied their freedom of decision making yet again. Marx argued that the successor stage to slavery was serfdom. This was based largely on his analysis of Europe. For African slaves, the first objective was to regain their own identity, with control over their life and work, and participation in decisions over their futures.

There are current forms of work organisation which are a matter for concern, and, in the view of the International Labour Organisation, deserve the label "slavery".

Race

The Transatlantic Slave Trade was not simply a matter of forced labour, in the absence of willing volunteers to go and work in the New World. It added a fundamental overlaying dimension of race. It was argued that black workers would be better physically suited to the conditions of plantation work. A supply of such workers was available, from Africa, under conditions which did not need to be observed by shareholders, consumers and citizens at home.

Through transporting millions of slaves, the Transatlantic Slave Trade created an ongoing global legacy of racial division, with the African Diaspora, and discriminatory attitudes, which were then further amplified by Empire. Patterns varied in different Empires, as we explore in the book.

Members of the general public are perhaps relatively familiar with the situation in the United States, which has dominated the international debate in recent years, but the Transatlantic Slave Trade was much more widespread, both in its activities and its impacts. It is not simply a matter of continued discrimination and prejudice based on skin colour. The proceeds of slavery and the Transatlantic Slave Trade made a major contribution to the wealth of Britain in the eighteenth century. As the book suggests, more research is needed.

This combination of work organisation, racial division, and Empire, has proved toxic. The lasting by-products will doubtless continue to complicate life in 2007. We cannot expect that our dialogue will be entirely calm, and expressed in rational terms at all times. Although it was a pragmatic approach to a problem of work organisation, chattel slavery was an assault on the identity of Africans, and the African Diaspora. The scale of deaths on the Middle Passage, and in the early months of work in the Americas, justify the use of the term "Holocaust".

Our objective is to arrive at approaches to reconciliation and healing, but this has to be preceded by a recognition of the enormity of what was done, primarily by people with skins of one colour to people with skins of another colour. In multicultural modern societies, we need to arrive at means of working together.

Business

This book deals with work organisation in the context of business and management. It seeks to explain how slavery, and the Transatlantic Slave Trade, came to form part of business strategy. This was often in a way that was not described on balance sheets or in annual reports, and may not have been discussed at company board meetings. Those who prospered most from the Transatlantic Slave Trade were often keen to avoid detailed discussion, and to focus on the straightforward business agenda. The Transatlantic Slave Trade enriched the business communities of Bristol, Liverpool and London, but without slaves being visible, as the trade was between Africa and the New World. Major banks such as Barclays and HSBC owed their foundation to the Transatlantic Slave Trade, which thus shaped the financial systems of London and the world.

The book argues that an understanding of slavery opens the way to breaking many other important silences around business and politics. On this basis, an alternative model of business is proposed, which locates the quantitatively driven process of business strategy within a moral framework. We prefer to base our model on working life, a context in which people collaborate, and develop particular forms of work organisation.

Adam Smith

This approach is not new. Adam Smith, when he set out the economic principles of business in "The Wealth of Nations" (1776), located them in the context of his earlier "Theory of Moral Sentiment" (1759), which expressed core beliefs of the European Enlightenment. He was an outspoken critic of slavery and of mercantilism, on both moral and economic grounds.

Smith argued the case for the division of labour, in terms of increased efficiency, productivity and profitability. He recognised that this could lead to boring and repetitive work, meaning that attention should be paid to the quality of life and leisure. This had implications for the owners of companies, and for government, who needed to ensure that the human needs of workers and their families were met.

Few would argue today in favour of slavery. In practice they often turn a blind eye to continued practices which fit that description, aided by business practices. Business can be used as an excuse for departures from ethical courses of action. On this basis, we might conclude that many of those who cite the work of Adam Smith, when arguing for radical approaches to free market capitalism, have not themselves read his work. Through their selective approach they have distorted his views, almost out of all recognition.

When Smith wrote, the right to vote in Britain was restricted to the wealthy. It was assumed that decisions would be made by the owners. Adam Smith was critical of managers who act as if they were the owners of enterprises, while in fact they are simply employees. He saw their self-interested conduct as contrary to the best interests of the enterprises and the workers.

Seamen

The Transatlantic Slave Trade operated at the expense of the slaves, but we should not neglect the treatment of the sailors. Many had been forced into crews working in the Transatlantic Slave Trade, where their travelling and living conditions were often little better than those of the slaves, with high death rates from transatlantic travel. Although the slave trading captains could make a prosperous living, moving from piracy to respectability, the life of a sailor was little better than slavery. This reminds us that the basis of slavery was control and the denial of participation. These considerations influenced the views of abolitionists, and the politicians who they sought to influence.

Abolition and Emancipation

The story of slavery and Citizenship is also a story of efforts to abolish the Transatlantic Slave Trade and end slavery, efforts which continue today. Control and participation at work, or their denial, affect the health and life chances of us all. Typically we make decisions without considering the wider implications, or we delegate decisions to others, outsourcing responsibility. The challenge of equity in health and safety at work continues. Many would argue for a form of citizenship at work, a situation where workers have a degree of control over their own work, and a chance to participate in decisions affecting their own futures. In the modern knowledge economy, it is argued, old approaches to management and control through vertical steering structures make little sense, and individual workers need to be enabled to work in teams and networks.

Positive Messages

Perhaps surprisingly, there are some very positive messages for work, and work organisation, from the history of slavery and its abolition. The talents, including leadership ability, of millions of Africans had been neglected. It became apparent that this was a fundamental error, part of the self-serving attempt to justify the practice of slavery. Despite being taken from their homes, and brought together in arbitrary combinations overseas, it proved possible to maintain elements of African culture, and to resist domination.

In particular, the successful slave rebellion in Santo Domingo, led by Toussaint L'Ouverture, demonstrated that the régime of slavery was far more fragile than had been realised. Slave owners had assumed that they could establish effective total control over their plantations, wielding hierarchical power. They neglected the potential for developing networking between slaves working on different plantations. In Santo Domingo, the slaves and former slaves were able to come together, develop leadership capacity, take control, and run their own country. Remarkably, they withstood military attack from the French, British and Spanish. Even today, the regiments say little about these defeats.

The slave rebellions demonstrated that it is possible to move from "steering society" to "network society", from following orders to working in partnership. It was this demonstration that slave rebellions could succeed, and could be sustained, that destroyed the myth of the docile contented slave population, which was maintained by proponents of slavery. As we explore in this book, slave rebellions were part of the networking movement which transformed industry and society, in Britain and across the world.

Non Governmental Organisations

Among the major actors in the story of the Transatlantic Slave Trade, slavery and Abolition are Non Governmental Organisations (NGOs). We should not imagine that the British Parliament decided to abolish the Transatlantic Slave Trade without an extended and highly effective campaign. Behind the rhetoric of William Wilberforce MP, the well-regarded Independent Member of Parliament for Hull, there were committed researchers and a network of campaigners. Particular lessons can be learned from the work of Thomas Clarkson and his Abolitionist colleagues, from 1787. In a concerted campaign, they were able to punch above their weight, establishing a landmark change.

We reflect on the concept that the abolition of the Transatlantic Slave Trade represented a "tipping point" in this history of human rights, and consider the impact on, for example, business ethics and corporate social responsibility. This impact concerns both the content of the change that was achieved, and the manner by which it was achieved.

Anti Slavery International, formed in 1839, based in London at Thomas Clarkson House, continues today with the struggle against slavery which was begun in 1787, drawing on insights and experiences of the African people and Diaspora communities. This book draws on the separate traditions of business and human rights campaigning, and seeks to address those who have worked in both traditions, as well as engaging a wider audience who seek to live and work in modern societies and economies. Rather than arriving at definitive conclusions about the past, about which so much more needs to be learned, we identify questions which still need to be asked, and seek to open up future dialogues.

World Citizenship

The present international context for dialogue and questions includes the United Nations Organisation, which recently cele-brated 60 years since its formation. The UN now provides a forum for all citizens of the world to meet as equals, especially through United Nations agencies such as the United Nations Educational, Scientific and Cultural Organisation (UNESCO). There have been a series of special anniversaries and designated years, marking progress towards the development of a world community.

This does not mean that all forms of slavery have now ended, or that injustice and inequality have been eradicated. Citizenship has a long way to go before we can claim to have achieved world citizenship. Dialogue, and openness to different points of view, are fundamental.

SILENCES

A Challenge

Historians face unusual challenges when researching the slave trade, and in particular the Transatlantic Slave Trade. Almost by definition, where people have reflected on their own actions with regard to slavery, they seem to have expressed disquiet. They have tried to give a favourable impression, by maintaining silences. We have to listen to the silences, and try to discern their meaning.

The distinctive feature of slavery and the Transatlantic Slave Trade has been the surrounding silence. Where there has been doubt about the morality of particular practices, records have been limited. Slaves are rarely literate, and slave traders do not enlighten their investors regarding details of their work, and the treatment of fellow human beings. In societies where the existence of slavery is taken for granted, such matters pass without comment. In modern societies, where explicit slavery would be considered unacceptable, difficult periods of national history may be neglected.

Given that there will be continuing limits to the evidence to be found, and in light of continued political sensitivities, we need to make sense of the silences. In some areas the book will provide more questions than answers. Following the outlawing of slavery, systematic status differences have continued. Social class is rarely discussed. It is preferable to imagine a world of democracy and equal opportunities. Democracies like to claim that they value freedom of information and freedom of speech. In most countries there will be practical limits to those freedoms. Where silence is systematically maintained, citizens are reduced to subjects. We are the slaves of our ignorance.

In the Southern states of the USA, the West Indies and Brazil, slavery was a daily fact of life. By contrast, in British polite society, it was rarely seen as a suitable topic for discussion. A similar view was then taken regarding the living conditions of the urban poor in Britain.

Silence could be linked to denial. Historians have investigated reports of numerous secret hiding places for slaves, for example in Bristol. Most British citizens would not have encountered slaves, so did not recognise that the Transatlantic Slave Trade, conducted offshore, was fuelling their own prosperity. Slave traders preferred to present themselves as successful businessmen and public benefactors.

Few of us pause to consider the potential long term implications of our actions. It is easier to concentrate on the short term. Slave traders did not have to think beyond particular transactions, buying and selling. Slaves were just a commodity. There was no discussion of a future where freed slaves might become citizens.

Life was typically solitary, poor, nasty, brutish and short. This made business easier. There were relatively few problems of ageing workers.

Breaking the Silence

There will be increasing discussion about the realities of the Transatlantic Slave Trade, with attempts to "break the silence". The Church of England has begun to address its own past involvement in slavery. There are debates in other European countries which had been involved in the Transatlantic Slave Trade, which Britain dominated. In the United States, the African Americans have been campaigning for the silence over the Transatlantic Slave Trade and slavery to be broken.

In 1768, the Danish slave ship Fredensborg was wrecked off the coast of Agder, in Southern Norway. In 1974 the vessel was recovered, providing evidence of Norwegian and Danish engagement in the Transatlantic Slave Trade. European countries, which today proclaim their commitment to decent work, have to come to terms with their own past. The Norwegian government funds the UNESCO Associated Schools Project network project "The Transatlantic Slave Trade: Breaking the Silence". Schools around the world, in places associated with the slave routes, are being linked.

What was going on?

Only black Africans were transported as slaves to North America. In North America only black Africans were slaves, and almost all black Africans were slaves. The racial legacy of the Transatlantic Slave Trade is thus hard to disentangle from the legacy of racial discrimination, which we have seen in other contexts such as the Belgian Congo under King Leopold II, and South Africa under Apartheid.

The situation in the Caribbean and Latin America was different. Following the arrival of Europeans, Portuguese, Spanish and French, local populations of native Americans died, many from European diseases. Death rates continued to be high, due to adverse working and living conditions. The plantation economies depended on ongoing imports of slaves, rather than developing a self-sustaining population of slaves. Slaves and owners mixed and intermarried, and it was often possible for slaves to buy their freedom. A complex mulatto culture developed, in contrast to the relatively black and white situation in the United States. The history of the different colonies also reflected the politics of the European colonial powers.

There are continued gaps in the story. There are silences, where the emerging truth is hard or impossible to reconcile with modern standards of morality and Human Rights. Because in many cases these silences go back for hundreds of years, they are hard to break. Fracturing the righteous façade exposes complex fulminating cans of worms.

In some cases, there are current and growing calls today for reparations, recognising past wrongs, and taking measures to effect change for the present and future. This campaign has been strongest among African Americans, concerned with the legacy of American slavery, and it must be addressed. We cannot relive or revisit the past, but we have to live with its consequences, and take it into account when planning for the future.

HISTORY

Public Understanding

The silences have been so deep, broad and long-established, that many people grow up in ignorance of salient facts regarding the background to our modern society. Education is supposed to socialise new generations of citizens, but the gaps are now becoming obvious. Students are taught by a generation of teachers who themselves have vital gaps in their knowledge and understanding. It may be time for the students to engage in the process of research to enable the re-writing of history.

In British schools, as recently reported by the Qualifications and Curriculum Authority, the secondary history curriculum has become very narrow. Most students learn about King Henry VIII, and the Tudor dynasty of monarchs, where there is a positive national story to be told. Then, all too often, there can be a gap, until we reach another popular topic, the rise of Hitler, which is seen as providing a straightforward example, from overseas, of how democracy can collapse into totalitarian dictatorship, resulting in genocide.

In between, we have the key period when Europeans explored (or "discovered") the world, the Transatlantic Slave Trade developed, and empires rose and fell. Typically there are separate school history courses which deal with the social and economic history of the period, with a focus on the British Industrial Revolution. Separate courses again consider European history of the period, with tensions between the Great Powers, culminating in the Scramble for Africa and the First World War.

In modern multicultural Britain, and increasingly multicultural Europe, what are we to teach about this missing period, and the missing links? Should the British Empire be regarded as a matter for pride? The bicentenary of the Abolition of the Transatlantic Slave Trade raises the question afresh. This book hopes to provide some of the answers, while posing more questions.

Official History

History can be a misleading guide. We should not expect accounts to be always neutral. In 1812 the UK and USA were at war. The

British burnt Washington. Who won the war? Each side, in their own history books, claims the victory. Each presents events in their chosen context.

Historians of the Second World War now emphasise the Holocaust, a process of genocide which almost eradicated Jews from numerous countries. Less information was available at the time. The truth is that the treatment of the Jews was not the reason for the involvement of the UK or the USA in the Second World War. There is still silence regarding what was known when, and by whom.

How are we to describe the Transatlantic Slave Trade? It combines elements of holocaust and genocide. It resulted in a continued Diaspora. It was a trade in people, driven by market forces, and for a long period not subject to regulation. It was conducted away from the public gaze. Despite the fact that millions of African slaves were transported, as part of the lucrative Triangular Trade, there was little discussion in polite society.

Who writes the history books? Typically the books have been written by the self-declared winners, with access to power, education and publishing. The balance is now changing.

Britishness and Citizenship

Despite our awareness of silences, official positions can be taken. Often they are hard to justify in terms of the historical evidence. Those who determine official positions may be ignorant of the history.

The discussion of the concept of "Britishness", in the speeches of several senior government ministers, reflects a concern to define a majority position and tradition, to which immigrants can be assimilated. It is partly in reaction to the realisation that British born young people can be alienated from established views and institutions, to the extent that they engage in acts of terrorism.

To date governments have not wished to recognise that their own policies and actions could have stimulated such adverse responses.

This debate has been influenced by the United States, which has long required a daily ceremony of saluting the flag, and reciting the oath of allegiance. The USA has always been predominantly a nation of immigrants. This has meant neglecting native Americans, and both slaves and their descendants. The USA has been built around the Constitution, and a legacy based on independence from what was seen as colonial rule.

France has long been conscious of national identity. The French Revolution provided the rhetoric of "Liberté, Égalité, Fraternité", which was retained after Napoleon Bonaparte's restoration of order after a period of chaos. All French political parties can locate themselves in the tradition of the Revolution.

In both the USA and France, minority groups can find it hard to feel included. Dissent can be taken to the streets.

The British would like to emphasise common values of tolerance, social justice, inclusiveness and the rule of law. In the context of 2007, it is perhaps natural to identify William Wilberforce MP as a leading figure, exemplifying British values. After all, as a Parliamentarian and Evangelical Christian, a member of the Clapham Sect, he devoted much of his life to the pursuit of causes which are compatible with "Britishness". His group laid foundations for Christian Socialism.

There is a need for caution. A triumphalist presentation of Wilberforce, with an over-simplified view of history, could serve to alienate a number of groups who need to be included in a sustainable Britain.

The problem is that politicians and civil servants tend to have a limited view of British history. It is not that they are suppressing the truth about the past. They may simply be ignorant, or unaware. One aspect of Britishness has been a focus on history from a British perspective. This is not unusual: most countries teach history in a way which reflects their own position.

The intriguing complication for Britain is that a small group of islands in North Western Europe built a world-wide Empire of Colonies, to which were added Mandates and Protectorates in the early twentieth century, after the First World War. British values and history were presented as a model around the world.

In the early twenty-first century, Britain continues to be a small group of islands in North Western Europe. The Empire has gone, with colonies having achieved independence, and in most cases membership of the Commonwealth. Since 1973, Britain has been a member of the Common Market and then the European Community and the European Union, working in partnership with countries who have been traditional rivals or even enemies.

National histories are written and published as a form of communication with the intended readers. When the context in which the readers live has undergone radical change, as it has done in Britain, there is a case for revisiting the history, and how it is presented.

The history of the Transatlantic Slave Trade, and of slavery, offers a remarkable opportunity to update our accounts of history. There are also dangers. One complication, for popular historians, is that individuals and governments tend to avoid talking about issues and events which they find embarrassing. It is often easier to accentuate the positive, to the extent that the negative passes without comment.

We have a classic example here with William Wilberforce and the abolition of the Transatlantic Slave Trade. The truth is more complex than the adulatory accounts which have been available since the biography by Wilberforce's sons, who were determined to establish their father's reputation. This is not to denigrate the contribution of this outstanding Parliamentarian and orator, but to seek a fuller picture.

Space, Time and Ideas

In order to understand the Transatlantic Slave Trade, and the issues of slavery and citizenship, we have to embark on a complex voyage across space and time, in which we encounter the movement of people and of ideas.

We cannot regard slavery as simply an historical phenomenon. It continues today, around the world, but in different forms. We will consider child labour, and forced labour in rural Brazil, Tibetan lack of self-determination, and slavery to ignorance in Nicaragua.

Furthermore, we should not consider slavery in isolation, but as part of a spectrum of approaches to work organisation, where control is in the hands of the owner, and the worker has no opportunity to participate in decision making. We will consider the restricted lives of Welsh quarrymen, and of groups of modern workers around the world. We explore the demand control model developed by Robert Karasek and Tores Theorell, which explains the stress which can result from particular forms of work organisation. This leads to an overview of the status syndrome, as explored by Michael Marmot. Poverty and a lack of power underpin modern forms of slavery, including hazardous child labour.

It is easy to look back over the history of slavery and the Transatlantic Slave Trade, and to imagine that the actors had full knowledge of what had happened before, and of what was going on at the time in other parts of the world. In fact, we must accept the limits of what was known, and by whom. News of events in one part of the world could take months to filter through. This was made clear in William Hague's biography of William Pitt the Younger, and Simon Schama's narrative of "Rough Crossings".

Even today, with all the advantages of communication, knowledge tends to be restricted and local. The British tend to know little about continental Europe, the USA know little about either, and the industrialised world knows and cares little about developing countries. Specialists tend to maintain limited dialogues, within their own communities. Opinions are therefore based on flawed assumptions and partial information. The book tries to provide intermediation between debates on work organisation, mobile work and healthy work.

It was of course easier to justify the Transatlantic Slave Trade if the focus could be on the profits for the trader and investors, and the resulting economic development in the regions purchasing the slaves. Thus it was convenient to talk about the Triangular Trade, covering the routes from North Western Europe to West Africa, to the Americas, and then back to Europe, aided by prevailing winds and currents. The conditions in which slaves were bought, transported and sold were little discussed, and typically arose at a safe distance from the home country. This in turn made it easier to argue that slavery was preferable to the prevailing conditions in Africa, a dark continent which few Europeans had visited. The level of knowledge has greatly increased, thanks to the work of C.L.R. James, Basil Davidson, Hugh Thomas, Robin Blackburn and Laurent Dubois.

COMMUNICATION

It has taken time for communication networks to link the developing countries themselves. The imperial powers acted as nodes, with the power to restrict information flows. This continued until the late twentieth century.

Similarly, discussions of the Transatlantic Slave Trade tend to concentrate on the Triangular Trade between the UK, West Africa and North America. Overall, North America was a relatively small player, compared with the West Indies and Latin America, where the plantation economy dominated, and slave imports were higher. However, communication and dialogue have been limited. The African Diaspora spanned the New World, but was handled in segments corresponding to the respective European Empires.

The British sought to act as lead traders of slaves to all the Empires, and for part of the eighteenth century enjoyed the monopoly contract to supply the Spanish Empire. The Transatlantic Slave Trade was a commercial business, with the trade in human beings complementing, and providing valuable income streams for, other activities at the early stages of the industrial revolution.

At home in Britain or France, where there were very few slaves, it was possible to continue life as if slavery did not exist. There was no need to discuss the economic benefits for the imperial power, and for industrialisation. The issue did not occupy centre stage in politics. Responsibility had been externalised.

In North America, by contrast, those who engaged in debates on slavery and the Transatlantic Slave Trade, did so on the basis of personal experience. Thomas Jefferson was all too well aware of the contradictions between the rhetoric of human rights, in the Declaration of Independence, and the ongoing reality of slavery. This was a matter of pragmatic politics, with property rights at the centre of attention.

Differences

In order to understand the silences, we need insights into the dialogues, and the obstacles which intervened.

There were clearly notable differences between the situations in British and French colonies. Furthermore, exchanges of experience between the two Empires have been limited. Even to this day, there are different approaches in Anglophone and Francophone Africa. The histories of slavery and Abolition in the two Empires are distinct, with few cross-references. The language and concepts are different. The continued international rivalries have deep roots, and profound collateral effects.

The French administered their colonies as overseas parts of France, alongside metropolitan France. Colonial citizens were French citizens. The British left control largely in the hands of absentee plantation owners. Their attention had been focussed on North America, until the loss of the United States. The British were less concerned with settlement than with trade. The continued prosperity of Britain was seen as linked to the growth of empire, in both West and East Indies.

In the French West Indies, where slaves constituted an overwhelming proportion of the population, it was thought easier to manage the situation by linking newly arrived slaves to others with the same local origins in Africa. By contrast, in the British West Indies and in the United States, slave owners tried to separate slaves from the same villages, so as to make them easier to manage. Slave networks were harder to build.

The French had an established system by which slaves could buy their freedom, or manumission. This often enabled relationships between slave owner and slave to be regularised through the completion of official documents. In British colonies, owners were white, while blacks were slaves: the system was simpler. There were sexual relationships between owners and slaves, but they were not regularised by law.

Revolution

To quote Chairman Mao, it is probably still too soon to assess the significance of the French Revolution. However, the decision by the French Revolutionaries in 1794 to declare slavery illegal had radical implications. Communications among slaves in the French West Indies meant that slaves were able to adopt the language of Revolution and Citizenship, and to declare their loyalty to the

Republic, flying the Tricolour, and enlisting to fight both mon-
archists and the British. The uprisings were credibly led, and
established governments which were led by former slaves, profess-
ing loyalty to Republican principles. Service in the armed forces
was a route to greater acceptance in society, and also meant access
to weapons.

The former slaves had made astute use of opportunities provided by political change in France, and demonstrated the effectiveness of their local networks as they established alternative
economic and political institutions. Their success challenged fundamental assumptions regarding the relative capabilities of black
and white people.

Histories of slavery in North America make little reference
to developments in the French West Indies. If one was to rely
on British accounts, slaves were simply the beneficiaries of
altruistic concerns of evangelical abolitionists, which were soon
adopted as government policy, reflecting the leading moral position of the British. Little mention is made of the dominant role
of the British in the Transatlantic Slave Trade in the century to
1807, or of the achievements of African slaves in fighting for their
freedom.

There is no doubt that the successful rebellion in Santo
Domingo, leading to the declaration of independence in Haiti, and
emulated by other French colonies such as Guadaloupe, engen-
dered fear among informed plantation owners in the Southern
States of the USA, and among those concerned with the American
constitution. It was more convenient to maintain the myth that
slaves were always docile and loyal, and that they were incapable
of organising themselves.

The period of alignment between Republican France and freed
slaves in the Caribbean was relatively short, as Napoleon re-
imposed slavery in 1803. The British establishment view was that
Napoleon had shown the necessary determination to restore order
in France after the chaos of the Revolution. The wheel had gone

full circle with successive transitions from slavery to Citizenship, and then to slavery.

Slaves as Pawns

During that same period, there were other higher profile stories, where the political stakes were seen as greater. The rivalry and warfare between Britain and France, and the American War of Independence, meant that the issue of slavery could be used pragmatically. The British used freed slaves to fight with them against the Americans. The French used freed slaves to fight against the British, who lost 60,000 in the war in the French West Indies, through fighting and illness. In neither case were these services rewarded by emancipation. Even when abolition of the Transatlantic Slave Trade was agreed by Britain and the USA in 1807, it was not accompanied by emancipation. That would have threatened property rights, alienating important political interests. Slavery was not abolished in Britain until 1833, when slaves were designated apprentices, and in USA abolition came as a pragmatic necessity during the Civil War in 1864.

Simon Schama's "Rough Crossings" links these different themes, but concentrates on the role of British abolitionists in seeking to alleviate the suffering of slaves sent to North America. There were well-motivated attempts to resettle in Nova Scotia and Sierra Leone. In each case, information was limited.

Principles of Capitalism

There are certain principles behind the operation of capitalist institutions which have facilitated the continuation of slavery. Individuals have sought to maximise personal financial returns. Limited liability has enabled businessmen to focus their attention on areas for which they could be held personally responsible. Effective businessmen have externalised areas of risk. The focus on financial performance made it easier to disregard human outcomes of business activity, which it is harder to quantify. Company directors have seen their responsibility as primarily to shareholders, whose value should be increased. As Smith noted, though themselves employees, they came to see themselves as in the role of owners.

Regarding business as a professional field in itself, rather than as an aspect of diverse activities, had led to the development of disembodied expertise. One theme of the Enlightenment had been an interest in human skill and expertise. The French Enlightenment reflected revolutionary commitments to the rights of man, and the abolition of slavery.

The myth of the detached objectivity of the professional accountant, and a model of corporate strategy based on financial engineering, have enabled businesses to flourish in areas of moral complexity such as the arms trade. The strategic manager benefited from remaining distant from operational details which might colour his judgement.

Making Sense of slavery

We should not assume that the people of a previous generation were fundamentally less "moral" than we are today. The modern "enlightened" student is challenged when trying to make sense of slavery. A similar problem arises with international outsourcing. The same fundamental question arises. In each case, apparently intelligent and decent people have been happy to be complicit in practices which the outside observer might today regard as morally unacceptable. In order to derive personal financial benefits for owners and managers, who have the power to make decisions, it has been seen as appropriate to create patterns of work organisation which deprive the workers concerned of basic human rights.

Slavery continued for decades after the abolition of the Trans-atlantic Slave Trade, and involved leading public figures who prided themselves on their personal morality. Campaigners argue that slavery continues today around the world, for example in the form of forced and hazardous child labour. We should not pretend that slavery has been abolished.

In a similar fashion, international outsourcing maximises the income and profits of owners and managers, moving work to regions where costs are lower and regulatory environments are weak. Workplaces that are out of sight may be regarded as out of mind, and not in need of inspection. This becomes a standard strategy for international human resource management.

The discussion is in terms of Control and Participation, with the objective of making sense of practices which have now been outlawed internationally, but were clearly previously seen as acceptable. Slavery is seen as an extreme case of a more general phenomenon of inequality and the exercise of power at work. It cannot simply be attributed to the actions of a small minority.

In general, business decisions are not made on the basis of full information, but are affected by what has to be made public. Business has always sought to make a profit. Many costs are not shown on the balance sheet, not discussed at board level, and not drawn to the attention of shareholders, other stakeholders, or the wider public. There is much that is not made explicit. If there is not a strong ethical framework, with means of enforcement of compliance, it is likely that business decisions will favour property rights over human rights. Power relationships need to be understood.

Towards Citizenship

To be freed from slavery does not in itself make someone a citizen. Citizenship involves having a measure of Control over one's life, and the opportunity to Participate in the decision making process.

The freedom comes with corresponding responsibilities, for one's own actions, and for others. In a democratic society we assume that individual adults have the right to vote for their political leaders. In return, they should accept the government who are chosen by the constitutional process.

Citizenship in the workplace is a more complex concept. It is likely to mean individuals having some autonomy regarding their own work. They expect to be informed and consulted, and to have the right to join trade unions or other associations.

There will be gaps between popular myth and practical reality. Even in countries where industrial democracy and participation are part of the consensus, in a modern complex society there is a danger that power will be held by a privileged minority.

What is to be done?

It is not sufficient to take a lofty moral stand. We need to come to an understanding of how intelligent decent people could act in this way. This involves a recognition that such conduct continues. Of course, injustice, inequality and unpleasant working conditions are not new. For centuries they might have been regarded as an inevitable part of life. There are now national, European and international laws and conventions. However, change does not happen by itself. Actions, or interventions, are required.

It might have been thought that the Enlightenment, with new priority being given to science, technology and the improvement of man and society, would have swept away such historic anachronisms as slavery, on the grounds that they were inconsistent with modern moral sentiment. We have to face up to the possibility that the new respect for the structures of science, predicated on assumptions about stability as derived from Newton's astronomy, enabled a new rationalisation of the status quo, which enabled it to be perpetuated. Furthermore, the erection of disciplinary structures made it harder for fresh ideas to assault the orthodoxy from outside the establishment. After decades of war in Europe, the call was for stability. Unfortunately the stability depended on drawing analogies with "the physics that never was". In the twentieth century economics, with the myth of equilibrium, provided rationales for behaviour which might be seen as severely deficient in human and moral terms. Quantification has been an invaluable means of obfuscating qualitative and moral issues. The myth of causal explanation has downgraded other modes of explanation, including epidemiology. Those in power have taken it upon themselves to determine what will count as evidence, to be taken into account when deciding policy.

If we remove the facades of stability and equilibrium, we are, it may be suggested, confronted with chaos. This has implications which go well beyond apparent anachronisms such as slavery and international outsourcing. Arguably it jeopardises the sustainable smooth running of society. Perhaps it would be better to leave well alone, and not ask awkward questions.

Emancipatory Action Research

The research required for this book has included Emancipatory Action Research, working in the tradition of the Committee to Abolish the Slave Trade, and learning from the experience of Clarkson and Wilberforce. It has meant active involvement in many campaigns, challenging authorities where necessary, and facilitating change. It is not enough to observe. Participation is required, with entry into new discourses.

Movement in the direction from Slavery to Citizenship, when it is achieved, is not always easy to sustain. Taking control of one's own life and work requires organisation and determination, and benefits from external assistance.

Non governmental organisations have played a vital role in this project, including Anti Slavery International, Amnesty International, the International Commission on Occupational Health, the World Psychiatric Association, the UK Work Organisation Network, and the Council for Education in World Citizenship.

CHAPTER 1

NATIONS AND EMPIRES

One day, when all our people were gone out to their works as usual and only I and my dear sister were left to mind the house, two men and a woman got over our walls, and in a moment seized us both, and without giving us time to cry out or make resistance, they stopped our mouths and ran off with us into the nearest wood . . .

. . . The people I was sold to used to carry me very often when I was tired, either on their shoulders or on their backs . . . Thus I continued to travel, sometimes by land, sometimes by water, through different countries and various nations, till at the end of six or seven months after I had been kidnapped I arrived at the sea coast . . . A slave ship was riding at anchor and waiting for its cargo.

. . . We continued to undergo more hardships than I can now relate. . . . Until at last we came in sight of the island of Barbados.

Edwards, P. (ed.) (1988) *The Life of Oloudah Equiano, of Gustavus Vassa the African*. London, Longmans, pp. 1–9, 11–14, 22–28, 84–87

MEMORIES OF EMPIRE

The modern reader is familiar with the stereotypes of Empire and slavery. There have been so many stories and films based on accounts of the Southern States of the USA, and the West Indies. Even if the films have been in technicolour, the characters have been fundamentally black and white.

The modern USA is still affected by the legacy of slavery, which was first instituted under the British Empire. As the USA takes on a global role, encountering people from other cultures around the world, and based on the "Project for a New American Century", we recognise many of the characteristics of Empire. Among these is the tendency to regard indigenous people, or local populations, as in some way immature, not fully able to determine their own future.

The British Empire continues to live on in the popular imagination, and it is commemorated in the continuing award of honours to hundreds of citizens. Memories are becoming hazy as to what Empire meant. It is generally agreed that Britain has lost its Empire, but has yet to define an agreed new role. There has therefore been some confused invocation of the memories of Empire. It was true that for a period the sun never set on the British Empire, but there is limited understanding of how the Empire was built, and how it was maintained. Understandably, there is a tendency for selective memories. We like to look back with pride, and to encourage younger generations to be aware of what went before.

For current African Diaspora communities, who have seen themselves as the victims of Empire, there has been little alternative but to look back in anger. The effort has been impeded by the absence of a stable platform in national institutions. There is no "African nation" as such. The peoples of West Africa, who had a tradition of Empires with strong distinctive cultures, were scattered and enslaved. Their descendants have inherited diverse perspectives, but have rarely been in a position to determine their own destiny. They often lack the necessary historical information to enable them to take pride in their past. This has weakened their sense of identity.

For most of Europe, the age of Empire is long dead. European engagement in the Transatlantic Slave Trade had largely been on the basis of private enterprise, and their colonial ambitions were relatively restricted. The British and French had the largest Empires, and still retain the greatest concern for their national identity and position. For example, they vigorously defend their permanent membership of the United Nations Security Council, resisting suggestions that their place could be taken by a representative of the European Union.

Workplaces are increasingly diverse and multicultural, bringing together individuals who locate themselves in different traditions and contexts. The workplace is an arena for interaction and debate, where issues of control and participation are centre stage. This book is concerned primarily with relationships in working life, and with demystifying conflicts and controversies. For slaves, owned as chattels, their working relationships are inseparable from the rest of their life. Where slavery is imposed by one race on another, and where those two races have different skin colours, the implications of the system are radical. The impact continues over generations. We have to tackle deep-seated issues of human rights.

Neither Empires nor slavery can be regarded as merely historical phenomena. They continue today, often in altered forms. This must be recalled as we encounter claims of citizenship, democracy, participation and equal opportunities.

SLAVERY AS EXCLUSION

Slavery has existed in numerous contexts over the centuries. Robin Blackburn (1988b) has argued that the slave is defined by the society from which he is excluded. The slave could not be a citizen of the Empire in which he was owned. He was regarded as isolated, an outsider, without a supporting family. He was subject to the authority of the master, and would often be tortured or abused. He was dehumanised, treated as an instrument.

In order for slavery to continue in a particular society, in some sense this involves the endorsement of the "free" population. There are difficult issues of responsibility, which we address in this book. Societies based on slavery had impacts on both masters and slaves. We have to reconsider what is meant by "freedom" in such cases. To what extent do those who regard themselves as "free", and as "citizens", have to accept responsibility for the enslavement of those excluded from Citizenship?

Slavery has taken place in most parts of the world at some time. The Transatlantic Slave Trade added an additional dimension of forced relocation. Trevor Phillips, Chairman of the UK Commission for Racial Equality, emphasised the impact of the transportation of slaves from one context to another. Slaves were taken from West Africa, deprived of their names, traditions, language and families. They were reduced to isolated individuals, or at best small groups with prior connections. On arrival in the Americas they were obliged to start afresh, in unfamiliar settings, and deprived of their liberty.

Phillips emphasised the scale of the Transatlantic Slave Trade, a precursor of modern globalisation:

> This was a huge process, probably the first great industrial-scale organization undertaken by Europeans. Leave aside the issue of morality, and abandon modern notions such as the idea that a human being cannot be treated as a piece of property, and you have the elements of every modern trade. There are millions of seemingly identical units (slaves); huge factories (the word plant, meaning factories and machines, has the same root as plantation), a close attention to reducing costs, the need for large amounts of financing, and literally cut throat competition. (Martin, 1999, p. 3)

We are confronting an enormous process, exhibiting man's in-humanity to man. It is time for it to be discussed. As Patrick Bryan, Jamaican historian, has argued:

> It is the people who refuse to discuss it who constitute the problem. (Martin, 1999, p. 45)

In 2007 it is no longer possible to refuse to discuss slavery. It would be helpful if the discussion could be well informed. These are not simply issues of remote history, but involve the central identity of many of those engaged in the processes of dialogue.

ANCIENT SLAVERY

The history of slavery can be traced back to ancient times. Although it had generally been an accepted state of affairs, the legal arrange-ments and moral justifications for slavery were often untidy and inconsistent, as if from the start it represented embarrassing un-finished business. Although the enslavement of others might have been seen as tolerable, nobody has ever wished to be a slave.

It was perhaps easier when life was organised in small nations, separate from the wider world. Traditional rules could cover the enslavement of others, typically originating from a distance, and with retribution unlikely. Slavery was a fact of life: it was nothing personal. There has not been a single time line: we can identify stages of development, from slavery to serfdom, and then on to further stages of economic and social development. Karl Marx described such stages in the mid nineteenth century: we can see examples of each stage in the world around us today.

Although slaves were treated as property, they could also gen-erally be held liable under the law, so at least their status as human beings was acknowledged. Christ did not talk explicitly about slaves, nor did St Paul protest against what was a widespread con-temporary phenomenon. Later translations of the Bible were able to make pragmatic adjustments to the texts, talking about "servants" rather than "slaves" when that seemed more convenient.

POWER

There has been "slavery" across the world for thousands of years, often following the conquest of one group, tribe or nation by another. Victory is often accompanied by claims of control over property, and the imposition of the victor's legal system. The defeated group are typically required to perform menial tasks, and to acknowledge their inferiority, with no prospect of social mobility to the highest levels of society. This continues today, restricting the freedom of individuals and groups. Property rights have normally prevailed over human rights.

Forced labour has, over history, been more common than free labour, with individual employment relationships a recent development. Serfdom was common across Europe, and was only abolished in Russia in the nineteenth century. Similar systems continued across Asia in the twentieth century.

In most of Europe, as serfdom faded away it was replaced by systems of social class, intended to condition expectations in agricultural and then industrial contexts. For most countries, individual autonomy of workers still remains a dream, rather than a reality.

Often it has been possible for slaves or forced labourers to achieve their freedom, either by serving a period of time, or by making a payment to the owner. This was seen as a natural progression. It provided the basis for colonial settlement in Australia and Canada, enabling individuals to make a fresh start and build a new life. Australians remember Britain as "the place the convicts came from".

THE PRE-COLONIAL CONNECTION BETWEEN AFRICA AND EUROPE

The Roman Empire spread across "the known world", including the coast of North Africa, with Roman citizens of many geographical origins. For centuries the rest of Africa remained unknown to Europeans. With the age of discovery and exploration, there were contacts with the coastal regions of the West, South and East, but the centre of the continent remained unknown. African history has generally been neglected, partly because of the multiplicity of languages, and the absence of a unified written culture. This has had a distorting effect.

The historical background for slavery must be freed from European stereotypes. We should recall that in fact Europeans, including the British, have often been slaves, for example captured by Barbary pirates, despite the claims to the contrary in "Rule Britannia". There have been great African nations and empires, with a key role for trade, including across the Sahara. Written records are scarce, but archaeology tells its own story.

Africa has occupied a particular place in the history of slavery. The historian Basil Davidson (1961, 1974) was committed to Africa, and its progress to independence and citizenship. He tackled the full span of African history with missionary zeal, determined to cast light on the dark continent, and to redress the imbalance which had previously prevailed. Too many histories of slavery and the Slave Trade had seen the issues from a European or American perspective, in ignorance of the ongoing situation in Africa. Davidson wrote for a non-specialist audience, and sought to make sense of many troubled centuries. During the pre-colonial period, Africa continuously suffered from a connection with Europe that was neither the equality that could open wide channels to the outside world, nor the sharp subjection that could provoke and stimulate the rise of African reassertion, political change and economic growth. These were years of isolation and paralysis, wherever the trade with Europe, essentially a trade in slaves, could plant its sterilising hand.

It is not straightforward to assess the full implications of the Slave Trade. In general terms, however, the impact appears to have been extremely damaging to Africa. Social structure was damaged, but this did not normally mean widespread depopulation.

Detailed economic analysis of African development over the centuries suggests that the relationship with Europe was consistently damaging. The argument is not entirely straightforward, for there were some benefits for Africa in engagement with international trade and overseas markets. We cannot simply argue that the European connection between 1450 and 1850 was a cause of economic stagnation, or that this stagnation grew worse after slaving became dominant around 1650. Even after the Transatlantic Slave Trade got into its stride Africans continued to weave textiles, smelt and forge metals, practise agriculture and carry on the manifold techniques of their daily life. With agriculture, there was even a gain from European contact. The ships from South America introduced new and useful crops that became of great importance to Africa: maize, manioc, pineapples and several other valuable foods.

The overall economic impact seems to have been consistently damaging. This is because although there were improvements in food supplies, the concentration on producing human beings for export had damaging consequences. After about 1650, with diminishing exceptions, African production-for-export became a monoculture in human beings. This damaged economic growth in coastal and near-coastal Africa. At the same time, the extension of European production-for-export of consumer goods gave the maritime nations of Europe their long lead in economic development.

Africa was now part of a fast-growing international trading system, the Triangular Trade, but was having to send end away the very men and women who would otherwise produce wealth at home. In exporting slaves, African states exported their own capital without any possible return in interest or in the enlargement of their economic system. Thus we see in slavery the foundations of Colonialism: the sale of consumer goods for the raw material of slave labour.

There was an ongoing process over the centuries. The Slave Trade, and then the crisis of its Abolition, were followed by Colonial invasion. All were aspects of a continuous process. The old Colonial partnership, which linked Europe and Africa, laid the foundations for the Colonial system.

Damage was done within Africa, as well as blighting international relationships. African political systems were corroded. Conservative elements in Africa were strengthened by engagement in the Transatlantic Slave Trade, and institutional change was impeded.

Looking back on the treatment of dissenting minorities, there is perhaps little to choose between European and African practices. It became easy for West African rulers to dispose of malcontents and trouble makers by selling them into slavery, so that they were transported overseas. Britain was doing much the same, transporting convicts.

Perhaps most corrosive impact of the Slave Trade was on European perceptions of racial superiority. This hastened the process of Colonial conquest, and lingers today. It is vital to address the truth today, before we can move on.

Davidson argues that behind the humiliation of the Slave Trade for Africans, there was the basis for continued self-belief. New relationships can be built. African Diaspora communities have wanted to regain confidence in their own past, healing the break in their history brought about by the Slave Trade. In 2007 they are reasserting their equality and unity with the rest of mankind. The objective is that, at last, the slaving chain of cause and effect, terminating in colonial subjection, should be broken.

Many orthodox histories have underestimated African resilience and creativity. We should not over-emphasise the extent of stagnation. There was repeated individual effort to meet new situations in new ways. With considerable skill and vigour, Africans learned or worked out techniques, and matched their wits against foreign partners and eventual enemies. Africans fought against capture and exile, the excessive power of chiefs, or invasion from abroad.

Change, including the Abolition of the Transatlantic Slave Trade and the freeing of slaves, should not simply be attributed to the efforts of middle class petitioners. It came from the work of countless slaves who refused to accept their fate, and rose in revolt against their masters, founded free republics in the Americas or died in the attempt. Africans demonstrated the capacity to organise themselves, and to overthrow oppressive rule. Once this is understood, the whole history of slavery and Abolition needs to be re-written.

SLAVERY

Slavery was not necessarily associated with racial differences. A particular form of work organisation did not necessarily have to determine social relationships. In principle there could be prospects of peaceful coexistence outside work, and scope for future change. For example, convicts sent to Australia as bonded labourers had the prospect of life as citizens once they had served their time. There could be a new start.

Black African slavery in North America was unusual, in that few slaves were allowed to achieve freedom. The slave owners and their political leaders, such as George Washington and Thomas Jefferson, did not have a vision of a future where black and white would live together as equals. Instead, for political purposes they were regarded as less than full human beings. It was simply assumed that any slaves who achieved freedom would leave the country. When the time came, the process turned out to be more complicated than had been imagined.

There are numerous continuing examples of slavery in the twenty-first century, based on centuries of oppression of one group, or race, by another. There tends to have been public attention to ethnic cleansing, the forced moving or murder of members of defeated groups, but less discussion of employment relationships and social order.

There are still many indigenous peoples who are seeking self-determination, as they wish to escape the control of powerful neighbours. Self-determination does not necessarily imply independence, but a measure of autonomy.

The Tibetan people have retained their distinctive Buddhist religion and culture for many centuries, and have resisted attempts by the Chinese occupiers of their land to eradicate their distinctive features. The Chinese have continued to regard Tibetans as an inferior national group within the Chinese Empire, often assigned the status of slaves, and there have been repeated acts of oppression. There would be little point in the Tibetans resisting in military terms, or engaging in a form of armed struggle. Instead, the Dalai Lama, accepted by the people as their reincarnated leader, has tried to create space for self-determination. He has enhanced self-respect among his people.

Slavery can thus be seen as a by-product of inequalities in power, and the absence of enforced international standards and international law. The consequences include implications for working conditions for individuals, who tend to be denied control over their own work and life. They lack the opportunity to participate in decisions about their own future. Political campaigns have emphasised the case for Democracy, and the right to elect a government.

Here we are particularly concerned with the workplace. Workers who lack Control, and the opportunity to Participate, tend to suffer damaging exposures, and may experience adverse health impacts.

Empires and slavery are frequently linked. The linkage does not just mean political subservience, but also unhealthy work. Where there is an extreme power difference between the strongest and weakest in a society, there are health consequences.

CITIZENSHIP

Many of our ideas of Citizenship derive from European culture. Discussion of "citizenship" evokes classical accounts of Periclean Athens, or Rome at the time of Julius Caesar. In small communities, there could be decisions by direct democracy, with votes accorded to citizens. This tends to focus on the rights of free men, and gloss over the fate of slaves. However, Roman Citizenship was achieved by people from diverse backgrounds. It was not simply the prerogative of white Italians. Successive conquered peoples provided the work force to meet the needs of Rome, with military sanctions available.

Citizenship has typically been determined by tribal and national identity. Many national borders today are a legacy of European empires, and do not reflect the previous national histories. Maps have further distorted perceptions, with the commonly used Mercator projection reducing the apparent size of Africa.

Rival colonial legacies continue, with anglophone and francophone countries remembering different histories. There are even alternative accounts of the Abolition of the Transatlantic Slave Trade and of slavery, with the French and British accounts each making little mention of the other, as they set out stories which presented their respective heroes in a good light. As public opinion came to find slavery generally unacceptable, this has presented challenges to national historians, who needed to anchor such views in mainstream opinion. In France, this meant the French Revolution. In Britain, it meant the Abolitionist movement.

TRIANGULAR TRADE

As the Transatlantic Slave Trade was part of the Triangular Trade, which brought great wealth to Europe, it was easy for attention to be diverted to the other stages, involving exports from Britain and other European countries, and imports from the Americas. It was the Middle Passage which provided the bulk of the profits, and was conducted away from public scrutiny.

The distinctive feature of the Transatlantic Slave Trade, where the "Middle Passage" in the eighteenth century was dominated by British slave traders, was in racial terms. Black African slaves were assembled at coastal ports by African slave traders, then transported to the New World by white European traders. The African slaves met the need for labour in the plantations. This need was made more urgent by epidemics which killed a large proportion of the Native American population. There was a shortage of white voluntary emigrant workers who could meet the growing needs for manpower.

We should not ignore the extremely high mortality rate among sailors on the triangular route. They were obliged to live and work in conditions not much better than those endured by the slaves, and, as details were published, this eventually affected public opinion.

EUROPEAN PARTICIPATION

A number of European countries participated in the Transatlantic Slave Trade, attracted by the profits available from supplying labour, and then transporting the products via the Triangular

Trade. International competition was an extension of rivalry in Europe, and overseas colonies, such as in the New World, provided venues for European warfare.

The Spanish found that they needed to import labour to work their mines in Latin America. Imported European diseases killed a large proportion of native Americans. Papal decrees made it clear that native Americans could not be enslaved, but there was no similar prohibition of enslavement of black Africans. A contract, the Asiento, was drawn up for the supply of slaves to the Spanish Empire, and international slave traders competed. In 1713, under the Treaty of Utrecht, the Asiento was awarded to Britain.

The Portuguese had led the early exploration of the coast of Africa, inspired by the ambitions of Prince Henry the Navigator. The Pope had then given them control of lands to the West in the New World, including Brazil. It seemed obvious that labour needs in the hostile environment of Brazil could be met from the slave trade in Nigeria and Angola. If necessary, there could simply be two-way links between West Africa and Latin America, with no intermediate stage of trade in manufactured goods from Portugal.

Italian traders, from the different city states, operated services for different European empires, providing slaves and transporting goods in return. This could be done on a commercial basis. Christopher Columbus, from Genoa, worked for the Spanish monarchy. There were many Florentine slave traders.

British sailors operated on a private enterprise basis, following the example of John Hawkins from 1562, raiding Spanish ports, attacking treasure fleets, and paying a proportion of their profits to the Crown. This provided the basis for the British navy, combining public and private agendas, but with no plans for long term investment. The British gained from their American colonies, but had to reconsider their plans after Independence. The Triangular Trade was a motor for developments in Britain and America, fuelled by imports of African slaves.

France maintained larger national navies, and expressed international ambitions. Around the world, the French and British were rivals. The French developed successful colonies in the West Indies, which depended on the continued import of slaves. They were less able to develop sustainable slave populations, in the adverse conditions of the Caribbean.

The Dutch had naval expertise, and ambitions to lead in world maritime trade. They developed trading routes to Africa, the West Indies and East Indies.

Sweden sought to dominate the Baltic, and to build associated international trade. This included modest trade in slaves.

The German states were not unified until the late nineteenth century, but were active in maritime trade.

Lithuania covered large territory in the centre of Europe, with ports on the Baltic, and some trading in slaves.

Denmark had a long naval tradition, in the Atlantic and the Baltic, and, during the period of the Transatlantic Slave Trade, ruled Norway. The discovery of the wreck of the slave ship Fredensborg cast light on Danish involvement in the slave trade.

Norwegian myths claim that Vikings discovered North America. Viking expansion covered much of Europe, with Viking settlers integrating with local populations over the centuries. From Atlantic coastal ports, Norwegian sailors could travel the world.

Belgium is a small country, but monarchs can have large ambitions. Modest engagement in the slave trade was later linked to the development of overseas colonies, as a means of increasing royal prestige.

THE LEGACY

In the twenty-first century, all of those countries need to be able to move on, completing the journey from slavery to Citizenship.

Slavery corrupted the slave trader and slave owner, as well as oppressing the slave.

Attitudes to other races, and in particular European feelings of innate superiority, were formed and moulded through experience of the Transatlantic Slave Trade. They were applied not only in Africa and the New World of the Americas, but were also carried over to the East Indies, for example by the British and French.

The Transatlantic Slave Trade involved collecting African slaves from dealers on the coast of West Africa, and transporting them to meet the needs of overseas markets. The same slave traders, such as the British, served the needs of many empires in the New World. It was a matter of supply and demand.

WEST AFRICANS SETTLE ACROSS THE WORLD

We can find Hausa and Yoruba slaves, who had originated in what is now Nigeria, working in Brazil, the French Caribbean and in North America. We might imagine an alternative history, whereby young Hausas and Yorubas could recall how their ancestors had travelled overseas to discover the world, and to contribute to economic development in several countries. They could locate this in the long history of trade across the Sahara, including a trade in slaves. Kano had been an advanced trading city for centuries before the New World was even discovered by the Europeans. Kano has continued the strong local tradition, little changed through the years of colonial rule.

In the past, histories of slavery and the Transatlantic Slave Trade tended to focus on particular countries and empires, defined in terms of where the victims of enslavement were taken to work. The frequent common origins of slaves, sent to work across several empires, have been neglected.

As we now consider the process of change, from slavery to Citizenship, we are struck by the differences. Scholars have tried to explain contrasting situations in modern race relations by reference to varying models of slavery. However, as Carl Degler argues in "Neither Black nor White" (1971), there was a similar legal framework in the two largest slave-holding countries, Brazil and the USA. The difference was that the laws were enforced in the United States, and used as the basis for racial segregation, whereas in Brazil mixed race relationships were commonplace, and provided a route out of slavery.

Particular aspects of the different European-based empires led to important differences. One obvious factor was language: Hausa and Yoruba slaves found themselves obliged to learn English, French, Spanish, Portuguese or Dutch, according to the requirements of their new masters. This led to them being reported in separate histories and literatures, with limited cross-references. A pragmatic compromise, found for example in Louisiana and the West Indies, was the evolving Créole language and culture. Créole is an international language, including the Indian Ocean islands of Mauritius and La Réunion, as well as the Caribbean islands.

USA

The tendency in the United States was to seek to separate slaves who had come from the same local region in Africa, to make the individuals easier to manage. It was harder for the slaves to develop a common culture, and to organise. Unusually, the slave population in the USA was able to reproduce, meeting the needs of the economy across the growing country, and thus avoiding reliance on illegal slave trading after 1808. Increasingly slaves were American-born, rather than recent arrivals from Africa. Families were able to be relatively stable, and many owners saw the economic benefits of an increasing slave population.

In the USA, only Africans were kept as slaves, and there was resistance to the idea of emancipation or manumission. Other needs for labour could be met by white indentured servants and voluntary emigrants, whose living conditions were not necessarily better, but whose legal status was superior. Where there was discussion of freeing of slaves, from the time of Thomas Jefferson, it was assumed that the freed slaves would be required to leave. In debates about the ending of slavery, which had been so divisive as an issue ever since the War of Independence, there were plans to relocate the former slaves, leaving the USA as a predominantly white nation. There was no plan for the former slaves to achieve the status of citizens. There were no half measures: each person was either black or white. If they were black, they would not be regarded as full participants in society, worthy of inclusion in history books.

The history of the USA tended to make little mention of local slave rebellions, such as by Nat Turner in 1831. There was certainly no discussion of the slave rebellions in the French Caribbean in 1793–1803. Typically slaves were denied access to arms, and even during the War of Independence, the War of 1812 and the Civil War, there was reluctance to change the status of slaves. The official view was that slaves were docile and compliant, preferring life in America to what might have faced them at home in Africa.

FRENCH AND PORTUGUESE EMPIRES

In the French Caribbean and Brazil, slaves were more likely to join others with the same origins in Africa. The slave trade continued until 1888 in Brazil, and there was less stability in which slave families could develop and grow.

However, there was an established system of manumission, which meant that the dividing line between black slaves and freed maroons, quadroons or mulattos became blurred. Status was typically linked to skin colour. Attitudes to relationships across the races were less rigid, and mixed marriages and sexual relationships were common. As a result, there was a large mulatto population, neither black nor white. There were relatively few voluntary emigrants from Europe.

In both the French Caribbean and Brazil there have been famous black citizens, chronicled in the histories. Implicitly, the assumption had been that, one day, possibly in the distant future, those who had come to the New World as slaves might achieve citizenship. Slaves had been allowed access to arms. In Brazil, the frequency of attacks along the coast, and the limited numbers of slave owners, made this a necessary defensive measure.

In Santo Domingo and Guadeloupe, in the French Caribbean, the French Revolution in metropolitan France provided the rhetorical foundations for slaves to claim the rights of citizenship. When they learned of the abolition of slavery in Metropolitan France in 1794, they were quick to proclaim republican loyalties, and to establish their own régimes. They were soon betrayed, in that Napoleon, when replacing the revolutionary government, also re-established slavery, thus reversing what had been seen as a slide towards anarchy.

Slaves found themselves as pawns in wars between the imperial powers, especially Britain, France and the USA. Promises were made, but often broken. Racial attitudes which had developed during the Slave Trade were slow to change.

WHY HAS THE TRANSATLANTIC SLAVE TRADE BEEN IGNORED?

Given the volume of human traffic across the Atlantic, and its economic significance for the nations concerned, it is perhaps surprising that so little has been written about the Transatlantic Slave Trade.

Herbert S. Klein, in "The Atlantic Slave Trade" (1999) suggested that the Transatlantic Slave Trade had been ignored by historians, because of its close associations with the prevailing ethos of European imperialism. There was a resulting lack of interest in a morally difficult problem, partly because of a claimed lack of methodological tools with which to analyse the complex quantitative data.

Scholarly research was ignored by a wider audience. When contemporary societies were split by racial conflict, the topic of the Transatlantic Slave Trade was too difficult to handle in a rational manner.

As he examined the pressures for abolition, Klein reached a somewhat cynical conclusion, which we explore further in this book. While the arguments against the slave trade may have had a moral origin, they were also based on the interests of European workers and capitalists, and not on any concern with the African slaves themselves. In a globalised world, such restricted approaches cannot be justified.

VIKINGS AND THE SLAVE TRADE

There are many possible relevant histories. The popular mythology is of Vikings sailing from Norway, and elsewhere in Scandinavia, in their longboats, and travelling well beyond the known world. A successful longboat depended on teamwork and discipline, with sails supplemented by oars. Modern discussions of reorganisation of the Norwegian armed forces reflect an ongoing ethos of participation and democracy. Raping, looting and pillaging are given less prominence. Longboats could travel up the Thames to Kingston and Hampton, where small boatyards remain in business. The Vikings have had a bad press in the UK, by and large. Their cultural achievements have been neglected, along with their discovery of America and colonisation of much of Europe. Their helmets did not even have horns.

THE TRANSATLANTIC SLAVE TRADE

The Transatlantic Slave Trade represented a dramatic contrast. The human cargo was packed tightly below decks, while the ships relied on their sails. The Triangular Trade depended for its success on full ships for each leg of the journey, servicing the West Indies and the American colonies. A full cargo of slaves would be loaded, and those that died could be thrown overboard during the "Middle Passage".

The Transatlantic Slave Trade has largely been ignored in the UK in recent years. This has changed, as the bicentenary of Abolition approached. A richer picture is being painted in television dramas, as insights are provided into the commercial aspects of the trade. It is clear that raping, looting and pillaging were an integral part of the Transatlantic Slave Trade and subsequent slavery. The proceeds of the Transatlantic Slave Trade and slave plantations funded many of the British aristocracy, but details of the trade, and of life on the plantations, were not discussed in polite society.

It is perhaps unsurprising that the Norwegian Government have funded the UNESCO Associated Schools Project flagship project on the Transatlantic Slave Trade. Apart from their own distinctive historical heritage, they have a longstanding commitment to international development and to human rights. They are aware of the fundamental importance of work organisation, and of the potential impact of action research interventions. Norwegians prefer consensus to conflict.

Norwegians played a minor role in the Transatlantic Slave Trade, and were not among the European leaders in the scramble for Africa. However, if you visit old houses along the Norwegian coast, such as in Orkanger, near Trondheim, you will find the stuffed heads of rhinos, turtles and antelopes mounted on the walls. slavery and Empire were global in their impact.

CHAPTER 2

THE TRADE IN PEOPLE
AND IDEAS

I must own, to the shame of my countrymen, that I was first kidnapped and betrayed by my own complexion, who were the first cause of my exile and slavery; but if there were no buyers there would be no sellers. So far as I can remember, some of the Africans in my country kept slaves, which they take in war, or for debt; but those which they kept are well, and good care taken of them, and treated well . . .

But I may safely say that all the poverty and misery that any of the inhabitants of Africa meet among themselves is far inferior to those inhospitable regions of misery which they meet with in the West Indies where their hard-hearted overseers have neither regard to the laws of God, nor the life of their fellow men.

Cugoano, O. (1787). *Thoughts and Sentiments on the Evil and Wicked Traffic of Slavery and the Commerce of the Human Species.* London, reprinted in H. McD. Beckles and V. Shepherd (2002) *Slave Voices: The Sounds of Freedom.* University of the West Indies. UNESCO, Paris.

BEFORE THE EUROPEAN
AGE OF DISCOVERY

African empires and economies had operated for centuries before the European "Age of Discovery". There were strong intellectual and economic foundations, many of which have been forgotten. We need to take account of diverse routes and cultural encounters.

The Sahara was a vital trade route, across an internal "ocean" of sand, traversed by camel caravans. There was traffic, both North – South and East – West, strengthened by Islam. This was more significant than activities around the Atlantic coastline, and meant that states looked "inwards" rather than "outwards".

Europeans had limited knowledge of what went on in Africa beyond the coasts of the Mediterranean and the Atlantic. Sailors, such as those working for Prince Henry the Navigator of Portugal, ventured ever further round the coast, but with no intention of settling or exploring inland.

The Chinese had developed great power and sophistication, but remained within their borders. They had little concern for what went on, in "barbarian" lands, beyond the limits of their empire.

With limited communication, the different worlds could share the planet, with few encounters. Today we look back on very different histories. From a British perspective, we can take as a basis the work of Hugh Thomas (1997), but this needs to be complemented with other insights.

RELIGIOUS ENCOUNTERS

While Europe slipped back in intellectual terms between the end of the Roman Empire and the start of the European Renaissance, the Islamic world grew. We should emphasise the strength of

Islamic culture, which cut across national borders, linking Africa, the Middle East and Asia. This did not separate religion from art, design, science, technology and politics. Islamic cultural pre-eminence was remarkable, and contributed greatly to modern Europe, as well as having a strong influence in Africa. The cities of Timbuktu and Kano were centres for Saharan trade and Islamic learning.

A new trend developed once Europeans were travelling around the world, engaging in what they termed voyages of discovery. In many cases Christianity accompanied trade and conquest. Christianity adapted to local circumstances, in what is known as syncretism, and was backed by military force and commercial development.

MEDIEVAL EUROPE AND SLAVERY

It would now be possible to call for a wholesale rewriting of school history books, dealing with a number of areas where there has been silence. European sailors who have long been praised as dis-covering Africa, extending the scope of the known world, were in fact at the same time engaging in the African slave trade from 1444, with Prince Henry the Navigator taking a 20% share of the proceeds. Africa did not need to be discovered. It housed many mature civilizations, with complex economies and political systems.

The history of servants and slaves also needs rewriting, as, in many countries, legal penalties could reduce a free man to the status of slave. Serfs had an intermediate status, with rights to property. Perhaps serfdom was a response by owners to a change in economic circumstances, and to new technologies which made slavery less relatively efficient. There has also been sensitivity over the use of language.

We need to clarify moral attitudes by the church. In 960, slavery was banned in Venice. On occasion enslavement of Englishmen was prohibited, while the French or Welsh could still be enslaved. In Italy, Spain and France, there came a time when slavery was no longer naturally viable. The change came later in England, after the Norman Conquest, but before 1200. The story was different in Southern Europe, bordering the Mediterranean, with wars between Christians and Muslims routinely accompanied by enslavement. In 1300 there were 30,000 Christian slaves in Granada.

Islamic laws included benign treatment of slaves. Slaves were marched to the Mediterranean from across Europe, as well as from across Africa, and two-way trade developed, involving slaves and other commodities. Slavery seemed less wasteful than execution, as a way of dealing with captives. Spanish law provided for marriage between slaves, and imposed restrictions on how they could be treated by their masters. Law in Genoa covered how many slaves could be transported on ships of particular designs.

There was a busy trade on the southern coast of the Mediterranean. Details are hazy, but Arab slave traders served a global market, with particular tastes such as black eunuchs.

ACROSS THE SAHARA

The trans Saharan slave trade developed from 1000 BC, but little was known about it in Europe. Slaves and gold were routinely traded. The Sahara was vital for the economy of West Africa, with African slaves used to undertake less desirable jobs, such as agriculture. Medieval West Africa included a dominant role for Muslim slave traders. In Bornu, 15 or 20 slaves could be exchanged for a horse. Slaves were the principal form of private property. The arrival of Portuguese slave traders in 1444 will have seemed a relatively conventional event, extending an existing trade.

PORTUGAL MOVES DOWN WEST AFRICA

European voyages of discovery were linked to trade, including trade in slaves. There had been earlier European ventures down the coast of Africa. It had been assumed that it was not possible to sail safely, although there were reports of great riches to be found. Those seeking gold often returned with slaves.

Reports of trade in slaves, gold and other goods encouraged the Portuguese to continue south by sea. Madeira and the Azores were taken as colonies, and used for dyes and wood. Slaves from Mauritania were taken back to Portugal, to be presented to Prince Henry. Trade with Africa was a Portuguese royal monopoly. New slaves were captured progressively further down the coast, but not all slaving trips were profitable. It became easier to buy slaves than to capture them: typically captives in war, used for heavy work, and sold on by African traders.

In the small coastal states of West Africa, slavery and the slave trade were not new. Katsina and Kano were major inland trading cities, with markets and metal industries. Portuguese society became accustomed to slave ownership as a mark of distinction, and there was also widespread intermarriage. Pope Eugenius IV had approved Prince Henry's expeditions in 1442; and in 1452 and 1454 Pope Nicholas V approved the enslavement of pagans. These derived from the need to act forcefully against Islam, after the fall of Constantinople.

The Cape Verde Islands were used to hold slaves from 1462, acquired through trade and some raids. A more complex trading pattern was developed. Madeira sugar was developed with slave labour, but sugar production on the Cape Verde Islands was unsuccessful. Slaves were used in Portugal, and rules were developed. Pope Pius II opposed enslavement of Christian converts. After Prince Henry, exploration continued southwards, accompanied by slave trading.

SPANISH SLAVE TRADE

Demand for slaves was growing in Spain, so raids commenced on the Portuguese West African coast, and then trade in slaves continued. Portuguese pressures in 1481 prevented the British from joining in. The Spanish used slaves to develop sugar in the Canary Islands.

Portugal developed Elmina, on the Gold Coast, and tried to control the slave trade. Sao Tome was used to settle expelled Jews, and sugar was developed. In 1485, Angola was reached, and then Congo. Slavery was well established, but not the Slave Trade. Dias rounded the Cape of Good Hope in 1487, with the West coast known, and soon slave trading included East Africa. The Portuguese did not travel inland, but linked with existing traders.

The Spanish continued to trade in slaves, joined by the Florentines, selling slaves in Valencia. Thus it was suggested that Amerigo Vespucci should sail to the New World for Portugal. This led to new outlets for the Florentine slave trade, serving the needs of a new market discovered by a Genoese, Christopher Columbus.

Columbus had lived in Madeira, worked as a sugar buyer for the Genoese, and visited Elmina. He saw slaves in the sugar plantations. He knew of the trade, but his early voyages did not carry slaves. He soon sent back Indian slaves from Santo Domingo to Seville. There were worries about their health, and the legal implications. Soon black slaves were taken to Spanish imperial possessions in the New World, but it was controversial. The key was the weakness of Indian workers on sugar plantations, compared with African slaves. The trade was regulated by the Crown, and driven by gold. King Ferdinand had no hesitation.

Slaves then accompanied Spanish conquests, by Velazquez, Balboa and Cortes. In Spain there was a debate about the treatment of the native Indians, but not about the African slaves. The collapse of the Caribbean population increased the need for the Transatlantic Slave Trade. Efforts to use local Indians continued to fail. The young King Charles V was asked to approve: he agreed.

The early Transatlantic Slave Trade was European, involving both Spanish and Portuguese sailors, and managed by Genoese bankers. Plantations developed across Santo Domingo and Puerto Rico, together with mining in Cuba, all using slaves, some supplied by German merchants. Soon there was direct trade from Africa.

Pizarro took slaves with him to Peru, and more went to Chile and Florida. The first slave rebellion was in Hispaniola in 1522, and a rebellion in 1533 led to a ten year guerilla war. There were further revolts in Cartagena in 1545, Santo Domingo in 1548 and Panama in 1552. In Mexico, escaped slaves lived as bandits from 1550.

Slavery was familiar in the New World, using captives from war. American Indian slaves could be treated as relations, not as dogs. African slaves were treated differently. Brazil was discovered in 1500, and at first offered a supply of slaves and redwood, sold in Seville by Italian merchants. Few African slaves were imported in the early years.

THE RENAISSANCE OF SLAVERY

Demand for African slaves in the New World continued, and the trade along the West African coast was lucrative. Direct involvement increased, as supplies via Benin and Sao Tome were inadequate. The focus switched to Congo, where the trade involved the local King Afonso, who conducted raids and organised markets, responding to new opportunities. Elmina continued to be important, and East African slave trading remained lucrative.

In Europe, the Transatlantic Slave Trade prospered in Portugal, Spain, Italy and Provence. Together with classical forms of artistic expression, the old institution of slavery had been revived during the European Renaissance, somewhat complicating the image of that period of cultural change.

GLOBAL SLAVE TRADE

The Saharan trade was strong until the end of the sixteenth century, providing a ready supply of slaves to the African coast. In 1525–50 about 1,800 slaves per year were shipped from Africa to the Americas or Europe; in 1550–75 2,500 per year. The proportion going to the New World increased, as demand increased in Brazil.

African slave traders played a vital role. Kofi Awoonor, former Ghanaian ambassador to UN, acknowledged:

> Let us accept that we were part of it. Because the acceptance of the facts will form part of the beginning of a new consciousness on our own part. We did take part. We would be less than human if we hadn't taken part, because the greed factor was there, and a lot of kingdoms made a lot of money. (Martin, 1999, p. 24)

The historian Dr Akosu Perbi (Martin, 1999) traced 35 slave markets in Ghana, providing evidence of a thriving trade. This has left a damaging legacy, with descendants of slave owners feeling guilty. Descendants of slaves are still angry.

Slavery and slave trading is a part of our human past, and was not the prerogative of a single racial group. The impact was not restricted to those who were directly involved. A global trade had global impacts.

EUROPEAN TRADE

Portuguese captains handled the capture or bartering along the coast, and took slaves to entrepôts, which were now well developed colonies. Slaves were sold on, for indirect transport, until the direct route was established at the end of the century. Portuguese traders also handled Spanish slaves, as human labour became a tradable commodity. Traders included Jewish converts to Christianity, and Spanish serving their Empire's needs. Traders broadened their range of goods.

At this time slavery was common in Europe. In 1550, 10% of the Lisbon population were slaves, and 7% in Seville in 1565. Slavery continued in France and Italy.

In the New World, African slaves worked in textile workshops, in agriculture and in mines, with new plantations being opened. American Indian slavery was outlawed.

There was little public criticism of slavery. Renaissance thinkers such as Michelangelo, Sir Thomas More, Erasmus and Machiavelli were silent. Pope Leo X spoke against the slavery of American Indians, but had his own African slaves in the Vatican. Pope Paul III proclaimed the abolition of slavery, but by this meant only American Indian slavery. Luther assumed that some men would be free, and some slaves. Slavery was accepted as part of the natural order of things.

There were some concerns over conditions for transport, and for feeding of slaves. Charles V demanded that slaves received an hour of Christian instruction per day, and ordered that they should not work on Sundays or feast days. In debates on Catholicism in the New World, there was no discussion of black Africans. There were no moral scruples. In 1557 de Soto argued that those who had been born free should not be kept as slaves. The argument was reported to Philip II, who ignored it. His concern was rather for the property rights of businessmen. De Oliveira argued in 1564 that the slave trade was evil, based on robbery and unjust wars. Traders responded that in buying slaves they were serving the best interests of humanity.

CONGO, ANGOLA AND BRAZIL

In Congo, where there had been a partnership approach to slave trading, in 1555 the Portuguese were expelled by King Diogo I, but a new King Alvare allowed their return. He was exiled by the rival Jaggas, and in turn sought Portuguese help. Portuguese control increased, and slavery increased. In Angola, the fortified town of Sao Paolo de Loanda was built, and after a war, became a regional base. The slave trade became firmly established, to the benefit of Brazil, and there was some improvement of local agriculture.

Portuguese diseases killed most local American Indians in Brazil, and others were maltreated. Life was regarded as expendable, as there was a ready supply of black slaves. 40–50,000 reached Brazil from Congo in 1576–91. It was assumed that imported slaves would die after 10 years, and be replaced, so there was no great concern regarding their treatment.

Brazilian sugar production increased, in single crop plantations. Refining was done in Europe. Many Africans had relevant agricultural skills and experience, and were visibly different, easily identified as slaves, by their colour. The European plantation owners grew rich.

UNITING SPAIN AND PORTUGAL

In the 1560s, the Spanish slave trade collapsed, with losses at sea, and royal debts. The Spanish relied on the Portuguese to provide slaves. It was assumed that African slaves were vital for the profitable development of Peru and Mexico.

In 1580, Philip II became King of Portugal as well as Spain, and commercial policies were merged. Spanish control of world silver was joined by control of gold, spices and sugar. The objective was then to restrict trade by the Dutch and English. Portuguese merchants were contracted to provide slaves. Monopoly contracts were sought, specifying the number of live slaves to be delivered.

This growing demand involved further development of the trade in Africa. Some 200,000 slaves were sent in 1600–25. City states began to develop in Nigeria, with numerous slaves. Kings had limited powers. Import of slaves to Europe was now ending, with most in Portugal. The focus was on meeting needs in the Americas.

OPPOSITION TO SLAVERY

In 1569 the Dominican friar Tomas de Mercado accepted the institution of slavery, but criticized the conditions in which the slaves were transported, and then obliged to live, and the associated trickery. Despite the fine words and promises, he argued that the treatment of slaves was barbarous This had no impact.

In 1573, the lawyer Bartolome Frias de Albornoz regarded slavery as unjustifiable, using arguments about Christianity. Fray Francisco de la Cruz responded that blacks were justly held captive, by reason of the sins of their forefathers. Fray Miguel Garcia refused to hear confession from owners of slaves.

It was generally assumed that the status quo had to be maintained. Philip III declared that all slave ships should carry priests. Official proprieties should be observed.

INTERNATIONALISATION

French pirates intervened from 1492, seizing gold from Elmina, and with a royal license by the 1530s to plunder shipping. In a major commercial innovation, the triangular trade began, with traders going to the Grain Coast for pepper, and to Rio de Janeiro for wood, also carrying slaves. After a pause for the Huguenot wars, French activity resumed in 1594, taking slaves from near Gabon to Brazil.

William Hawkins was the first English adventurer involved, in the 1530s, followed by Thomas Wyndham. Both were primarily concerned with gold, not slaves. The Portuguese increased escorts, and complained that their Papal monopoly was being broken.

In 1562 John Hawkins initiated the English slave trade on a regular basis, testing the weakness of the Spanish, and with strong political and business support, including support from Queen Elizabeth I. He raided Portuguese slave boats, and stole the slaves. A second voyage, in 1564, raided Sierra Leone and Venezuela, returning via the French colony of Florida. The third voyage involved 6 ships, 2 belonging to the Queen. They took slaves in Africa, captured a Portuguese slave ship, crossed the Atlantic and burned Rio de la Hacha. They were trapped in Veracruz, and lost several ships before reaching home, their reputations intact. In Britain their reputations were as sailors and courageous explorers, serving as royal admirals in time of war. Internationally they were regarded as pirates, growing rich by robbing others, with the shameless support of the monarchy.

The Portuguese had allowed peaceful trading for gold by the English, but were more concerned about the Spanish. This position modified with the union of Spain and Portugal.

The Dutch were involved from 1592, attracted by the prospect of easy profits, first dealing with gold, then with slaves. They were working with German partners and developing trade with Brazil, taking raw sugar to Holland to be refined. They were effective traders on the African coast. The Dutch West India Company, founded in 1607, secured a 12 year monopoly of Dutch trade in 1621, and wanted to encourage the emigration of agricultural labourers. The company initially opposed the slave trade, but there were active Dutch slave traders in business by 1620.

The Portuguese were more worried by slave revolts in New Spain in 1607–11 and in 1612. The Spanish were jealous of the monopoly, and tried to renegotiate contracts. The Portuguese millionaire Elvas became responsible for legal slave trading, and expanded the business. Corruption and smuggling increased, but the Crown wanted the Transatlantic Slave Trade to increase, for financial reasons. Slaves were secured through trade, war or tribute, which meant engaging in local African politics.

The Dutch West India Company planned an attack on Brazil in 1623, and developed their own plantations. Slave trading seemed essential, through war with Portugal, and through trading. In 1637, the Dutch took Elmina, and in 1641, Luanda.

The Danes joined the competition from 1625, with a slow start. It had become an obvious option for European countries with maritime traditions.

The French had roots in Canada from 1603, and in the Caribbean from 1625, with a company formed in 1627 and tobacco plantations in Guadaloupe. At first slave labour was not used; this changed by 1640–45, with the needs of sugar plantations in inhospitable conditions.

English settlers were in Bermuda from 1609, then Virginia and Massachusetts, with several Caribbean possessions by 1632, including Barbados, Antigua, Nevis and Montserrat. Slaves seemed necessary in order to develop successful economic activity. They were supplied by the Dutch from 1619. King James I had licensed Robert Rich to trade in slaves between Guinea and Virginia. Hawkins had continued slave trading, and the revival of English trade included trade in slaves, often with guaranteed income to the Crown. British naval activities were largely privatised, as the government were reluctant to commit to the expenditure required for a royal fleet at time of war.

The first African slaves were seen in North American colonies in the 1630s. At first, white indentured servants were used, but the conditions of transport and of work were harsh, and slaves seemed better able to deal with the climate. Unlike indentured servants, African slaves were not to be offered eventual freedom.

WILLIAM SHAKESPEARE: "THE TEMPEST"

Shakespeare's "The Tempest", was first performed in London in 1611, as accounts were received of life in the New World. It was recognised that there would be "Rough Crossings" from Europe, on the long voyage across the Atlantic, and that the New World provided a place of refuge for those who had been engaged in political battles in Europe. In the Americas, artificial societies were being established, brave new worlds.

As an historian for a popular audience, Shakespeare provided a depiction of the key events of British history, not only from the perspective of royalty, but giving insights into the views of the common man. As a writer of tragedies and comedies, he set out and illustrated the rules which underpinned the order of things. There was little scope for social mobility, but often opportunities for laughter.

Towards the end of his career as a playwright, Shakespeare wrote "The Tempest", in which Prospero, a man of books, is ruler of his own island, which he had taken from the natural owners. Despite all his books and abstract knowledge, he depended on the practical knowledge of Caliban, who he treated as a slave. They had a working relationship.

Prospero acknowledges his dependence on Caliban:

> We cannot miss him. He does make our fire,
> Fetch in our wood, and serves in offices
> That profit us. What, ho! Slave! Caliban!
> Thou earth, thou, speak!

However, he maintains that rigid discipline is required in order to secure obedience:

> Thou most lying slave.
> Whom stripes may move, not kindness! I have used thee,
> Filth as thou art, with human care, and lodged thee
> In mine own cell, till thou didst seek to violate
> The honour of my child.

Among the themes which can be extracted from the play are the encounters between different forms of knowledge, personified by Caliban and Ariel. Caliban was physical and untutored, while Ariel was ethereal and intellectual, implementing the ideas of their master Prospero.

Despite them sharing the island for 12 years, each as apprentice to the other, Caliban, deprived of control over his own island, had made little progress on language, and Prospero had not advanced in practical skills. Furthermore, they had failed to establish a reasonable discourse. Prospero's daughter Miranda had grown up to despise Caliban:

> Abhorred slave,
> Which any print of goodness wilt not take,
> Being capable of all ill! I pitied thee,
> Took pains to make thee speak, taught thee each hour
> One thing or another. When thou didst not, savage,
> Know thine own meaning, thou wouldst gabble like
> A thing most brutish, I endowed thy purposes
> With words that made them known. But thy vile race,
> Though thou didst learn, had that in't which good natures
> Could not abide to be with. Therefore wast thou
> Deservedly confined into this rock, who hadst
> Deserved more a prison.

Caliban reciprocates.

> You taught my language, and my profit on't
> Is, I know how to curse. The red plague rid you
> For learning me your language.

Shakespeare was a master of dialogue. Through Caliban, he gave insights into a section of society with whom dialogue was not possible. Such slaves and lower orders were regarded as subject to the whims of their masters, and their maltreatment was regarded as natural. Prospero and Caliban had forgotten their common humanity, which makes discourse possible. Each needed to master common concepts, combining language and practice.

"The Tempest" ends without deaths or suffering for the major characters, who had been manipulated by Prospero.

Now I want
Spirits to enforce, art to enchant;
And my ending is despair,
Unless I be relieved by prayer,
Which pierces so, that it assaults
Mercy itself, and frees all faults.
As you from crimes would pardoned by,
Let your indulgence set me free.

The reality of international travel and slavery was very different. Millions died. Actions were remembered as crimes over many generations. As long as there was not parity of esteem, resentment could continue.

SPANISH AND DUTCH RIVALRY

The Spanish tried to maintain control of the Transatlantic Slave Trade, but suffered losses to the Dutch. The Spanish Inquisition damaged Portuguese slave trading which had been undertaken by Jewish converts to Christianity, who were burnt in public for pretending conversion. The scale of the slave trade remained modest until the 1640s, when sugar took over from tobacco as the dominant crop in the Caribbean. There were also English and other European slaves, held in Morocco.

Chaos in Spain and Portugal in 1640 ended Spanish control over the Slave Trade, and left plantations in Brazil and Peru in need of black slaves. The Dutch led an illegal slave trade, reflecting their strength in Europe and possessions in Africa and the East. The Portuguese responded with slave trading from Mozambique, and, regaining their independence, expelled the Dutch from many African bases. Trade in slaves increased, with 200,000 in 1626–50.

The English and French Caribbean became important consumers for slave imports, and the Dutch still dominated the trade, developing Congo and Curacao. The Dutch had settlements in North America until 1664, using slave labour. When New Amsterdam fell to the English, the Slave Trade switched to Barbados and Guadaloupe.

The Caribbean, for Europeans, became a base for sugar and slavery, handled by royal monopoly trading companies and mercantilist systems, placing controls on the activities of the colonies. Planters protested, and slaves and other goods were smuggled on a large scale.

The demand for sugar in Europe had spread from the rich to the poor, providing a ready and growing market for the products of the plantations. Working conditions in the plantations were harsh, and the Dutch dominated the supply of slaves. After earlier failures, the French Company of the Western Islands was founded in 1664, including trade in slaves, with Danish assistance. The Sénégal Company, from 1673, was more effective, but soon went bankrupt. Louis XIV preferred to buy the necessary slaves from the Portuguese, and used slaves as troops for his navy. The supply of slaves was jeopardised by a Muslim revolt in 1673.

LEGAL BRITISH SLAVE TRADE

Expansion in Barbados and Massachusetts seemed to require increased regular supplies of slaves, so in 1651 the Guinea Company was formed by Samuel Vassall, active in London, Massachusetts and Virginia. In 1660 the Royal Adventurers into Africa was formed by Prince Rupert, with prestigious private investors, including the philosopher John Locke in 1663. They sought to rebuild English forts in Africa which had been damaged by the Dutch and the Swedes. Slaves represented a quarter of the initial business. As the company gained in efficiency, the Dutch were challenged, and war followed, where the Dutch prevailed. There was a call for free trade in slaves, and new trading companies were formed.

In 1672 the Royal African Company was formed, taking over earlier assets, and adding new investment. Slaves were important from the start, with a license for 1,000 years, and a strong royal connection, together with plantation owners, leading City figures and John Locke. It was a joint stock company, with a need to borrow and make high profits on each voyage. Led from London, it was challenged from Bristol, with sugar refineries. By the end of the century, 60% of the company's income came from slave trading. 90,000 slaves were exported by 1689. 75,000 were sold to British North America 1673–1725. Plantation owners also used slaves from Barbados and purchased from Spanish traders, while New York traded with pirates. Slave trading was big business, across the Atlantic and within the Americas.

The Royal Africa Company prospered, and added trade with the Baltic for Swedish iron and amber, while textiles and metal goods were made in England, stimulating manufacturing industry. The foundations of the Triangular Trade were laid, involving a network of supply and distribution chains.

The Glorious Revolution of 1688 meant that the Royal Africa Company lost favour, and faced new competition. Independent traders were allowed to operate. Bristol and smaller maritime towns competed, together with Dublin and Limerick. North American colonies continued to buy slaves from the West Indies, with major expansion of African slaves from 1690. Maryland legislated to allow slavery in the 1670s, including Christian slaves. John Locke advised Carolina on the constitutional status of slaves.

EUROPEAN WEALTH FROM SUPPLYING SLAVES

The Spanish slave trade, and Spanish colonies, had crumbled, leaving reliance on Dutch, French and English traders, without producing a flow of tax income to the Spanish Crown. They bought from the English, Jamaica and the Dutch, and then bought from Barbados to supply Peru. The Spanish favoured using Genoese agents, and Dutch Sephardic Jews, with reliance on the Amsterdam market. Overall, 60,000 slaves reached Spanish America 1650–75. King Charles II of Spain regarded the slave trade as absolutely necessary. The moral dimension was recognised, but not faced. In 1690 an Order in Council in London allowed Barbados and Jamaica to trade in African slaves with Spain.

In Brazil, about 350,000 African slaves were imported in 1650–1700, with the trade dominated by Portuguese merchants, and growing links between Angola and Brazil. The market grew with the discovery of gold in Brazil. 150,000 slaves were imported in 1700–10.

Swedish and Dutch traders combined in 1649 to trade in slaves, tobacco, sugar, ivory and gold. The Duke of Courland (Lithuania) was involved in slave trading in 1651 in Gambia and Tobago. In 1651 the Danes had ambitious plans, and seized Swedish establishments in Africa. The Elector of Brandenburg (Germany) planned to take slaves from Angola, and Germans were active in 1685–1720. Profits appeared assured, so the number of trading nations increased.

By 1700 the national companies were largely failures, so the royal monopolies were relaxed. The West African coastline was crowded. The Gold Coast had settlers from Holland, England, Denmark and Brandenburg, with Portuguese, English and Dutch settlements further south. Only Portugal was interested in developing African colonies. In 1675–1700 about 600,000 slaves were exported, largely to the Caribbean. European trade had an impact on the regional economy of West Africa, and on political systems. Conquest of rival states was encouraged, as the victor could enslave the vanquished. The Slave Trade drove local African economies, where the most lucrative product was human labour.

The Spanish and Portuguese companies staggered on, but without control. There was a period of uncertainty. New deals on slave trading were done with France, under Louis XIV. Widespread illegal slave trading continued. The English sought to exclude the French, and sell to the Spanish, with a draft contract in 1707. English and French rivalry grew. The French explored a "European Common Market in slaves". There was in effect joint European exploitation of Africans.

SLAVERY AND THE TRIANGULAR TRADE

The British grew more enthusiastic about slavery as the basis for the business of gunmakers, cutlers, dyers, sailmakers, weavers, iron makers, serge makers and flannel makers. The International Slave Trade was recognised as the potential engine to drive economic development, linked to the Triangular Trade. Thus, in 1713, the Treaty of Utrecht enabled the British to supply slaves to Spanish America.

The resulting trade in the eighteenth century transformed the economic and social history of Britain. The profit was derived from the Middle Passage, conducted at a safe distance from scrutiny by critics, as slaves were transported from Africa to the Americas.

SLAVERY AND ENLIGHTENMENT

There were those who felt guilty. William Pitt the Younger, in the House of Commons in April 1792, speaking in favour of Abolition of the Transatlantic Slave Trade, declared that "No nation in Europe has plunged so deeply into this guilt as Great Britain". The result of the Transatlantic Slave Trade, to which he referred, had been economic transformation in Britain. However, the nature and extent of this transformation requires further exploration.

The privilege of handling the Spanish slave contract was sold by the British government to the British South Sea Company, with the objective of clearing the British national debt. The deal was supported by Daniel Defoe, and provided an income stream to Spain. There was opposition from Jamaica and Bristol. The plans went ahead on an international industrial scale, with aims to secure a monopoly. Queen Anne and George I were shareholders, as was Jonathan Swift.

The company did not succeed as planned. Presents were given to governors, instead of duties. Jamaica and other participating colonies maintained their independence. Private traders wanted to continue without control. Pirates operated with considerable cruelty. Trade was interrupted through war in Europe, and with Spanish insistence on slaves coming directly from Africa, to avoid charges of heresy. Company property was seized in 1727.

In 1720 there was speculation in the South Sea Company shares, involving the royal family, 462 MPs, 100 members of the House of Lords, Alexander Pope, Sir John Vanburgh, John Gay, King's College Cambridge and Lady Mary Wortley Montagu. Few considered that the company was based on the Transatlantic Slave Trade. If challenged, they would see employment by Christians in the Americas as preferable to rule by godless princes in Africa. Thomas Guy sold his shares just before the crash, and made a fortune, which endowed Guy's Hospital. Others, including Sir Isaac Newton, were ruined. The company survived, and sold 64,000 slaves in 1715–31.

Sir Isaac Newton was the prophet of Enlightenment Science, convinced that there could be a rational explanation for everything. He argued that the universe should be seen as stable, taking astronomy as the model. Society could be seen as divinely ordered and hierarchical, with each knowing their place. Having accepted that slavery was scientifically and morally acceptable, based on personal financial motivation, the establishment intellectual foundations of the Enlightenment were fractured, with implications for the subsequent history and philosophy of science.

Slavery is a defining issue for the Enlightenment, and undermines the complacent foundations of rationalism and modern science. Denis Diderot and his French Encyclopaedist colleagues appreciated the importance of practical skill, and challenged simple hierarchical views. Adam Smith expressed his opposition to slavery and the slave trade.

SLAVE TRADING AS BUSINESS

European nations, after long periods of war, were seeking economic development. The slave trade provided an obvious way of accelerating the process.

In France, the South Sea Company experience was repeated with the Mississippi Company, again involving slave trading. John Law put together the Mississippi Company, the Company of Sénégal, the French East India Company, the China Company and the Company of Africa, to form the New Company of the Indies, floated as a "mighty salvation" for France. In 1720, having added more companies, the paper value collapsed, but the company continued, selling slaves.

In the early eighteenth century the British Transatlantic Slave Trade grew immeasurably, with ships from Bristol, London, Liverpool, Whitehaven, Lancaster, Chester and Glasgow. From 1721–30, the British carried 100,000 slaves to the Americas.

The French Transatlantic Slave Trade was affected by their failing to secure the Spanish contract, and the trade was concentrated on five ports, linked to exemptions for French manufactured goods. Nantes was the main port, with Irish and Dutch merchants also involved, and local sugar refiners. Cotton and glass manufacturing also developed. Bordeaux was also active. French law covered slaves in France, but their stay was limited to three years. The black population increased. In 1721–30 the French shipped 100,000 slaves.

The Dutch remained major slave traders, with colonies in South America, and the Dutch West Indies Company carried 3,500 in 1715–31. Independent firms were also active.

The Danes were keen to follow the British example of commercial success. In 1725 their West India Company allowed slaves to be brought in by private traders. In 1733 they increased their Caribbean possessions, and switched from cotton to sugar. Fortunes were made.

The Austrian Netherlands joined the trade with the Ostende Company in 1723, but one crew of 100 were themselves captured in 1724 and sold into slavery in Algiers.

The Portuguese formed a monopoly company in 1724 to serve Brazilian gold mines, and used English manufactured goods. The trade was largely horizontal with Brazil, with Angolan slaves from inland. Diamond mining depended on slaves.

North American colonies had been slow to engage in slavery, until plantations in the Carolinas needed labour for rice and indigo, and Virginia for tobacco. Small farmers failed, and plantations offered an answer. Their needs for slaves were supplied from Britain, with caution about possible rebellions.

It was argued that slaves had better lives in North America than in the West Indies. Slaves outnumbered whites in South Carolina, where they grew rice based on seed imported from Madagascar. North Carolina, Virginia and Pennsylvania also imported slaves. There were complaints about colonial duties. British traders stepped up marketing, with demand from Rhode Island. American slave trading began from Newport in 1725, first owned by Barbados merchants, trading in rum. Providence was involved from 1736, with New York trailing behind.

Markets were broader than the Americas: the Moroccan Sultan Mulai Ismail maintained a slave army of 180,000 in 1700, and

Egypt also bought African slaves. The trade in slaves was certainly not restricted to the Transatlantic Slave Trade, although that was the focus of attention in the eighteenth century.

INDUSTRIAL REVOLUTION

The Industrial Revolution began in the eighteenth century, and continued until the recent shift to deindustrialisation. There was new politics, new warfare, medical advances, and sugar. Beet sugar had not been developed, so West Indian plantations were vital to meet increasing public demand as wealth and expensive tastes spread. Sugar was a key import for both Britain and France, meeting a massively increased demand, and producing large profits for plantation owners. From 1700–09 the per head consumption of West Indian sugar was 4 pounds; by 1780–89 it was three times as much, and by 1800–09 it was 18 pounds per head. In 150 years British consumption per head had risen 2,500%. All of this depended on African slaves.

Tobacco was also expanding. It was cultivated in Virginia. In the 1650s, 65,000 pounds of tobacco was shipped to England. Just over 10 years later, this rose to over 1,000,000 pounds per year. This had been the work of white indentured labour from Britain. By 1700 this supply had ceased. The plantation owners turned to slave labour.

Britain dominated the Transatlantic Slave Trade in 1740–50, taking over 200,000 slaves, of which 60,000 went to Virginia and the Carolinas. The motor for future economic growth was being built across the Atlantic.

The British Empire was in effect a superstructure of American commerce and naval power, on an African foundation. The Transatlantic Slave Trade was opened up on a club basis. In the 1750s Britain took another 200,000 slaves, and the French 90,000. Britain captured key French anchorages in Africa.

Britain was not alone in seeking to benefit from slave trading. Spain continued to produce sugar, and therefore needed slaves, provided via Cuba, buying from the Caribbean. A Catalan company resumed activities with Africa.

North American slave merchants rapidly became wealthy, developing international partnerships. Profit margins were 10% on slaves, compared with only 5% on other produce. Rhode Island, which did not use slaves itself, led the trading, with shipbuilding and many overseas holdings in Jamaica and elsewhere in the West Indies. Trading was active in Maryland and New York, as was Massachusetts and Pennsylvania. In 1750 Georgia legalised slavery, and trade boomed. The different states each found the necessary formula for economic growth, many relying on slavery.

Britain's victory in the Seven Years War in 1756–63 gave it ownership of the French sugar islands of Guadeloupe and Martinique, together with their slave suppliers in Africa. Havana then fell to the British in 1762, with an initial lucrative slave trade monopoly for John Kennion. The Triangular Trade boomed. The Treaty of Paris meant the return of these territories, with Britain retaining a few new sugar islands and securing Florida. Louisiana passed to Spain. The French response was to seek to develop their colonies without reliance on Britain, and with a key role for slavery.

The Transatlantic Slave Trade flourished in 1763–78, when France entered the American Revolutionary War against Britain. Coffee, tea, jam and chocolate were popular, and production depended on slaves. Britain carried 250,000 slaves in 1761–70, largely from Liverpool. West Indian society flourished for the planters, at the expense of the slaves.

France took over as leading sugar producer, and stepped up slave trading, using larger boats. Nantes, Le Havre, St Malo and Honfleur were active in slave trading. Louis XV was delighted. Trade was with Loango and Santo Domingo.

Brazil saw slavery as vital for continued economic development, as many American Indians had died or escaped. Sugar and tobacco came from plantations, relying on Portuguese slave trading companies, who were operating a transatlantic business from Luanda and Benguela.

The Spanish still wanted to work through a monopoly contract, via Puerto Rico. Now, instead of buying from Africa, they tended to trade with Jamaica and other suppliers of slaves in the Americas. Cuba was taking a dominant role.

The British shipped slaves to Florida, but little was produced from local plantations. Richard Oswald owned the first ships, and traded in Gambia and Jamaica before retiring to Ayr.

CHRISTIANITY AND SLAVERY

The slave trade took many forms. The Transatlantic Slave Trade relocated millions of Africans, making profits for the masters of the trade. Operating between continents, the trade could be treated simply as business, with difficult issues externalised, and the slaves not visible to most British citizens. British and European shareholders could concentrate on the financial results, and were spared the ordeal of encountering slaves on their home territory.

Christians have traditionally believed that their service to God provided the basis for their freedom and citizenship. This has led to a stress on obeying rules, and taking vows of obedience. This approach to service was undertaken by free will, and sometimes discussed in terms of enslavement. It contrasts with the horrors of chattel slavery, which were kept from the attention of the European population.

However, the position of the Church regarding slavery was ambiguous: the Pope had declared that native Americans should not be enslaved. Successive Popes maintained silence regarding enslavement of black Africans. It was argued that slavery offered a route to Christianity and salvation for benighted Africans, whose life at home was presented as worse than their fate in the

Americas. This argument benefited from the limited exposure of the British, and other Europeans, to the realities of slavery. Committed Christians, of all denominations, saw nothing inherently wrong about slavery and the Transatlantic Slave Trade, right until the late eighteenth century. Ignorance was bliss, and enabled the flow of profits to continue without imposing strain on the conscience.

One route from slavery to Citizenship has been through faith, through accepting that individuals by themselves could not remove the institution of slavery. Accepting that life is not all that there is, and that a place in heaven could await the good Christian, could provide a peaceful solution. However, this may be interpreted as a case for accepting the status quo, and has often been advocated by those for whom the status quo was comfortable. John Newton was a slave trader for many years before becoming a Christian minister and hymn writer, but for some years after his conversion he was not a prominent campaigner against the trade, in which the Church of England was deeply involved.

Others have been emboldened by their faith to stand up against injustice. The moral certainty of the religious leader has provided a rallying point for followers whose individual strength was insufficient. The preacher John Wesley, founder of the Methodists, wrote and spoke against slavery and the Transatlantic Slave Trade. He preached a social gospel, and called for social inclusion.

We are left with a number of unresolved paradoxes. Whereas opinion formers in the twenty first century would find it impossible to offer a public defence of slavery, the situation was clearly different in the eighteenth century, even in the Christian Church.

The situation should be recognisable for those concerned with business ethics in the twenty first century. There are areas of business activity today, such as the arms trade, tobacco, alcohol or asbestos, where it may not be advisable to probe beneath the surface if one wishes to enjoy profits with a good conscience.

CONCLUSION

For over five hundred years, European prosperity and economic development were linked to the exploitation of Africans as a source of slave labour, providing the motor for growth. This unbalanced relationship was relatively manageable while the continents were largely separate, and news was slow to travel.

In light of the contradictions between the principles of Christianity and Democracy, which are seen as central to European civilisation, and the practice of chattel slavery, there is unfinished business to be resolved before world citizenship can be achieved. It is not simply a matter of economic exploitation. Doubt has been cast on the moral content of both Christianity and the Enlightenment. Europe's claims to civilisation, and a civilising mission, are left tarnished, to say the least.

CHAPTER 3

ECONOMIC DEVELOPMENT

Happy, Happy lad! What a fortune is thine! – Look around to see the
miserable fate of almost all our unfortunate colour – superadded to
ignorance, – see slavery, and the contempt of those very wretches who
roll in affluence from our labours. Superadded to this woeful catalogue
– hear the ill-bred and heart-racking abuse of the foolish vulgar.

King, R. et al. (ed.) (1997) *Ignatius Sancho on Black Slavery in London.*
London, National Portrait Gallery

It is tempting to look for simple explanations. However, it would
be a mistake to argue that slavery was an inevitable accompaniment
to capitalism. Slavery pre-dated capitalism, and caused major
debates among the economists and theoreticians.

DISCONTINUITY

It is important to understand how slavery could have a place in the
workplace and economic development. Economic development

does not always proceed smoothly. There can be major dis-continuities, requiring fresh strategies. These need to be presented to decision makers in terms which satisfy adherents to old ways of thinking. Arguments can be made in terms of change, and presented as temporary or transitional. This is a way of claiming new criteria against which decisions are to be considered.

At the point of transition between economic phases, or paradigms, there are difficult decisions to be made. Entrepreneurs will seek to proceed, tackling new challenges, and giving partial accounts of their activities.

The workplace is not separate from society as a whole. It is an arena for public health and for developing collective approaches. It is an environment for learning. Every workplace is a "knowledge workplace", with different kinds of knowledge deployed in various ways. The Enlightenment Encyclopaedists saw the importance of practical knowledge, complementing theoretical knowledge which tended to be emphasised by academics.

THE BUSINESS CASE

It is not difficult to identify the business case for the Transatlantic Slave Trade. The establishment of colonies in the New World enabled new crops to be grown, and new minerals to be extracted, resulting in exports. As the communities grew, they could also be consumers of goods manufactured in Europe. This led to a demand for labour, and laid the foundations for a flourishing Triangular Trade whose profits helped to fund industrialisation at home in Europe.

There were few native Americans available, and many soon died of European diseases. Normal use of voluntary immigrant labour or indentured servants encountered difficulty, as insufficient numbers of European workers were being freed from agrarian work. The Pope had ruled that native Americans could not be enslaved.

African slaves provided an answer: there was an apparently inexhaustible supply. There was an existing system of African slave traders, the Atlantic Ocean currents flowed in the right direction, and the Transatlantic Slave Trade could generate healthy profits from buying and selling. There was the additional bonus of profits from cargo carried on the other two parts of the round trip.

For Britain, which was developing overseas colonies and sought to maintain international naval power, the arguments were distinctive. The benefits of participation in the Transatlantic Slave Trade could be seen in terms of increased domestic wealth and employment in the home country. The trade in slaves could be conducted offshore, away from public view, and at limited expense. It was easy for businessmen and ordinary citizens to disregard what was taking place out of sight, and just enjoy the benefits.

THE LEGAL SITUATION

The legal situation of slaves in England remained ambiguous. Lord Chief Justice Mansfield tried a number of key cases, some of them instigated by Granville Sharp. There was an apparent contradiction between British domestic liberties, in which the country took pride, and slavery.

Sir William Blackstone published "Commentaries on the Laws of England" in 1765. In the first edition he wrote:

> A slave or a Negro, the moment he lands in England, falls under the protection of the laws, and with regard to all natural rights becomes eo instanti a freeman.

It is clear that he was placed under pressure by plantation owners and their supporters in England. Thus the second edition reads:

> A slave or a Negro, the moment he lands in England, falls under the protection of the laws, and so far becomes a freeman; though the master's right to his service may probably still continue.

The law remained far from clear. However, there was a continuing series of cases. The slave Jonathan Strong, who was in England, in a case in 1765, was saved from being returned to slavery after being badly beaten. James Somerset, in a case in 1771–1772, was saved from being taken out of England as a slave. The greatest public response was to the case of the slave ship Zong (1783), where 132 slaves were thrown overboard, so that the owners could claim insurance. In the last case, Sharp lost the case, and the slaves were ruled to have been the owner's property. Reports of the cases served to raise awareness. Concern was further raised when Sir William Dolben and some associates visited a slave ship on the Thames, and this resulted in legislation to regulate the carrying of slaves to Africa, which became law in 1788.

The British colonies in the West Indies were not ruled as a group, but each had links to Britain. They relied on a basis of English law, and the working assumption was that this law did not prohibit slavery. The British government reserved the right to control the slave trade, and disallowed an attempt by the Jamaican local Assembly in 1774 to limit the import of slaves. In general, the laws were interpreted in the interests of the plantation owners, many of whom also had Parliamentary seats at Westminster. The position of slaves was set out in the 1674 Act of Jamaica:

> All Negroes legally bought as bondslaves shall here continue to be so and further be held and judged and taken to be goods and chattels and ought to come into the hands of Executors . . . as other assets do, their Christianity or any Law, Custom or Usage in England or elsewhere to the contrary not withstanding.

In Barbados in 1680, the island was dominated by the plantation owners. Two hundred each had properties worked by more than 60 slaves. The biggest planter had more than 1,000 acres. The second biggest, Christopher Codrington, owned more than 600 acres. His land funded the establishment of All Soul's College, Oxford, and his estate was inherited by the Society for the Propagation of the Gospel in 1710.

PRIVATE ENTERPRISE

It was important economically to imagine that the Slave Trade was simply a matter of business. "Free trade" was a useful principle on which to campaign, while avoiding definitions of what was meant by "freedom", or the details of the "trade" in human beings.

The British entry into the Transatlantic Slave Trade, and their subsequent domination of the supply of slaves to the different European empires, was a matter of private enterprise. As long as the government of the day received a share of the spoils of privateering, they were generally happy to turn a blind eye to details of the activities which provided the income. This was the established basis on which navies had been organised and financed. The defence of the realm was largely in private hands.

So much of the history of the island depended on chance: the wind and weather were the best defence against invasion. All being well, great profits could be derived from modest investments.

Adam Smith argued that where advantage could be gained through using skilled and committed workers, slavery would be uncompetitive and unsustainable. Slave labour cannot compete with a motivated free workforce, equipped with appropriate work organisation and technology. Where work requires the exercise of knowledge, this implies active voluntary commitment. Thus the advance of industrialisation meant the decline of slavery. The contexts for the work of slaves varied, in different parts of the New World.

Adam Smith, whose "The Wealth of Nations" (1776) is frequently cited as the basis for modern business, located his account of capitalism in a framework of well-developed moral principles. In "A Theory of Moral Sentiment" (1759) he outlined "A mercenary exchange of good offices according to agreed valuation".

> . . . All the members of human society stand in need of each other's assistance, and are likewise exposed to mutual injuries. Where the necessary assistance is reciprocally afforded from love, from

gratitude, from friendship, and esteem, the society flourishes and is happy. All the different members of it are bound together by the agreeable bands of love and affection, and are, as it were, drawn to one common centre of mutual good offices.

This does not sound like capitalism based on market forces alone, or a society which includes slaves who are regarded as less than fully human.

But though the necessary assistance should not be afforded from generous and disinterested motives, though among the different members of the society there should be no mutual love and affection, the society, though less happy and agreeable, will not necessarily be dissolved. Society may subsist among different men, as among different merchants, from a sense of its utility, without any mutual love or affection: and though no man in it should owe any obligation, or be bound in gratitude to any other, it may still be upheld by a mercenary exchange of good offices according to an agreed valuation.

He argued that we need a basis on which to exchange services. Justice is a precondition for sustainable social relationships. Agreed valuations depend on shared access to knowledge.

Society, however, cannot subsist among those who are at all times ready to hurt and injure one another. The moment that injury begins, thee moment that mutual resentment and animosity take place, all the bands of it are broken asunder, and the different members of which it consisted, are, as it were, dissipated and scattered abroad by the violence and opposition of their discordant affections. If there is any society among robbers and murderers, they must at least, according to the trite observation, abstain from robbing and murdering one another. Beneficence, therefore, is less essential to the existence of society than justice. Society may subsist, though not in the most comfortable state, without beneficence; but the prevalence of injustice must utterly destroy it.

There is such a thing as society. It is not just a matter of individuals and their families. It is hard to see how the Slave Trade and slavery could operate in the moral environment sketched by Smith. Rather, the inherent injustice of slavery could be seen as endangering society as a whole.

> Though nature, therefore, exhorts mankind to acts of beneficence, by the pleasing consciousness of deserved reward, she has not thought it necessary to guard and enforce the practice of it by the terrors of merited punishment in case it should be neglected. It is the ornament which embellishes, not the foundation which supports the building, and which it was, therefore, sufficient to recommend, but by no means necessary to impose. Justice, on the contrary, is the main pillar that upholds the whole edifice. If it is removed, the great, the immense fabric of human society, that fabric which, to raise and support, seems, in this world, if I may say so, to have been the peculiar and darling care of nature, must in a moment crumble into atoms.

He opposes over-burdensome regulations, but argues the case for justice. This has moral foundations. Slave traders evaded justice, in part by ensuring that details of their actions remained unobserved.

> In order to enforce the observation of justice, therefore, nature has implanted in the human breast that consciousness of ill desert, those terrors of merited punishment, which attend upon its violation, as the great safeguards of the association of mankind, to protect the weak, to curb the violent, and to chastise the guilty. Men, though naturally sympathetic, feel so little for an other, with whom they have no particular connection, in comparison of what they feel for themselves; the misery of one, who is merely their fellow-creature, is of so little importance to them in comparison even of a small conveniency of their own; they have it so much in their power to hurt him, and may have so many temptations to do so, that if this principle did not stand up within them in his defence, and overawe them into a respect for his innocence, they would, like wild beasts, be at all times ready to fly upon him; and a man would enter an assembly of men as he enters a den of lions.

It was clearly important to protect British citizens from the knowledge of the details of slavery, which provided so many products from which they benefited. As long as the British citizen was kept in ignorance of the realities of the Slave Trade, it could continue.

Adam Smith found slavery explicable, but morally unacceptable. He argued that it could never be as effective as the use of paid labour, which was provided on the basis of contracts which should be freely entered into. Smith was a moral philosopher. One problem has been that many of the readers of "The Wealth of Nations" have chosen not to locate it in the moral framework of "A Theory of Moral Sentiment".

THE BRITISH SLAVE TRADE

There was much to concern Adam Smith. The British were not simply minor players in the international slave trade. They dominated it during the eighteenth century. British prospects for growth looked good, with colonies in North America and the West Indies, meaning that exports largely went outside Europe. By 1750 half the British exports to Africa were re-exports from Europe. In the 1730s British ships took 170,000 slaves. British contraband annoyed the Spanish, and led to war. Bristol declined, as Liverpool grew.

London

London was the key port for the financial transactions associated with the slave trade, and handled 75% of sugar imports. It was the base for the Royal African Company, which held the monopoly of trade from 1672 to 1698. It administered trading posts on the West African coast, and was responsible for seizing any English ships, other than its own, involved in slaving.

During the eighteenth century other ports took on leading roles, but London continued to benefit. The financial might of the City of London, and the expanding system of docks, represents a lasting legacy. From 1721–30 the British carried 100,000 slaves to the Americas.

The leading trader was MP and Governor of the Bank of England, Humphrey Morice. He pioneered medical treatment, and measures against scurvy. In the 1730s Bristol became the leading slave port, and Liverpool overtook London. Jamaica had become the leading colony, overtaking the smaller Barbados.

The West India Company played a continuing role in the development of London, as is shown in the Museum in Docklands, and the statue to Robert Milligan, remembered as a merchant and civic benefactor, rather than as a slave trader. Lord Mayor William Beckford (1709–70) is remembered with a statue in Guildhall. He had a home at Fonthill, near Salisbury, and kept 22,000 acres, and Drax Hall, in Jamaica.

Slavery provided the foundations for the banks established by Alexander and David Barclay, and by Francis Baring, who earned £7,000,000 from slave trading.

There are numerous sites associated with the Slave Trade (Pocock, 2000). The Countess of Home, with a fortune from plantations in Jamaica, lived in Portman Square, where her house became the Courtauld Institute of Art. Also in Portman Square were the Beckford family (plantation owners and a Lord Mayor of London), Admiral Lord Rodney and Mrs Edwin Lascelles, with a fortune from Barbados. A walking tour of the West End could include homes in Wimpole Street, Queen Anne Street, Baker Street and Cavendish Square.

Around London are further sites with a revealing history. Sion House was bought by Monserrat merchant Nicholas Tuite in 1749. The importance of coffee, a product of slave plantations, is shown by the fact that by 1700 there were 3,000 coffee houses in London, the most famous in the area of Covent Garden: Bedford Coffee House, Child's Coffee House, Piazza Coffee House, Slaughter's Coffee House, Somerset Coffee House and Turk's Head Coffee House.

Bath

Fashionable members of London society also had houses in Bath, funded by estates in the West Indies (Pocock, 2003). The Pulteney family developed the Bathwick estate. William Beckford, son of the Lord Mayor of London, moved to Bath after the collapse of his fortunes. William Pitt the Elder was MP for Bath; Pitt the Younger lived in Bath in 1802, and was aware of local concerns in Bristol about threats to the slave trade. William Wilberforce lived in Bath for a time, and Josiah Wedgwood opened a showroom there in 1772. The atmosphere changed in Bath with a financial crash from 1792. New resorts such as Cheltenham and Brighton rose in popularity.

Jane Austen and her family lived in a series of houses in Bath, before returning to Hampshire. Her father was trustee of a plantation in Antigua, and her godfather James Langford Nibbs was a plantation owner. Her two brothers Francis and Charles were sailors who rose to the rank of Admiral and Rear Admiral, over long careers. They had worked with Nelson, who saw himself as a defender of the slave trade, because of the importance of the West Indies to the British economy, bringing in 80% of overseas income. Jane Austen was clearly concerned with the issue of slavery. Her novel "Mansfield Park" was informed by her knowledge of the Knight family, with Godmersham Manor in Kent, and plantations in the West Indies. The novel reported silence on the subject of slavery, when the issue was raised by Fanny Price. In 1812 it was difficult for a family which was at the time associated with plantations to make critical comments. Jane Austen declared to her sister Cassandra, in a letter on 24 January 1813, that she had been "in love" with Thomas Clarkson, who she knew as the author of "The History of the Abolition of the Slave Trade", published in 1808. Francis and Charles were both involved in naval actions to enforce the prohibition, and Francis reported his horror at the conditions they found on a Portuguese slave ship, en route to Rio de Janeiro.

Bristol

After 1698, Bristol was able to use its position as an Atlantic port to become a major player in the slave trade. For 50 years it was Britain's main slaving port. It grew in population and wealth, and became England's second city. Georgian properties were developed in Queen Square, Dowry Square, St James Square, King Square and Orchard Street.

Bristol was an expensive port to use; the harbour suffered extremes of high and low tide, and as ships became larger they had difficulties on the Avon.

Thomas Goldney was an Bristol entrepreneur, active in the slave trade, who worked with Abraham Darby, one of the pioneers in the early Industrial Revolution at Ironbridge. Through the work of individuals, the slave trade fuelled investment in the new industries.

The slave trade, and the associated triangular trade, provided opportunities even for the smallest business in the area, as was noted by John Cary:

> A trade of the most advantage to this kingdom of any we drive, and as it were all profit, the first cost being little more than small matters of our own manufactures, for which we have in return, gold, elephants' teeth, wax and negroes, the last whereof is much better than the first, being indeed the best traffic the kingdom hath, as it doth occasionally give so vast an employment to our people both by sea and land. (Martin, 1999, p. 49)

Abraham Elton was able to build several successful careers, as a mariner and copper trader, merchant venturer, and then mayor of Bristol.

The Slave Trade enabled Bristol to be transformed into a leading port and a major city, with proud civic buildings. Successful businessmen such as Edward Colston of Bristol, with engagement in the slave trade, West Indian plantations and the Royal Africa Company, could present themselves as public benefactors, while the nature of the trade which provided their wealth was not discussed. The many statues and plaques in his memory omit any mention of the slave trade. He owned a fleet of ships which traded with St Kitts', and a sugar refinery in Castle Park. The Codrington family owned another sugar refinery. The Wills tobacco industry began in Bristol 1768–88.

The homes of slave traders and privateers have been preserved (Pocock, 2003): Thomas King, Edmund Sanders, Joseph Holbrook, Henry Bright, Woodes Rogers, Henry Webb and James McTaggart.

Liverpool

The Slave Trade was central to the growth of Liverpool, complemented by local industries for export: linen, glass, metal, leather and shipbuilding. Slave trading began in 1690, specialising in the Spanish empire. Using geographical location, and with the Isle of Man as a warehouse, the trade grew each year.

Foster Cunliffe was a leading slave trader, and mayor three times, with an office in Maryland. The local MPs were largely slave traders, founding dynasties. Lancashire cotton was exported, selling to Africa and North America. Shipbuilders were also slave traders. There was limited trade in Africans to England, with public advertisements of sale.

Liverpool's port charges were much lower than Bristol's; with its long deep waterfront it was a much more efficient port and could accommodate larger ships. The demand for slaves carried in

Liverpool ships rose. Slaves were delivered primarily to Barbados, Jamaica and Virginia.

By the 1780s nearly twice as many Africa trade vessels were clearing each year from Liverpool as London and Bristol combined. By the end of the eighteenth century, Liverpool had over 60% of the British trade, and 40% of the European trade. Liverpool's net proceeds from the African trade in 1783–93 were over £12m, from 878 voyages and the sale of 300,000 slaves. In 1807, on the eve of Abolition, 1,283 slaving vessels were cleared from British ports, of which 1,099 were from Liverpool. Liverpool had almost established a monopoly.

J. Wallace, in 1795, noted that investing in the Slave Trade provided opportunities for all, encouraging a form of popular capitalism.

> Almost every man in Liverpool is a merchant, and he who cannot send a bale will send a bandbox. The attractive African meteor has so dazzled their ideas that almost every order of people is interested in a Guinea cargo. It is well known that many of the small vessels that import about a hundred slaves are fitted out by attorneys, drapers, ropers, grocers, tallow-chandlers, barbers, tailors etc, some have one-eighth, some a fifteenth, and some a thirty-second.

Arthur and Benjamin Heywood built a bank based on servicing the Slave Trade: this was later taken over by the Bank of Liverpool, Martin's, and then Barclays. Thomas Leyland transported 3,500 slaves to Jamaica between 1782 and 1807. He was a mayor of Liverpool and founded a bank which was taken over by Midland, now HSBC. John Gladstone was a successful slave trader, and father of Prime Minister William Ewart Gladstone.

Liverpool city centre displays the legacy of slavery, with numerous buildings and monuments (Pocock, 2001). The abolitionist MP William Roscoe (1753–1831), is buried in Renshaw Street Unitarian Chapel. Bluecoat School was funded by a group of slave traders, and built 1716–17. The Town Hall was built by slave traders Joseph and Jonathan Brooks. Even Penny Lane, made famous by the Beatles, was named after the slave trader James Penny, and there are debates about whether the name should be changed. Every time that we hear "the barber shaves another customer", we may be reminded of the slave trade.

TRADING IN HUMAN LABOUR

People who had been free, citizens (or at least not the property of others) in their own countries, had been abducted, transported overseas, and put into slavery. As slaves, they were thus classified as lower than the lowest classes. This argument is complicated by the fact that the Transatlantic Slave Trade was not simply a matter of raiding the coasts of Africa, but involved a complex trade in people, including across the Sahara. In the name of business, human labour was reduced to a commodity, to be bought and sold. As far as slave traders and slave owners were concerned, slaves were seen in terms of their potential for labour and for breeding. Previous skills, experience and knowledge were of no interest.

Although few slaves came to Britain, it has been calculated that at the end of the eighteenth century there were 1 million slaves working 3,000 hours per year unpaid, in overseas plantations, producing sugar, tea and coffee. The population of England was 5 million. There were black communities in London, Bristol and Liverpool, but colour bars inhibited their development and integration.

CAPITALISM AND SLAVERY

Eric Williams, who was later Prime Minister of Trinidad and Tobago, in "Capitalism and slavery" (1944) analysed the links between the Transatlantic Slave Trade and the early development of capitalism. He argued that in the UK, great banks were founded and great businesses were based on the profits of the slave system.

Williams analysed the rationalisation of slavery in terms of issues such as climate, which usefully clouded the fact that slavery was a political and economic institution. Once it became less economically vital, he argued, it became prudent to abolish it. As Williams put it "The Negroes had been stimulated to freedom by the development of the very wealth which their labour had created".

Williams summarised his conclusions:

1. The decisive forces in the period of history we have discussed are the developing economic forces.
2. The various contending groups of dominant merchants, indus- trialists and politicians, while keenly aware of immediate inter- ests, are for that very reason generally blind to the long-range consequences of their various actions, proposals and policies.
3. The political and moral ideas of the age are to be examined in the very closest relation to the economic development.
4. An outworn interest, whose bankruptcy smells to heaven in historical perspective, can exercise an obstructionist and disrup- tive effect which can only be explained by the powerful services it had previously rendered and the entrenchment previously gained.
5. The ideas based on these interests continue long after the inter- ests have been destroyed and work their old mischief, which is all the more mischievous because the interests to which they corresponded no longer exist.

There are largely unexplored implications of Williams' argument that the profits of slavery funded the first industrial revolution in the UK. This would mean that the official myths of how the UK led the way to economic development, through success in agrarian innovation, and the harnessing of natural resources such as coal, iron, water and wool, have left out something fundamental. Whereas other countries had to reform their financial systems, and overcome obstacles of education and social class, in order to industrialise sustainably, the British were different. The Transatlantic Slave Trade provided an income stream just when it was needed, to kick start the process. Transformation of the enabling infrastructure was postponed.

Slavery fitted well with the British class system, and even with aspects of life in independent schools, many of which were funded from the profits of the Slave Trade. A feeling of natural superiority, backed by money, could secure access to the ruling class, and work could then be delegated or outsourced to others, with the added refinement of recruiting another group to act as middle managers, dealing with operations, and leaving superior beings to deal with "strategy".

Slaves contributed vastly to Britain's rise as an industrial nation. Slavers needed ships; crews needed provisions; traders needed goods to barter for slaves: fetters, chains, padlocks, guns, pots, kettles; plantations needed machinery; rum factories needed bottles. Cotton picked by slave labour in New England was manufactured in Lancashire and sold on the colonial market, mostly Africa. Investors loaned money to slavers, bankers banked their profits, insurers insured their ships and cargoes. Slavery, and the Transatlantic Slave Trade, were good for business.

INVOLVEMENT IN THE TRIANGULAR TRADE

Goods from Britain, as the industrial revolution developed, were transported to West Africa. These included guns, shackles and muzzles manufactured in Birmingham, and textiles from Lancashire. In West Africa the cargo was offloaded, and replaced with slaves, which were transported to the Americas on "the middle passage". On the final stage of the journey, ships brought luxuries for the coffee houses, such as coffee, sugar, chocolate and rum, together with raw cotton for processing in Lancashire.

The journeys on all three stages were aided by prevailing winds and currents. Merchants expected a high rate of return on their investments. Sailors gambled that they would survive enough voyages to be able to take early retirement. As for the slaves, they were simply cargo, supplied to North America, the West Indies and South America.

Small local banks were established, to handle the finances of the Triangular Trade and local merchants. With amalgamations, banks founded in Bristol and Liverpool became, for example, Barclays and HSBC. They provided a remarkably effective and efficient system for raising and deploying funds with minimum disclosure. The key transactions were off the balance sheet in Britain, so did not need to be discussed with shareholders or tax-payers. The banks received the profits, and were able to assist their clients to gain maximum economic and social advantage.

From a business and public relations perspective the Transatlantic Slave Trade had many advantages. The slaves did not come to Britain. The key revenue earning stage of the Triangular Trade, together with the plantations which produced sugar by slave labour, were overseas, out of sight. Enough plantation owners had seats in the House of Commons to ensure that their business was not threatened. The commercial arguments were in terms of competitiveness. Slaves were property, and were not considered to have human rights. Their labour came free, but was everywhere in chains.

THE ECONOMIC IMPACT OF SLAVERY

There is an opportunity for research by local historians of all ages. The impact of slavery has been understated in the published literature, whether we consider books, or guides to stately homes. Recent discussions of the Slave Trade have highlighted the roles of key ports such as London, Bristol and Liverpool, but have failed to grasp the extent to which the slave trade financed Britain as a whole, affecting both public and private sectors.

There have been widespread calls for apologies to be offered. Andrew Hawkins, a descendant of William and John Hawkins, the sailors who started British engagement in the slave trade, went in chains to Banjoul, in Gambia, to apologise.

British Prime Minister Tony Blair has indicated that he sees no case for an apology. The debate in Bristol on 10 May 2006, discussing whether the City of Bristol should apologise for its role in the Transatlantic Slave Trade, concentrated on the role of the city in the slave trade, and voted against an apology. They neglected to consider the wider role of Britain as a whole.

A common argument is that individuals cannot sensibly accept responsibility for the actions of their ancestors. However, it is apparent that many of those who are happy to distance themselves from responsibility for the past have very little understanding of what happened. They do not recognise the depth of feeling among the descendants of slaves, and the factual evidence on which it is based.

The Transatlantic Slave Trade was not just a matter of isolated atrocities committed by maverick sea captains and their brutalised crews. It was integral to the Triangular Trade, driving British economic and social development. To the extent that there was an economic, social and political system in Britain, it was all affected.

BLACK PLAQUES

It is not always easy to trace the route taken by the money. Those who were personally involved in slavery did not want to discuss the details. On the other hand, they were keen to be remembered as leading local citizens and civic benefactors. Schools, town halls and monuments proclaim their virtues, but do not dwell on the source of their wealth. The people of Bristol and Liverpool are now coming to terms with the origins of the funds for many of their public buildings, including schools. A similar reassessment is needed in the City of London. Having unearthed new details of the past, a profound moral question arises. What, if anything, is to be done? Who were the founders of local schools and hospitals in the seventeenth and eighteenth centuries? What was the source of the money?

We could institute a new system of "Black Plaques", to be awarded to institutions or buildings with previously undisclosed links to slavery. We could start with a closer investigation of the various properties managed by the National Trust, whose buildings had often been funded from West Indian fortunes.

One purpose of gaining wealth, by means which were not to be discussed in polite company, was to secure social advancement. In the eighteenth century numerous ostentatious Palladian mansions were built, often funded by the fortunes of Jamaican heiresses. As with William Beckford's Fonthill Abbey, the origins of the money in the profits of the Transatlantic Slave Trade were hidden. Visiting your local stately home, are there gaps in the historical account which may now be explained? How was it that there were so many extravagant country houses built across the country, by individuals and families who did not seem active in business in Britain? There are numerous cases from which we could choose, from the rich British national heritage of stately homes dating from the eighteenth century, many of them now in the care of the National Trust.

Clandon Park

Elizabeth Knight was heiress to a considerable fortune from Jamaica, where her father owned several sugar plantations and was a successful slave trader. She married Thomas, the second Baron

Onslow (1679–1740) and her fortune enabled him to rebuild Clandon Park, near Guildford. In addition, the family used the balance of the estate to purchase the land where Guildford Cathedral, Surrey University and Onslow Village now stand.

Thomas' younger brother Arthur was the third of the Onslow family to hold the office of Speaker of the House of Commons. Arthur (1691–1768) was Speaker for 33 years, and introduced the keeping of records of Parliamentary business. His portrait hangs with that of Richard (1528–71) and Richard, first Baron (1654–1717), the earlier Onslow speakers, in the Speakers' Parlour at Clandon Park. In 1801, George Onslow was created the first Earl of Onslow.

The combination of Jamaican money and English social standing was powerful and far from unusual. The novels of Jane Austen (such as "Mansfield Park"), and the Brontës, give fictional examples, with little reference to detail.

Apart from these passing biographical details about Elizabeth Knight, the visitor to a superb Palladian country house would see no reference to slavery, beyond the ceiling in the Marble Hall, by Giuseppe Artari, who depicted slaves breaking out from the ceiling and into the entablature in the manner of Italian baroque painters and sculptors. The house is now open to visitors, and laid out as it was in 1778, when an inventory was made of the rooms and contents.

After the injection of the Jamaican money through the marriage to Elizabeth Knight, the family fortunes of the Onslows suffered a decline. The family became unable to maintain Clandon Park as a family home. The 6th Earl sold the house to his aunt, the Countess of Iveagh, who presented it to the National Trust in 1956. The house now hosts the collection of eighteenth century furniture and porcelain which was a bequest of Mrs David Gubbay, who had spent much of her life in India, before moving to London.

As the visitor walks around the stately home, in the care of the National Trust, local residents provide a wealth of detail of the

Onslow family and the Gubbay collection. Around the house, the well-kept gardens in the style of Capability Brown include a Maori House from New Zealand, where an Onslow was Governor-General, and a grotto. The visitor in 2006 is given almost no indication of the link between the stately home and its sordid source of funding. The guide merely remarks "Elizabeth Knight, whose Jamaican fortune may have prompted the construction of the house".

David Dabydeen argued

> There were two grand tours. There was the English gentleman who makes his grand tour to Italy and to France, to bring back home artifacts of that civilization, which are mostly sculptures and paintings. And there was the other simultaneous grand tour, which is of Africans from the West Coast of Africa to the Caribbean and to the New World plantations. These two grand tours were intimately entwined. The first grand tour could not have existed without the second. (Martin, 1999, p. 130)

We have to begin to redescribe the basis of what it was to be considered educated in the eighteenth century.

Eynsham Hall

Eynsham Hall, near Witney in Oxfordshire, was built in the 1770s by Robert Lacy and his son Willoughby. The Lacy family were active in the West India Company, and the Willoughbys had been leading settlers in Barbados, with the royal warrant and the title of Governor. Apart from building Eynsham Hall, Willoughby Lacy invested in the Drury Lane Theatre, in partnership with David Garrick, Garrick's brother, and James Lacy. The gardens at Eynsham Hall are laid out in the style of Capability Brown, and the interior furnishings showed the influence of Robert Adam, although there is no evidence of Adam working at Eynsham Hall. Both country homes and the London theatre benefited from finance derived from slavery.

The Coffee House Challenge

It is often argued that the slave trade involved only a small minority of the British population in the eighteenth century. It is true that relatively few British went to sea, and indeed mortality rates among sailors were high. However, the products of the Triangular Trade, to which the slave trade contributed, were in universal demand.

Fashionable London society was based on consuming the products of slave labour internationally: coffee, tea, sugar, chocolate and rum. Ideas could be exchanged, between leading society figures who had been investors in the South Sea Company. With the prospect of large assured profits, few asked about the basic activity of the company, which was selling slaves to the Spanish Empire.

Those who drank in some 500 coffee houses around London took their luxuries for granted. Their successors today have begun to support Fair Trade, in opposition to modern forms of slavery and exploitation. This builds on the example of the boycott of sugar, organised by the abolitionists in 1792.

Whereas straightforward documentary evidence regarding the slave trade can be in short supply, much can be learned from contemporary poetry, which, as in the case of Cowper, manages to make a serious point while retaining, in the last couplet, a sense of humour.

> I own I am shocked by the purchase of slaves,
> And fear those who buy and sell them are knaves;
> What I hear of their hardships, their tortures and groans,
> Is almost enough to drive pity from stones.
>
> I pity them greatly, but I must be mum,
> For how could we do without sugar and rum?
>
> (William Cowper "Pity for Poor Africans" (1787))

SOCIAL CAPITAL

Britain was the first country to experience an industrial revolution, which involved processes of social capital formation and agglomeration in building new companies and factories. Perhaps in parallel was social capital formation in Non Governmental Organisations (NGOs), finding new ways of working together. Individual expressions of concern are less effective than concerted activities with a foundation of research. Here good offices are exchanged based on shared valuations and beliefs, in a non-mercenary interpretation of Adam Smith.

The key was to develop an idea, building an organisational structure, and making change; in short: entrepreneurship. This has meant individuals realising that they could make a difference. They could escape from external control in building a new company or movement, and enable a broader level of participation.

The industrial revolution involved a transition from slavery to employment. The abolitionist movement represented a transition from individuals as subjects to individuals as citizens. Conventionally these two processes have been considered separately. Here we link the two, considering work organisation, and citizenship in the workplace.

THE ENGLISH ENLIGHTENMENT

From the outside, the British establishment and the industrial revolution may have been seen as united, and governed by orthodoxy. In fact, internal divisions continued.

Scientific and industrial advances in eighteenth century England were being made by dissenting entrepreneurs from the provinces. This was a new generation, distinct from the slave traders and plantation owners who used their wealth gained overseas in order to buy social position and property in England. The new entrepreneurs had much in common with their Quaker predecessor John Bellers, and shared moral assumptions with Adam Smith. The English Enlightenment was not, like the contemporary movements in France or Scotland, driven by academic theory from the old universities. On the contrary, dissenters were barred from attending Oxford and Cambridge, where statements of Anglican faith were required. The English Enlightenment was diffuse and pragmatic, with a strong element of rejection of the establishment. The Lunar Society, based in Birmingham, cultivated links with Thomas Jefferson and Benjamin Franklin in North America, and with Jean Jacques Rousseau in France.

The two groups both made use of the same banks, but their life experiences, beliefs and objectives were different. The industrial working class and the urban middle class were distinct again. With limited communication between the classes, and an absence of democracy worthy of the name, the obscenity of slavery and the Transatlantic Slave Trade was allowed to continue off shore. Money from trade, and in particular from sugar plantations and the slave trade, allowed one to buy a place in society.

It was only with the American Declaration of Independence that the issue of slavery came to public attention. How, it was argued, could the Americans claim beliefs such as "life, liberty and the pursuit of happiness", while continuing to own slaves? Having posed such questions, the uncomfortable fact of British dominance of the Transatlantic Slave Trade received attention. Dissenters felt shame, and sought to distance themselves from associations with the trade.

JOSIAH WEDGWOOD

Josiah Wedgwood was a pioneer in the industrial revolution, with a humble background as a working potter. A self-made man, whose fortunes were bolstered when he married his cousin, he built a world-leading pottery company which sought to break the mould. Among his favourite projects was the campaign to abolish the Transatlantic Slave Trade.

Joseph Priestley, Thomas Boulton, James Watt and the Lunar Society, many of them Unitarians, bridged the gap between business and social concern. Wedgwood was a master of the science and technology of pottery, testing numerous alternative combinations of materials to produce memorable products. Wedgwood worked with the leading artists of the period, such as James Flaxman. He tried to catch the attention of the leading opinion formers, such as royalty, and then made their favourite products available to a wider audience, at premium prices.

He is remembered particularly for Jasper, Queen's Ware, and the Frog Service which was made for Catherine the Great of Russia. His product range included ornamental items and medals. Among these was the medal created for the Committee for the Abolition of the Slave Trade, depicting a kneeling slave, with the motto "Am I not a man and a brother?".

Wedgwood wrote to James Watt in 1788:

> I take it for granted that you and I are on the same side of the question regarding the slave trade. I have joined my brethren here in a petition for abolition of it, as I do not take a half measure in this black business. (Uglow, 2002, p. 11)

On 29 February 1788 he wrote to Benjamin Franklin:

> This will be an epoch before unknown to the world, and while relief is given to millions of our fellow creatures immediately the object of it, the subject of freedom will be more canvassed and better understood in the enlightened nations. (Uglow, 2002, p. 412)

Wedgwood's colleague Erasmus Darwin was shocked when he encountered manacles, made in Birmingham and sold for use with African slaves. He wrote to Wedgwood on 13 April 1789:

I have just heard that there are manacles or gags made at Birmingham for the slaves in our islands. If this be true, and such an instrument could be exhibited by a speaker in the House of Commons, it might have great effect. (Uglow, 2002, p. 413)

In what has widely been termed the age of revolution, the sympathies of the dissenting entrepreneurs lay with American Independence and the French Revolution. Wedgwood and his colleagues were concerned to build a better modern world, and not merely to perpetuate the existing system which they saw as corrupt and unjust. Their efforts were devoted to the manufacturing industry, supported by an emphasis on empirical scientific research. They networked across the economic sectors and disciplines, with the unifying theme of debates in the Lunar Society.

Clues to Wedgwood's political affiliations can be found in his pottery, which included portraits of John Wilkes. This did not mean that Wedgwood was a political radical in the conventional sense: he valued his connections with royalty, both in Britain and Russia, and was proud to describe himself as the Royal Potter.

LIGHT FROM THE LUNAR SOCIETY

There has been a shortage of detailed published historical material on the slave trade, and its impact in the UK, as if people were ashamed. Leading traders, when they made donations to their communities, disguised the origins of the money (Edward Colston in Bristol, Robert Milligan in London). We hear the sound of silence from the establishment. Even today there is reluctance to discuss this area of the past. The more we listen to the silences, the richer the symphony which emerges, with complex rhythms and harmonies.

What seems to emerge, from behind the scenes, is what we would today probably call a "Community of Practice", linking networks in otherwise disparate fields. This fits Manuel Castells' account of "network society" challenging "steering society", but two hundred years ago. With the Lunar Society, we encounter a remarkably modern agenda, which is currently discussed in terms of "the new production of knowledge" (Gibbons et al., 1994) and the "re-thinking science" (Nowotny et al., 2001). Wedgwood certainly engaged in action research: he tested new approaches, and reflected on the outcomes.

Wedgwood worked with a close knit group of dissenting industrial innovators, who had been excluded from the old universities on the basis of their Unitarian beliefs, and had little fellow-feeling with the ruling establishment. They formed new partnerships, developing new products, creating new markets, in what we might call the industrial revolution. Wedgwood's partner Thomas Bentley met Rousseau in Paris. Jefferson and Franklin were in correspondence with the Lunar Society. Wedgwood sold pottery, and Thomas Clarkson campaigned for abolition of the slave trade, in all three countries. Wedgwood served with Clarkson and William Wilberforce on the Committee for the Abolition of the Slave Trade, producing the famous medal.

When Clarkson, a prize winning Latin scholar at Cambridge, became exhausted from his efforts (the campaign of his pioneering organisation took 51 years) he tended to go and relax with Samuel Taylor Coleridge and William Wordsworth in the Lake District, when Coleridge complained of his "enslavement" by opium. Coleridge and Wordsworth wrote poems and letters in praise of Clarkson, Wilberforce and Toussaint L'Ouverture.

The impact of slavery can be seen in eighteenth and nineteenth century poetry, in the absence of more conventional democratic means of expression. In addition, some 400,000 people signed petitions for abolition, and participated in the boycott of sugar in 1792, raising awareness in the urban coffee houses which depended on the products of slave labour.

ARGUMENTS ON SLAVERY
AND CAPITALISM

Eric Williams (1944) argued that slavery and the Transatlantic Slave Trade financed the early stages of capitalism in Britain, and that abolition of the slave trade came when it was economically and politically convenient for the British establishment. This ties in with modern interpretations (James, Blackburn and Dubois) of Toussaint L'Ouverture, whose rebellion succeeded in humiliating the French, British and Spanish armies, and demonstrating that passive compliance by slaves could not be assumed.

There had been a history of slave revolts in British colonies, each of which attracted violent retribution. In Barbados in 1675 6 slaves were burnt alive, 11 beheaded, and 25 more executed. In Antigua in 1735–36 86 slaves were executed, 77 burned to death, and others hanged. In Jamaica in 1760 400 slaves were killed, and 100 executed. A revolt in Tobago in 1774 met with a response of mutilation and burnings.

Toussaint L'Ouverture's revolt in the French West Indian island of Santo Domingo had a radical impact on British policy. It is estimated that the British Army lost as many as 100,000 men in the West Indies in 1793–1802. British troops failed to quell the slave army, who were seen as threatening to destabilise colonies across the Americas.

Pitt the Younger was astute in his management of Wilberforce, and his pragmatic deployment of abolition of the Transatlantic Slave Trade as a weapon in the war with France, changing the pace of the Parliamentary campaign according to external circumstances. There was little public discussion of the deaths of British troops in the French West Indies, failing to defeat slave armies, as did the French and Spanish armies. This view is somewhat at odds with the recent account of Pitt by William Hague, which depicted Pitt as regretting his failure to abolish the slave trade.

As for the major actors in early British capitalism, the picture is interesting. Adam Smith was opposed to mercantilism and slavery. Wedgwood and his Lunar Society colleagues were horrified by slavery, but awareness only really grew from 1776, with the American Declaration of Independence, with its inherent contradictions over slavery. Wedgwood's partner Thomas Bentley tried to extricate himself from business relationships with slave traders. James Watt shared Darwin's concerns regarding Birmingham metal products which were used as shackles and gags for slaves. The industrial pioneers recognised the importance of constructive work organisation if they were to optimise the success of their businesses.

Committed workers would be better than slaves, if the objective was to build sustainable business, using the best available knowledge. The theme of control and participation is explored in detail in this book.

As for the early English working class, their conditions of work and living were not always markedly better than those of slaves. There were few slaves in Britain, and limited information. They lived as domestic servants, or in distinct communities, for example in Bristol, Liverpool and London. There appears to have been little overlap between the working class movements and abolitionism, but on the other hand the faces on Wedgwood pottery, sold to the aspiring middle classes rather than to industrial workers, included John Wilkes. There were a few African members of the London Corresponding Society, which was at the core of radical thinking. It was difficult for multiracial engagement to develop, as a colour bar was imposed to restrict access to education and training, for example through apprenticeships. Attempts, encouraged by Marx, to bring these strands together in British Chartism, with related movements across Europe in 1848, came to little.

Current official accounts of Abolition have been woefully inadequate, and have had damaging psychological consequences for the African Diaspora communities. Abolition was not simply a matter of philanthropy. Africans struggled for their freedom, sought to engage in processes of change, and have long deserved their Rendezvous of Victory. The networking approaches deployed by L'Ouverture to build a nation and armies, from slaves on separate plantations, represent a classic example of social capital formation and self-determination. Denied literacy by their slave owners, they deployed oral tradition and tacit knowledge. They demonstrated that knowledge goes beyond what is captured in the form of explicit documents.

The prevailing silence about slavery and the Slave Trade in Britain has had another consequence. The British people have also been denied a proper historical account of their own economic and political development. The same oppressive system of control has restricted the freedom of both slave and worker.

SLAVERY AND THE TRANSATLANTIC SLAVE TRADE

In the United States, the continuation of the Slave Trade beyond 1808 was not essential for the continuation of slavery, as the slave population was reproducing itself, with the children of slaves inheriting their parents' status.

Slavery and states' rights were divisive issues leading to the American Civil War. Principled positions came later. Pragmatism was dominant. Abraham Lincoln was committed to doing whatever was necessary to save the Union, and concluded that slavery had to be abolished. Following the Civil War, the period of Reconstruction showed that the attitudes which had underpinned slavery had not been destroyed through war. Racial prejudice continued.

Freedom has continued to be relative, with long legal and political battles over civil rights in the USA. Constitutional amendments abolishing slavery and setting out equal rights were then challenged using arguments based on property law. The arguments over civil rights became blurred, as it was maintained that different groups could be separate but equal. Even today, the descendants of slaves constitute a permanent under class. This was revealed afresh in the chaos following Hurricane Katrina in 2005, and the desolation of New Orleans. Poor black residents did not have cars or other means of escaping when the hurricane warning came. Their homes have been given low priority in the recovery and reconstruction efforts. We must anticipate a new generation of blues songs about the disaster, complementing the documentary "When the Levees Broke: A Requiem in Four Acts", directed by Spike Lee.

The situation was different in the West Indies and Latin America, where families were less established among slaves, death rates were higher, and the economies continued to depend on slave labour on plantations. There were smaller white populations, and a greater level of intermarriage. Economic change could therefore lead to unemployment and poverty for former slaves. Work as an employee is often hard to find, so subsistence farming was common. The legacy of slavery and empire could mean an ambition to migrate to the imperial home country.

Britain abolished slavery in 1833, taking effect in 1838, but did not achieve the universal adult franchise until the twentieth century. Access to power was controlled. Social class, less visible than skin colour, remains a determining factor. One legacy of the former British Empire has been the flow of immigrants, descended from former slaves, or from the countries from which the slaves were taken. History is ever present.

In the rest of Europe, slavery was not simply a transatlantic and racial phenomenon. Serfdom continued in Russia until the late nineteenth century, as a continuation of a form of feudalism which had vanished from the rest of Europe. It continues around the world today. In Europe there was a graceful shift from serfdom to social class difference.

The different European nations had participated in the Transatlantic Slave Trade to varying extents, and have since found themselves seen as favoured destinations for emigration. Patterns of migration continue. There is an undiscussed past history to be explored.

BUSINESS DECISIONS

Decisions, both in business and in politics, are not generally made on the basis of full information, equally accessible to all concerned. Typically some actors wield more power and influence. Where information is available on the profits derived from a particular trade, but not on the details of how it is conducted, there will be pressure to respond to the available information. Knowledge is not spread equally, and it is manipulated by those in power. This is not new, but it is now more widely realised. There are no simple answers. The injustice and inequity have been spectacular and systematic.

At company level, the business accounts need to be clear, showing the quantifiable benefits of making particular decisions. The accounts are prepared for a formal audience. One problem is that health, learning and other human consequences of economic activity are hard to quantify, and may simply be dismissed as "soft" factors, not taken into account in business decisions.

If labour is not in short supply, it may be easy for decision makers to approve policies and practices which involve high levels of turnover, attrition and wastage. In the case of the Transatlantic Slave Trade and slavery, it could be argued that the employment of sailors was conducted on a similar basis. White sailors were not always treated much worse than black slaves. Similarly, the armed forces did not rely entirely on volunteers. It was understood that press gangs were used to recruit.

It may be thought convenient to keep particular costs off the balance sheet, to strengthen the apparent case. Providing extra space for passenger cargo on the Middle Passage, for example, could be presented as an extravagance. Rather than making complex projections about the long term, it can be tempting just to show current transaction costs. How otherwise could one apportion costs in an acceptable manner?

Slave traders were accustomed to taking out insurance policies to cover their cargoes on particular voyages. This could, on occasion, make it financially advantageous to throw the human cargo overboard, rather than complete the voyage and sell at a loss. The case of the Zong in 1783 captured the public imagination.

As slaves were regarded as property, rather than human beings with human rights, it is not surprising that life and death decisions could be made, based on commercial considerations. On a long slaving voyage, with an uncertain market for slaves on arrival, captains might decide that it would be financially advantageous to throw surplus slaves overboard, and claim the insurance payment. The argument depended on asserting that water supplies were running low, and that this difficult decision had saved other lives. In the case of the Zong, 132 slaves were thrown to their deaths. Reports spread by word of mouth through the African community in Britain. The incident was reported, and the captain was taken to court. His view that the slaves were his property was upheld by the judge, but the longer term impact on the campaign for abolition was considerable. Granville Sharp pursued the case, and J.M.W. Turner immortalised it in an oil painting.

In the twenty first century we are experiencing further discontinuities. We may gain insights into each, from study of the other. We see modern equivalent cases, such as the deaths of Chinese cockle-pickers swept away by tides in Morecambe Bay, and railway workers killed by defective wagons. A particular case, such as the Zong, can catch the imagination and help to change the course of history.

PUBLIC IMAGE

Overseas activities provided the basis for mutual benefits, especially if support could be given to the myth of British greatness. The morale of those at all levels of society in Britain could be raised by accounts of imperial grandeur.

Despite their limited finances, British monarchs liked to appear to be strong. Overseas possessions helped to suggest a significant presence on the world stage, while not involving royal attention or investment. North America was colonised by individuals in the name of government, rather than by government. The same was true of Africa and India. Some victories were won by unconventional means, and without direct expense being incurred by government. There was tacit agreement that few questions should be asked.

Business depends on gaining competitive advantage. At sea, out of sight of witnesses, it was possible to take advantage of the efforts of others, attacking foreign fleets and taking prizes. The business was risky but profitable.

THE BRITISH ROLE

British merchants laid the foundations for Empire around the world. All of the key factors of production were located elsewhere, but typically carried in British vessels. Of 6 million African slaves transported in the eighteenth century, some 2.5 million were transported in British ships, which were seeking to supply the needs of plantations across the Americas.

It has been easier for historians to relate to the concept of Britain as campaigners for liberty against the evils of the international slave trade, rather than to recognise the scale of British engagement in that trade. Typically such awkward facts are simply omitted.

SOCIAL CLASS

Relying on slavery meant separating work from society. Slaves are not seen as citizens. Their masters are seen as citizens, but not as workers. This paved the way for the enduring social class system.

The outcomes of the Transatlantic Slave Trade in the UK included a reinforcement of the social class system. Those merchants whose fortunes had been made from the slave trade could seek to join the upper classes, whose lives of leisure are described in novels such as Jane Austen's "Mansfield Park". Their ambition was that their children would not follow them into trade. As far as possible, the source of the family money should not be disclosed: it was, after all, considered more honourable to have inherited wealth than to have obtained it through trade. Their descendants are today's upper middle classes, often happily oblivious to the origins of their family wealth. When the silences over slavery and the Transatlantic Slave Trade are being broken, that will require the re-writing of many family histories. New editions will be needed for guidebooks to many stately homes.

INDUSTRIALISATION AND UNDERDEVELOPMENT

Part of the profits from the Transatlantic Slave Trade were invested in the new factories of the industrial revolution, where often little attention was given to the working and living conditions of the workers. Management was about deriving maximum output. The designs of early factories resembled the floor plans of slave ships.

Given the distance which businessmen preferred to keep between themselves and the sordid realities of slavery and plantation life, this could be maintained in the industrial world of owners, managers and workers in factories. It was easier to manage a business based on the simple realities of income and expenditure, keeping clear of operational detail.

The forced removal of millions of Africans of working age removed a key resource from African economies, restricting their capacity to develop. It is hard to quantify the cost to Africa of the African Diaspora, just as it is hard to quantify the human cost of Leopold II's activities in the Congo.

We might compare the impact in Africa of the modern epidemic of HIV/AIDS, which is removing a large proportion of the generation of young adults, distorting demographic patterns, changing roles of individuals and their family relationships. UNESCO have estimated that the demographic consequences of the Transatlantic Slave Trade included a halving of what would have been the expected population in 1850. The removal of active young adults left a long legacy.

STAKEHOLDERS

To discuss the Transatlantic Slave Trade and slavery in terms of stakeholders, ethics and corporate social responsibility gives rise to difficult questions. Clearly, the Transatlantic Slave Trade and slavery could only proceed on the basis that the views and interests of the slave need not be considered. In essence, the slave was not seen as fully human.

The set of stakeholders was more narrowly defined, with most power in the hands of owners. It was often thought best for families and communities to be kept in the dark regarding the nature of the business transactions which led to a flow of income. This was made easier by conducting the buying and selling of slaves off shore. The profits from sugar plantations could be celebrated and consumed without making it explicit that slave labour was an integral part of the business operation.

In polite society it was not thought proper to discuss trade, from whence the funds for polite society had been derived. On the other hand, it was assumed to be proper for a man of business to be driven by the requirements of business, thus precluding wider consideration of "softer" factors.

KNOWLEDGE

With slavery, the knowledge and skill of the individual slave is discounted, as it is assumed that he will remain inferior, with no route to equality or parity of esteem. The myth of inferiority had to be maintained in order to justify this block on otherwise normal patterns of human resource development.

Individual slave owners knew that the assumption was false, but kept their silence for reasons of self interest. They often had slave mistresses and children. They were denying their own personal responsibility for the sake of social standing.

Older slaves were a source of traditional wisdom on the plantations, taking forward African oral tradition. This, with the distinctive music, continued despite limited literacy.

CITIZENSHIP AND ENLIGHTENMENT

Citizens are not inherently inferior to their leaders or rulers. They are not subjects. Monarchies, whether absolute or constitutional, preserve the elements of slavery and subjection. The myths of hierarchy, stability and continuity are sustained.

Since the English Civil War, the virtual structures of relative social status have been maintained, inhibiting citizenship. The order of things is, behind the scenes, imagined as unchanging. For John Bellers, and his successors in the Lunar Society, the answer was citizenship in the workplace.

Slavery fits into the order of things, where everyone knows their place. The presence of defined slaves makes it easier to give status to others. In a world of stability, slavery can seem a natural element of creation. To disturb stability could bring chaos and revolution. Thus, in order to confirm the longed-for stability of Europe after the Thirty Years War, with a manufactured veneer of science, other races were sacrificed.

There was pressure to establish order in the disciplines, as well as in politics. In catering for the needs of élites, there were casualties. Enlightenment philosophers defined the limits for slavery, but slave traders and businessmen did not read. The Encyclopaedists explored the nature of work, and appreciated the importance of skill. Adam Smith emphasised the moral foundations for business.

FROM HENRY TO HITLER

In order to understand what happened between Henry and Hitler, we have to explore the series of language games which were played.

The Tudor approach to foreign policy placed great reliance on the security of an island nation from attack by continental powers. As maritime exploration opened up access to new worlds to the West, South and East, a presence at sea became pivotal to a world role. There was, however, limited knowledge available regarding the nature of the activities at sea, which was central to the British role over the 350 years between the death of Henry VIII and the start of the twentieth century. Before the First World War, Germany was concerned to match British naval strength. After the First World War, Hitler's rise to power included assertions of Germany's right to operate as a great power, alongside Britain.

In the interim period, there was a shift from a naval strategy based on individual entrepreneurs, financing their activities from piracy in the name of their monarch, to a British navy which ruled the waves. British monarchs did not enjoy absolute powers. They had limited financial resources, and Elizabeth I led the way in seeking to benefit from wars between European rivals, who could thus advance the British interests at their expense.

British pragmatism meant making a virtue of the outcomes of individual initiatives. The British crown did not finance piracy, but they received a percentage of the spoils. They did not prescribe a policy of colonial settlement, but they were happy to assume the mantle of increasing imperial power.

The British Empire was, in essence, a do it yourself operation, where the veneer was presented as reality. At no stage was there a programme of long term investment in the development of the Empire. It was, rather, a process of spin doctors presenting fragments of evidence from around the world as a cohesive imperial picture. Because each stage of extending the Empire was conducted on commercial grounds, details could be withheld on the grounds of commercial confidentiality. Those operating on a business basis were concerned to maximise income, while incurring the minimum expenditure.

Opportunism and short-term entrepreneurial enterprise were vital, in the absence of long term government policy and investment. Sea captains depended on privateering, which was seen by their victims as piracy, in contravention of international law. Where they identified overseas settlements as a basis for growth, this was again on a private sector basis. There was a need for labour in the prospective colonies, and this was met by the slave trade. Economic development in the small island at home was intensifying, meaning that few volunteers were available to work overseas.

From an early stage, the British outsourced the management of their Empire. Whether to the South, the West or the East, the new Empire needed to draw on international expertise. Complementing the African slave trade there had been the Indian outsourcing business, vital for managing colonies in Africa and Asia.

Without the Indian presence, it would not have been possible for a small island to operate a global empire.

Once the Second World War came, and Britain under Churchill were fighting Germany under Hitler, the spin doctors could present the case in national and patriotic terms. It was therefore argued that Britain was an island race, and would never be slaves. However, in practice the war effort depended on financial and political support from the United States, and manpower from the Empire.

This summary account has lost some of the favourite themes of the British Empire. The mythology was of an Empire over which the sun never set, with a civilising mission whereby immature peoples could be prepared for autonomy and self-government. The myth contained elements of reality, and underpinned the missions of generations of colonial administrators. Behind the Empire, however, there is a resounding silence. It has not been addressed, or broken.

PRODUCTS FROM SLAVERY

Silence and denial have not been confined to the Transatlantic Slave Trade. It is not the only case where the emerging truth is that systematic behaviour in the past, which is continuing today, has irreversible and enduring consequences. Crops and businesses associated with slavery and the slave trade have had enduring impacts.

Tobacco

One of the major crops which used slave labour on plantations was tobacco. Today it is understood that there are links between tobacco smoking and cancer, but the trade continues. As sales fall in industrialised countries, there is a growing market for cigarettes in developing countries.

It is argued that jobs depend on the continued cigarette business. Tobacco companies are reluctant to address issues of cancer, or to discuss the extent of medical evidence. Instead, they seek to associate their brands with sports and arts events, which are seen as publicly acceptable.

In practice, both manufacturing employment and customers are now largely in developing countries, where health information is less available. Profits continue to be received in industrialised countries.

Alcohol

The medical consequences of alcohol consumption are well known. However, alcohol production is profitable for companies, and provides valuable tax income for governments.

Alcohol has become part of normal culture, in many countries. Arguably if it were now to be discovered and introduced, it would be more heavily regulated. Instead, due to vested interests, there are voluntary codes of practice. When legislating on the recreational use of drugs, governments tend to disregard alcohol, which is seen as an acceptable part of the status quo.

Arms Trade

One of the most successful industries in the UK is arms, manufacturing weapons for sale. The defence industries provide employment in the UK and overseas. It is argued that competitors would take the business if UK companies were to withdraw. It is therefore vital to maintain a strong market presence.

There is silence about the nature and use of particular weapons such as land mines and cluster bombs, which are subject to control under the Geneva Conventions.

The traditional argument has been that the defence industries are integral to the defence of the nation, and that it would be unpatriotic to oppose continued support, intervening in the market. It has been maintained that technical excellence in the defence industries constituted a resource for use in the civil sector. In the UK, experience of successful transfer from defence to civil sectors is scarce.

Asbestos

The medical consequences of exposure to asbestos have been known since 1935, but the manufacture and use of asbestos have continued. There is a long delay between exposure and cancer diagnosis, which complicates the allocation of responsibility. There is no cure for asbestos-related illness.

Epidemiologists have predicted the scale and timing of asbestos-related illnesses, and can analyse their likely occurrence among asbestos workers, their families and communities. Often these are in developing countries, where medical and welfare services are limited. Insurers for asbestos manufacturers have sought to minimise their compensation claims by denying proof of their responsibility.

REASONS FOR SLAVERY

Modern discussion of slavery is coloured by moral positions: it is hard to find anyone to speak in favour, yet many condone practices which might be seen as consistent with slavery.

Study of the reasons for the rise and fall of the Transatlantic Slave Trade reveals that most decisions were taken on economic grounds, reflecting the self-interest of those concerned. At the peak, the Transatlantic Slave Trade involved major business interests across the UK, and many Quakers were slave owners. Prime Minister William Ewart Gladstone's father was a slave trader and slave owner. It was considered unpatriotic to attack a trade on which the country depended.

British mercantilists saw a lucrative income from the Triangular Trade, and lobbied hard against any attempts to curtail it. The flow of profits funded the initial phases of the Industrial Revolution, complementing the availability of an industrial workforce due to increased efficiency in agricultural production.

Once the Industrial Revolution matured, steam power and new machines enabled factory production, surpassing the outputs of slave labour overseas. At that stage the colonies in the West Indies were proving an expensive drain on resources. As the new American colonies gained in strength, and then achieved independence, the West Indies was seen as generating losses rather than profits. Investment switched to the East Indies.

Adam Smith argued against mercantilism and slavery. Once the West Indies were no longer profitable, so Eric Williams argued, their lobby lost influence, and the rhetoric of free trade could be introduced. Once this turning point was reached, slavery could safely be attacked on moral grounds. However, among the reasons for doing so was the wish to eradicate rival colonies where slavery remained viable and an economic challenge was posed.

By discussing slavery in business terms, the moral issues could be disregarded. As the business interests had secured seats in Parliament through rotten boroughs, it required successive Parliamentary reforms to shift the balance of opinion. Discussing business as a system continues to enable the avoidance of difficult ethical and moral issues. They can be ruled out of consideration because they involve issues of soft data, which cannot be handled by finance directors.

It is perhaps telling that, at this stage in the early twenty first century, we can see the recurrence of certain aspects of the slave trade, but with different patterns of physical mobility. Entrepreneurs feel able to outsource functions to where they can be performed more cheaply. Alternatively, they are happy to bring in casual labour, to be sacked as soon as their efforts are no longer needed. Gangmasters provide the cheap labour for farms, and for cockle picking, even for airline catering for use around the world. It may have been possible to get away with such conduct in the past. It is harder to do so today.

What is going on? Business process re-engineering gloried in the power of analytical approaches which saw business in terms of processes. The focus was on the bottom line, on short term results. People could be discounted, as soft factors do not impress financial decision makers. It is now being recognised that people are the key resource for any organisation. That includes slaves.

CHAPTER 4
....

EMANCIPATION

The Good Lord who created the sun which gives us light from above, who rouses the sea and makes the thunder road – listen well, all of you – this god, hidden in the clouds, watches us. He sees all that the white man does. The god of the white man calls him to commit crimes: our god asks only good works of us. But this god who is so good orders revenge! He will direct our hands; he will aid us. Throw away the image of the god of the whites who thirsts for our tears, and listen to the voice of liberty which speaks in the hearts of all of us.

Boukman, the priest leader, in Fick, C. (1990) *The Making of Haiti: the Saint Domingue Revolution from Below.* Knoxville, Univ of Tennessee Press, pp. 92–9.

THE SEARCH FOR SIMPLICITY

Many previous writers have tried to present a simple account of the abolition of the Transatlantic Slave Trade. British school textbooks present the heroic campaign led by William Wilberforce from 1787. African Diaspora groups point to the achievements of slave rebellions, such as that led by Toussaint L'Ouverture in Santo Domingo in 1791. Eric Williams saw the abolition of the Transatlantic Slave Trade by the British in 1807 as being linked to the changing economic circumstances, which meant that the slave trade was no longer essential for the British West Indies, while it remained vital for the French West Indies.

As so often in history, there are elements of truth in each of these accounts. Emancipation was not simply an outcome of moral conviction by a middle class campaign group. However, it was not strongly linked to campaigns by the new industrial working class, working in solidarity with their African brothers. It represents a remarkable achievement for a small Non Governmental Organisation, but raises many fundamental questions.

EMPOWERMENT

We should be cautious about accounts of change which dwell on how a previously subservient group was empowered, often implying that the real credit for any change resides with the superior group. Genuine empowerment is when a group takes control of its own future. After years of asking, the move is made, as if by right.

Slavery in the United States was not simply a life sentence. As the status of slave was inherited, it meant that the sentence would continue over the generations. In that context, it would be empty to talk of empowerment within the system of slavery. The choice was between escape and rebellion.

From the early days of the American colonies there had been concerns over security. In states where white settlers were outnumbered by African slaves, the issue was more urgent. Given that there was no plan to move toward a multicultural society, any

Africans who ceased to be slaves would have to leave the country. As each slave represented a valuable asset to the owner, there were measures to prevent escape, and draconian punishments for runaways who were caught.

The issue of slavery was brought to a head in the American Civil War. Indeed slavery was presented as a major cause of the civil war. However, this did not mean that victory for the Union, and the Amendment to the Constitution which declared slavery illegal, meant that American former slaves of African descent, and their descendants, could expect to enjoy equal civil rights.

Empowerment of African Americans required initiatives from the community. It became clear, during the period of reconstruction after the Civil War, that divisions remained, and old attitudes would take time to change. In Alabama, Booker T. Washington founded the Tuskegee Institute, with the objective of developing a new generation of leaders in the African American community. Among the early students was a young nurse, great aunt to Condoleezza Rice, now Secretary of State and a former Academic Dean at Stanford University. She is a third generation product of Tuskegee.

THE LUNAR SOCIETY

This book argues that there was an international link between emancipation, enterprise and revolution, which has been underestimated in previous accounts. At the heart of the British Industrial Revolution there was a distinctive approach to enterprise and innovation, which was based on an intellectual revolution which we may call the "English Enlightenment". This had international dimensions, providing links to France (Rousseau), and the Americas (Jefferson, Franklin and L'Ouverture). At the core of what we could regard as a movement was a commitment to liberty and an abhorrence of slavery, combined with an awareness of the complexities involved in change.

This was not a movement based on grand theory, or led by the ancient universities. Quite the reverse. The Lunar Society comprised a network of practical businessmen, with a common background as Unitarian dissenters, which excluded them from Oxford and Cambridge Universities. They were not interested in the classical civilisations and theology, but were fascinated by the potential application of empirical science, in which they engaged, and the implications for business and society.

Members of the Lunar Society were appalled by the atrocities of the Transatlantic Slave Trade, which emerged in the wake of the American Declaration of Independence in 1776. The case of the slave ship Zong, in 1783, when 132 slaves were thrown overboard to their deaths by a captain seeking insurance compensation, caught the public imagination. In a famous court case, the captain escaped punishment, as the slaves were regarded as his property, and without human rights.

The Lunar Society dissenters saw the depravity of slavery as linked to the corruption of the ancient universities, where All Souls College Oxford was funded by the slave trade, King's College Cambridge invested in the South Sea Company (selling slaves to the Spanish Empire), and the Church of England owned slaves. The Lunar Society developed network links with radical thinkers in North America and France, and were able to distil their own variety of revolution. These were practical men, engaged in industrial production, and developing new businesses by synthesising previously separate areas of thinking and research.

CLASS CONFLICT

Counterfactual analysis is both difficult and dangerous. However, in the presence of so much silence over great issues, it must be attempted. Why, given that the industrial working class in Britain faced similar deprivation of control and participation to that experienced by African slaves, did they not make common cause? Why was the British Industrial Revolution a story of entrepreneurs and economic change, rather than public political upheaval?

Slaves were largely kept out of mainland Britain, so news of their conditions was suppressed. African slaves and British workers rarely met. Had they done so, racial stereotypes would have doubtless complicated matters. It is not that there had been no such contacts. There were black communities in London, Bristol and Liverpool. Working class British sailors had often been taken as slaves by the Barbary pirates, and then, if they were fortunate, released after payment of a ransom. Slavery was an occupational hazard. Sailors who chose to engage in the slave trade risked appalling conditions, and high mortality rates, in order to have the chance of earning a fortune.

The Lunar Society, and other radically inclined industrial entrepreneurs, did not extend their radicalism to the point of establishing common cause with the workers. They referred back to the late seventeenth century work of dissenting Quaker economist John Bellers, who argued for co-ownership and social inclusion. However, in the workplace they saw the need for order, leading by example.

The Lunar Society were practical philosophers, engaging in scientific research and aware of the vital importance of human skill. Wedgwood and his colleagues had much in common with Diderot and the French Encyclopaedists, in the breadth of their interests. Diderot took his library to Empress Catherine the Great of Russia, who also commissioned the "frog" dinner service from Wedgwood. They sought to set the fashions, but were not themselves part of the establishment.

At the same time, life in the British establishment continued as if nothing had changed. The injection of funds from slavery and sugar plantations enabled aristocratic landowners to maintain their standard of life, albeit at the cost of marrying lower born heiresses to finance their stately homes. Their seats in Parliament and their country houses were secure. The career structure was in place: a conforming Anglican background led to classical studies and then a career in the law, the church or the army, if a career were needed. Trade was out of the question for a gentleman.

Delays in reforming the House of Commons meant that radical changes, such as the abolition of the Transatlantic Slave Trade, could not command a majority as long as it was contrary to the interests of the plantation owners. This meant that extra-Parliamentary means had to be deployed, linked to detailed understanding of the working of the political system.

The abolitionist movement, like the Lunar Society, spoke for those who had lacked power in the past, but would soon take centre stage. They demonstrated the difference which can be made by individuals. In a campaign which had to be sustained for over 50 years from 1787, the only survivor of the original committee, Thomas Clarkson, saw the emancipation of slaves in 1838.

MORALITY

It is hard to find anyone today who will give arguments in favour of the slave trade or slavery. Such arguments would not be seen as "politically correct". We must address the challenge of explaining the historical phenomena in clear economic terms. We need to make sense of the participation of so many leading figures who claimed to be enlightened thinkers. Support of the Slave Trade was apparently politically correct until 1807.

There were vocal opponents, such as Oliver Goldsmith, in "The Traveller" (1764);

> When I behold a factious band agree
> To call it freedom when they themselves are free;
> Each wanton judge new penal statutes draw,

Laws grind the poor, and rich men rule the law;
The wealth of climes, where savage nations roam,
Pillag'd from slaves to purchase slaves at home;
Fear, pity, justice, indignation start,
Tear off reserve, and bare my swelling heart"

There is no reason to believe that moral standards are generally higher in the twenty-first century than in the past. On this basis, we need to reflect on current practice, and not simply assume that the slave trade and slavery are simply matters of history. Slavery continues in various modern forms today.

It also appears that decisions regarding Abolition were not taken on primarily moral grounds, though subsequent justifications have been given in moral terms. In other words, the reasons for decisions may require further explanation. Here we set the scene, and investigate thinking in the United States and France, before returning to the traditional narrative of British abolition. In a turbulent time in the Age of Revolutions, it is not appropriate to keep merely to a narrative in one country. Tom Paine worked in all three countries. Abolitionist campaigners such as Thomas Clarkson maintained close links in all three countries, whose fate was linked. They planned strategies on a global scale.

DEMOCRACY

There was a curious paradox. Those countries from Northern Europe who were most advanced in the development of ideas of democracy and individual freedom were also the leaders in establishing the most exploitative system of slavery that the world has ever seen. Democracy for the slave owners was sustained by the denial of freedom to the slave. This contradiction did not escape the attention of leaders and writers.

In order to cope with this inconsistency, one approach was to ensure that the two worlds, "old" and "new", were kept apart.

This was perfectly possible in days when travel and communication were difficult. It presents more difficult challenges today, when nations like to look back on their histories with pride, and when it is assumed that information is readily accessible. Businessmen were able to benefit from operating in both geographical worlds. Shareholders and voters were normally domestic, while activities based on slavery were conducted offshore, away from public scrutiny. The same could be said to apply today. The workers who were exploited and enslaved were typically not seen by the owners: they were bought in Africa, sold in the Americas, and only the profit was seen on European soil.

Discussion of "the rights of man" was somehow understood as applying only to the European population. Thomas Paine does not mention slavery. It was rarely suggested that slaves should simply be freed. Indeed, had this practice been widespread, the moral credibility of the politics of slavery would have been shattered. Slaves themselves played little visible part in the British abolition movement. The strategists judged that their closer involvement would have been unhelpful. We argue, however, that the proven success of slave rebellions, especially in the French West Indies, had a profound impact.

ABOLITION MOVEMENT AND ABOLITIONISTS

In the eighteenth century the British benefited from slavery and the Transatlantic Slave Trade more than any other nation. They were meeting the perceived need for slaves in the American colonies, and developing lucrative plantations in the West Indies, and they had enjoyed the role of monopoly supplier of slaves to the Spanish Empire.

It was also the British who led the struggle to abolish the system. Christians had been complicit in the slave trade, and churches had benefited from it; yet it was Christians who were in the forefront of the abolition movement. We need to try to understand their change of mind.

Some have proclaimed Abolition as a great victory for distinctively British morality. This simple view is presented by Sherrard in "Freedom from Fear: the slave and his emancipation" (1959). This is

> a story which should be a source of pride to all Englishmen, and yet is too little known.

He maintained that English leadership was morally superior:

> . . . England is the only country which has consistently and firmly upheld the ideal of individual liberty; and now that the cause of freedom has passed from her hands into the keeping of a conglomeration of talkative nations, slavery is raising its head once more in subtle guise and renewed strength.

With some ingenuity, credit is given to the British for improving conditions in the trade which they dominated:

> That Britain at the beginning of the eighteenth century should have been no wiser and no better than other nations is not a matter for surprise. It is much more significant that, owing to certain elements in the British character, the transfer of the trade into English hands was to prove the first effective step towards its abolition. (Sherrard, 1959, p. 51)

A further creative move is to blame African traders, rather than the British:

> The main charge should be leveled not against the merchants in England, nor their agents in America, but against the methods of capture adopted in Africa, the conditions obtaining in the middle passage, and the treatment which the slaves received at the hands of their masters across the Atlantic. These matters concern the slave rather than the trade. (Sherrard, 1959, p. 58)

Emancipation could constitute a serious threat to the property rights of the slave owners in the West Indies, who were also voters and Members of Parliament at home in Britain. Political power and voting rights were based on property, and only a small minority of the population had the vote in Parliamentary elections. The great campaigner William Wilberforce had purchased his Parliamentary seat in Hull, and knew government ministers by being part of the same university-educated élite.

SLAVES AS PAWNS

Slaves did not count as full human beings for purposes of designing systems of political representation. This could cause complications for the designers of constitutions, such as in the United States, where the respective powers of the new states needed to be balanced, while the extent to which they depended on slaves varied.

The detailed political history from the American War of Independence in 1776–83, and the French Revolution in 1789, to the British Abolition of the Transatlantic Slave Trade in 1807 is enlightening. It casts a different light on the Transatlantic Slave Trade, which was part of a complex set of relationships involving Britain, France and the United States.

Decisions were made by a small group of the political élites. A different story was presented for public consumption in each country. This is not surprising, as each country was grappling with competing concerns. Slaves had no votes, and no rights. They were seen as a commodity, traded for economic reasons. They were an accidental reality, and not part of a long term plan. The British, French and Americans used black slaves as pawns in a game of geopolitical chess. Each nation now has their own history of Abolition, in which they claim credit for enlightened thinking, and tend to downplay the contribution of the slaves themselves, who fought for their freedom, and for the freedom of other Africans.

THOMAS JEFFERSON

Thomas Jefferson, revolutionary thinker, diplomat and then President of the United States, was well aware that his radical calls for freedom in the American Declaration of Independence were inconsistent with the continuation of slavery in North America. His preferred solution would have been to free slaves where possible, but to send them out of the United States, which he saw as destined to remain a white country. His view did not prevail in those states where slavery was valued, seen as economically vital, and politically convenient. Jefferson himself appears to have fathered children by slaves, borne out by recent DNA evidence.

Jefferson drafted elements of the Declaration of Independence which were struck out by Congress. Here he linked slavery with the discredited rule of the British king:

> He has waged cruel war against human nature itself, violating its most sacred rights of life and liberty in the persons of a distant people who never offended him, captivating and carrying them into slavery in another hemisphere, or to incur miserable death in their transportation hither. This piratical warfare, the opprobrium of infidel powers, is the warfare of the Christian king of Great Britain. Determined to keep open a market where men should be bought and sold, he has prostituted his negative for suppressing every legislative attempt to prohibit or to restrain this execrable commerce. And that this assemblage of horrors might want no fact of distinguished die, he is now exciting those very people to rise in arms among us, and to purchase that liberty of which he has deprived them, by murdering the people on whom he has also obtruded them: thus paying off former crimes committed against the liberties of one people, with crimes which he urges them to commit against the lives of others. (Jefferson, 1944, p. 25)

These clauses were removed in response to pressure from South Carolina and Georgia, and from Northern states, who had few slaves themselves, but were engaged in the slave trade. Pragmatism overruled principle.

There was debate as to whether slaves should be regarded as equivalent to freemen, when calculating populations and liability for taxation. Even at the early stages of relations between the states, slaves had an arithmetical role.

There had been no mention of Negroes in Virginia from the foundation of the state in 1607 until the arrival of Dutch slaves in 1650. The British then continued the slave trade, which continued to independence. Slavery continued to be controversial:

> Nothing is more certainly written in the book of fate, than that these people are to be free; nor is it less certain that the two races, equally free, cannot live in the same government. Nature, habit, opinion have drawn indelible lines of distinction between them. It is still in our power to direct the process of emancipation and deportation, peaceably, and in such slow degree, as that the evil will wear off insensibly, and their place shall be filled up by free white labourers. If, on the contrary, it is left to force itself on, human nature must shudder at the prospect held up. (Jefferson, 1944, p. 51)

Under the law of Virginia, slaves were treated as property:

> Slaves pass by descent and dower as lands do. Where the descent is from a parent, the heir is bound to pay an equal share of their value in money to each of their brothers and sisters. (Jefferson, 1944, p. 52)

It was proposed "to make slaves distributable among the next of kin, as other movables." (Jefferson, 1944, p. 255)

It was suggested (but not included in the new Virginia legislation) that all slaves born after the Act should be emancipated, with a view to them moving to live elsewhere.

Rather than recommending the incorporation of blacks into the State, it was argued that the races were different. It was acknowledged that the treatment of slaves makes them less likely to respect the law:

> The man in whose favour no laws of property exist, probably feels himself less bound to respect those made in favour of others. (Jefferson, 1944, p. 261)

When freed, he is to be removed beyond the reach of mixture. (Jefferson, 1944, p. 262)

It was therefore likely that if slavery continued, it would be at the expense of violence against individuals, tensions between the states, and possible eventual civil war or secession.

GEORGE WASHINGTON

George Washington, who had commanded the rebel forces in the American War of Independence and became President, also experienced considerable private disquiet regarding slavery, which seemed inconsistent with the public rhetoric of freedom (Wiencek, 2004). On his death he instructed that all of his own slaves should be set free. One of these, West Ford, it is suggested, may have been his own son by a slave. Interestingly, his wishes were not fully observed, and families were divided and sold.

Both Washington and Jefferson were acutely aware of the ambiguities in their positions. They conducted a successful campaign for independence based on arguments for life, liberty and the pursuit of happiness. Both were familiar with the institution of slavery. Both owned slaves, and recent evidence suggests that they were indeed familiar with female slaves, possibly fathering children by them.

The separate states of the USA were determined in their assertion of independent states' rights. They were not prepared to be forced into the abolition of slavery when it appeared important for their economic survival.

In a sense Washington and Jefferson had inherited the failure of the British to plan for the future. The slave trade had grown as economic opportunities provided a market. New colonies had established their own policies. None of them had envisaged a future with freed slaves.

SLAVES AS FAMILY

The British and French politicians were able to distance themselves from the realities of slavery, which did not have a significant presence on domestic soil. Just as there was a tradition of using foreign mercenaries in warfare, so slaves were deployed as part of necessary processes of economic transition. In some cases slaves were armed in wartime. It was difficult to enforce subsequent disarmament. Entry into the slave trade had been for commercial reasons. There was no exit strategy. When trade moved into other areas, politicians were relieved, and could make a virtue of what had often been an economic change.

Americans did not enjoy the luxury of distance. Wherever they stood on the issues of the slave trade and slavery, they had encountered slaves in their own personal lives. Often the relationships had been extremely close, in a manner which could prove embarrassing if disclosed. There were clearly numerous cases where relations between slave owner and slave went beyond employment. Widespread mixed relationships challenged, or at least complicated, arguments for any moral basis for the system of slavery. As abolition led to emancipation, the problem of race relations in a multicultural society emerged.

SLAVE REBELLIONS

Toussaint L'Ouverture became leader of the slave rebellion in Santo Domingo in 1791. A brilliant military leader, he led his slave army in defeating the French as well as the invading Spanish and British. He became de facto governor of the colony. When Napoleon attempted to restore slavery in the French colonies, Santo Dominguo returned to war. In 1803, having been promised safe conduct, Toussaint was tricked by Napoleon's forces and imprisoned in France.

Wordsworth's sonnet to Toussaint L'Ouverture (1803) located Toussaint's work in a wider global perspective.

Though fallen thyself, never to rise again,
Live, and take comfort. Thou has left behind
Powers that will work for thee; air, earth and skies;
There's not a breathing of the common wind
That will forget thee; thou hast great allies;
Thy friends are exultations, agonies,
And love, and man's unconquerable mind.

Slaves in the French West Indies showed that they were well able to organise, rebel, run a national government, and resist foreign armies, including the British, French and Spanish. This challenged conventional assumptions of European superiority, and exposed the fragility of control by slave owners. The slave leaders found that when they responded to the French abolition of slavery in 1794, they faced repression by Napoleon Bonaparte, and the re-imposition of slavery by force. This served to expose the emptiness and partiality of white European rhetoric about the rights of man. The rights of man counted for little if they came into conflict with property rights.

Henry Brougham's "Inquiry into the Colonial Policy of the European Powers" (1803) found:

... the fruit of our iniquity has been a great and rich empire in America. Let us be satisfied with our gains and, being rich, let us try to become righteous – not indeed by giving up a single sugar cane of what we have acquired but by continuing in our present state of overflowing opulence and preventing the further importation of slaves ... The experience of the United States has distinctly proved that the rapid multiplication of the Blacks in a natural way will inevitably be occasioned by prohibiting their importation ... the structure of West Indian society will more and more resemble that of the compact, firm and respectable communities which compose the North American states. (Brougham, 1803, p. 69)

Looking at Haiti, he declared:

> When a fire is raging windward, is it the proper time for stirring
> up everything that is combustible in your warehouse and throwing
> into them new loads of material still more prone to explosion? . . . in-
> dependent of any other considerations against the negro traffic, the
> present state of the French West Indies renders the idea of continu-
> ing its existence for another hour worse than infamy. (Brougham,
> 1803, p. 69)

A COLONY OF CITIZENS

As Dubois (2004) has shown, in the French West Indies, there was
a determined attempt by slaves to move directly to citizenship,
using the rhetoric of the French Revolution. The minority of
educated slaves were able to follow developments in Metropolitan
France, but with a time delay built in due to the need to cross the
ocean. During the turbulent revolutionary period, this often meant
responding to one policy in the West Indies, while it was being
changed in France.

> The fight over slavery and emancipation during the revolutionary
> period was a global affair. It involved political debates and alliances
> on both sides of the Atlantic, military conflicts not only in France
> and Britain but also in Spain and the United States. Its economic
> disruptions reshaped patterns of production in the Caribbean,
> opening the way for the dramatic expansion of Cuban sugar in the
> early nineteenth century as well as the Louisiana Purchase. These
> broader developments were driven by the revolution within the
> societies of the French Caribbean, where slaves, gens de couleur,
> and some whites took to heart the possibilities embedded in repub-
> licanism, and ultimately brought about the most radical social and
> political transformation of the Age of Revolution. To understand
> the larger history of democracy – of its contentious meanings, its
> unstoppable divagations – we must expand our historical vision and
> incorporate, as a central part of this history, the ideals and actions
> of those who produced emancipation from within slavery. (Dubois,
> 2004, p. 430)

Once slavery was declared to be abolished in France, and slaves had the experience of organising their own society, it became clear that previous arguments about their inherent inferiority were without foundation. Toussaint L'Ouverture told his colleagues that they had the ability to lead, and they found that this was true.

> Slavery was an affront to the ideal that all people were born with certain natural rights, and the triumph of 1794 was in instituting a political order worthy of the claims of universalism despite its profound danger to the reigning order of the day. That slaves succeeded in their revolts was a remarkable enough achievement of the period; that their revolt ultimately was embraced by the French Republic and transformed into a new political order is just as notable. But this radical order fell prey to other visions. Productivity and profit were seen as dependent on racial hierarchy and slavery, and dreams of racial equality collapsed as racial solidarity became the basis for the defence of liberty. The struggle of slaves enabled political principle to overtake, but not defeat, the forces of inequality. The insurgents left a legacy of possibility that long remained – that still remains – unfulfilled. (Dubois, 2004, p. 430)

Although the success of the slave rebellions in the French West Indies prompted the restoration of slavery by Napoleon, the impact around the world was such that no slave owner, anywhere in the world, could rely on his slaves remaining docile.

SILENCING THE PAST

The history of slavery, and its abolition, tends to have been written by whites, who have typically discounted the impact of slave rebellions, which suggests that abolition was achieved, at least in part, by the efforts of the slaves.

Michel-Rolph Trouillot (1995) was concerned to explore curious silences in history, with particular reference to the history of slavery, and the active role of slaves in bringing about abolition. Like Robin Blackburn, he noted the marginalisation of the successful slave revolt in Haiti, suggesting that it complicated simple assumptions regarding European superiority and African immaturity. As a Haitian academic teaching in the United States he could see the difference between what had happened, and what was said to have happened. Trouillot went further, taking additional examples of what he termed silences in the mainstream accounts.

> Silences enter the process of historical production at four crucial moments: the moment of fact creation (the making of sources); the moment of fact assembly (the making of archives); the moment of fact retrieval (the making of narratives); and the moment of retrospective significance (the making of history in the final instance). (Trouillot, 1995, p. 26)

Conventional historical methods will not work in such circumstances.

> These moments are conceptual tools, second level abstractions of processes that feed on each other. As such, they are not meant to provide a realistic description of the making of any individual narrative. Rather, they help us understand why not all silences are equal and why they cannot be addressed − or redressed − in the same manner. To put it differently, any historical narrative is a particular bundle of silences, the result of a unique process, and the operation required to deconstruct these silences will vary accordingly. (Trouillot, 1995, p. 27)

The major European empires have developed their own histories, which enable them to preserve their myths of superiority.

> The general silencing of the Haitian Revolution by Western historiography . . . is due to uneven power in the production of sources, archives and narratives. But if I am correct that this revolution was unthinkable as it happened, the insignificance of the story is already inscribed in the sources, regardless of what else they reveal. There are no new facts here; not even neglected ones. Here, I have to make the silences speak for themselves. I do so by juxtaposing the climate of the times, the writings of historians on the revolution itself, and narratives of world history where the effectiveness of the original silence becomes fully visible. (Trouillot, 1995, p. 28)

Historians today are left with a problem, in that the records include large areas of silence.

> Power is constitutive of the story. Tracking power through various "moments" simply helps emphasise the fundamentally processual character of historical production, to insist that what history is matters less than how history works; that power itself works together with history; and that the historians' claimed political preferences have little influence on most of the actual practices of power. A warning from Foucault is helpful: "I don't believe that the question of "who exercises power?" can be resolved unless that other question "how does it happen?" is resolved at the same time. (Trouillot, 1995, p. 29)

Trouillot argues for the creation of an alternative history:

> The play of power in the production of alternative narratives begins with the joint creation of facts and sources for at least two reasons. Firstly, facts are never meaningless: indeed, they become facts only because they matter in some sense, however minimal. Second, facts are not created equal: the production of traces is always also the creation of silences. Some occurrences are noted from the start; others are not. Some are engraved in individual or collective bodies; others are not. Some leave physical markers; others do not. (Trouillot, 1995, p. 29)

Building histories out of silences is far from easy:

> The unearthing of silence, and the historian's subsequent emphasis on the retrospective significance of hitherto neglected events, requires not only extra labour at the archives – whether or not one uses primary sources – but also a project linked to an interpretation. This is so because the combined silences accrued through the first three steps of the process of historical production intermesh and solidify at the fourth and final moment when retrospective significance itself is produced. (Trouillot, 1995, p. 58)

Having considered the case of a single slave who became a colonel and built a castle, Trouillot tackled the Haitian Revolution. In 1790, the French colonist La Barre assured his wife that life was safe and peaceful. The Negroes were tranquil, obedient, and freedom for them was a chimera. A few months later, the most important slave insurrection in recorded history broke out.

Trouillot remarks:

> When reality does not coincide with deeply held beliefs, human beings tend to phrase interpretations that force reality within the scope of these beliefs. They devise formulas to repress the unthinkable and to bring it back within the realm of accepted discourse. (Trouillot, 1995, p. 72)

He continues:

> The contention that enslaved Africans and their descendants could not envision freedom – let alone formulate strategies for gaining and securing such freedom – was not based so much on empirical evidence as on an ontology, an implicit organisation of the world and its inhabitants. Although by no means monolithic, this world-view was widely shared by whites in Europe and the Americas, and by many non-white plantation owners as well. Although it left room for variations, none of these variations included the possibility of a revolutionary uprising in the slave plantations, let alone a successful one leading to the creation of an independent state. (Trouillot, 1995, p. 72)

He explores the link between colonisation and racism, and thus lays the foundations for European empires.

> Colonisation provided the most potent impetus for the transformation of European ethnocentrism into scientific racism. In the early 1700s, the ideological rationalisation of Afro-American slavery relied increasingly on explicit formulations of the ontological order inherited from the Renaissance. But in so doing, it also transformed the Renaissance worldview by bringing its purported inequalities much closer to the very practices that confirmed them. Blacks were inferior, and therefore enslaved; black slaves behaved badly, and were therefore inferior. In short, the practice of slavery in the Americas secured the blacks' position at the bottom of the human world. (Trouillot, 1995, p. 77)

The longer the myths of racial superiority and inferiority were allowed to be given credence, the greater the problems would be when it came to Abolition, emancipation and equal opportunities.

THE CHURCH OF ENGLAND REFLECTS

The Christian Church has had a complex history with regard to slavery. In the twenty-first century, the modern Church of England is able to cite biblical references to support the case against slavery. There are standard texts, from Genesis onwards, which to the modern reader might seem unambiguous and conclusive.

It has been conventional to refer to the image of God:

> So God created humankind in his image, in the image of God he created them; male and female he created them.

> Genesis 1. 27

The Bible sets out a covenant between God and Man:

> God said, "This is the sign of the covenant that I make between me and you and every living creature that is with you, for all future generations: I have set my bow in the clouds, and it shall be a sign of the covenant between me and the earth. When I bring clouds over the earth and the bow is seen in the clouds, I will remember my covenant that is between me and you and every living creature of all flesh; and the waters shall never again become a flood to destroy all flesh".

> Genesis 9. 12–15

There are frequent references to freedom and liberation:

> Thus says the LORD, the God of Israel, "Let my people go, so that they may celebrate a festival to me in the wilderness."

> Exodus 5. 1

Justice and peace are promised:

> Then justice will dwell in the wilderness, and righteousness abide
> in the fruitful field. The effect of righteousness will be peace, and
> the result of righteousness, quietness and trust forever. My people
> will abide in a peaceful habitation, in secure dwellings, and in quiet
> resting places.
>
> Isaiah 32. 16–18

Christ in his incarnation brought these themes together:

> Let the same mind be in you that was in Christ Jesus, who, though
> he was in the form of God, did not regard equality with God as
> something to be exploited, but emptied himself, taking the form of
> a slave, being born in human likeness.
>
> Philippians 2. 5–7

Christianity offers hope of a world beyond what is visible:

> The Spirit of the Lord is upon me, because he has anointed me to
> bring good news to the poor. He has sent me to proclaim release
> to the captives and recovery of sight to the blind, to let the oppressed
> go free, to proclaim the year of the Lord's favour.
>
> Luke 4. 18–19

Engagement in Christianity offered the prospect of change for sons
of God:

> Do not lie to one another, seeing that you have stripped off the old
> self with its practices and have clothed yourselves with the new self,
> which is being renewed in knowledge according to the image of its
> creator. In that renewal there is no longer Greek and Jew, circum-
> cised and uncircumcised, barbarian, Scythian, slave and free; but
> Christ is all and in all!
>
> Colossians 3. 8–11

Mankind was presented as being united through Christ:

He is the image of the invisible God, the firstborn of all creation; for in him all things in heaven and on earth were created, things visible and invisible, whether thrones or dominions or rulers or powers – all things have been created through him and for him. He himself is before all things, and in him all things hold together. He is the head of the body, the church; he is the beginning, the firstborn from the dead, so that he might come to have first place in everything. For in him all the fullness of God was pleased to dwell, and through him God was pleased to reconcile to himself all things, whether on earth or in heaven, by making peace through the blood of his cross.

Colossians 1. 15–20

Christ offered reconciliation:

For the love of Christ urges us on, because we are convinced that one has died for all; therefore all have died. And he died for all, so that those who live might live no longer for themselves, but for him who died and was raised for them. From now on, therefore, we regard no one from a human point of view; even though we once knew Christ from a human point of view, we know him no longer in that way. So if anyone is in Christ, there is a new creation; everything old has passed away; see, everything has become new! All this is from God, who reconciled us to himself through Christ, and has given us the ministry of reconciliation; that is, in Christ God was reconciling the world to himself, not counting their trespasses against them, and entrusting the message of reconciliation to us. So we are ambassadors for Christ, since God is making his appeal through us; we entreat you on behalf of Christ, be reconciled to God. For our sake he made him to be sin who knew no sin, so that in him we might become the righteousness of God.

2 Corinthians 5. 14–21

However, despite the apparently consistent Biblical position regarding sin and reconciliation, the position of the Church of England was compromised in previous centuries. Christians were involved in the slave trade and in slave ownership. Eventually Christians were at the forefront of the abolition movement, but the lead was first taken by Methodists and Unitarians.

Churches as institutions benefited from the proceeds of the Transatlantic Slave Trade, and then were compensated at the time of abolition. The initial Christian response to the horrors of transporting, trading and owning slaves, as the details became more widely known, was to ameliorate the abuses rather than abolish the system. It is not clear to what extent the Churches, and their members today, have been aware of the part played by the Church in slavery. Many Church leaders have found the emerging truth extraordinarily difficult to deal with, especially if they are working with multicultural congregations including African Diaspora communities.

It can be helpful to consider individual cases. Church communities, like all human institutions, can be imperfect. It is well for each age to examine its activities and values. The Christian tradition until the eighteenth century was that chattel-goods and trading slaves for slavery was acceptable to God, and that Christians were entitled to get rich from its proceeds. Plenty of biblical texts could be cited showing how the existence of slavery went unchallenged. So the way that the Bible is used in each generation, including the present day, is called into question. We might ask what evil elements of today's society go accepted and unnoticed, which future generations will condemn?

ABOLITION MOVEMENT AND ABOLITIONISTS

Whatever conclusions we form about the abolition of the Transatlantic Slave Trade, it is clear that it was not exclusively a British issue. However, as the British had come to dominate the slave trade in the eighteenth century, British decisions could have a global impact.

In 1765 Granville Sharp befriended a runaway slave named Jonathan Strong and consequently was closely involved in securing the famous legal ruling of 1772, abolishing slavery within England (the Somerset case, relating to the slave James Somerset). He became first chairman of the "Society for Effecting the Abolition of the Slave Trade", was a tireless abolitionist and also part of the founding group of Sierra Leone. Sharp laid the legal foundations for the campaign. He had published a pamphlet in 1769, setting out the case against slavery: "A Representation of the Injustice and Dangerous Tendency of Tolerating slavery; or of admitting the least Claim of Private Property in the Person of Man, in England".

> The perpetual service of a slave cannot, with propriety, be compared to the temporary service of an apprentice, because the latter is due only in consequence of a voluntary contract, wherein both parties have a mutual advantage; but in the former case, there is no contract, neither can a contract be even implied, because the free consent of both parties cannot possibly be implied likewise; and, without this, every kind of contract (in the very nature and Idea of such an obligation) is absolutely null and void. (pp. 163–164, Oldfield, 1998, p. 31)

A survivor of the "Middle Passage", Olaudah Equiano managed to buy and retain his freedom in spite of being cheated many times. He made a living as a hairdresser in London and educated himself, and became an associate of Granville Sharp. In 1789 he published his autobiography, and then sold the book throughout Britain, undertaking lecture tours and actively campaigning to abolish the slave trade. As he wrote, in "The Interesting Narrative of the Life of Olaudah Equiano, or Gustavus Vassa the African", London, 1789,

> After all, what makes any event important, unless by its observation we become better and wiser, and learn "to do justly, to love mercy, and walk humbly before God"?

Ottobah Cugoano was a slave brought by a merchant to England where he was set free. He played an important role in the case of Henry Demane, a black man due to be shipped to the West Indies as a slave. He worked with Granville Sharp, and in 1787 published an account of his experiences, "Thoughts and Sentiments on the Evil and Wicked Traffic of the Slavery and Commerce of the Human Species".

> Is it not strange to think, that they who ought to be considered as the most learned and civilized people in the world, that they should carry on a traffic of the most barbarous cruelty and injustice, and that many . . . are become so dissolute as to think slavery, robbery and murder no crime?

Slaves were more than just items of property. Slavery touched on basic principles of freedom and democracy, supposedly cherished by British politicians, as well as by freedom fighters in North America and revolutionaries in France.

Capel Lofft, in his "A Summary of a Treatise by Major Cartwright, entitled The People's Banner against undue Influence: or, the Commons' House of Parliament according to the Constitution" (1780), wrote:

> To be free is to be in a condition of giving assent to the laws of the state, either in person, or by a representative . . . To be enslaved is to have no will of our own in the choice of law makers; but to be governed by rulers whom other men have set over us.

THOMAS CLARKSON

After winning the 1785 Latin prize on slavery at Cambridge, with the essay "Is it lawful to make slaves of others against their will?", Thomas Clarkson met Granville Sharp and some Quakers, and together they formed the Society for the Abolition of the Slave Trade. In his 1786 "Essay on the slavery and Commerce of the Human Species", Clarkson wrote:

If liberty is only an adventitious right; if men are by no means superior to brutes; if every social duty is a curse; if cruelty is highly to be esteemed; if murder is strictly honourable, and Christianity is a lye; then it is evident, that the African slavery may be pursued, without either the remorse of conscience, or the imputation of a crime. But if the contrary of this is true . . . it is evident that no custom established among men was ever more impious; since it is contrary to reason, justice, nature, the principles of law and government, the whole doctrine, in short, of natural religion, and the revealed voice of God. (Wilson, 1989, p. 15)

Thomas Clarkson published a series of essays on the Slave Trade, stressing that the inhumanity on which it was based was in contradiction to the professed ideals of kings and politicians alike. The essays were given to the Spanish King, to new British Members of Parliament, and widely circulated in France.

Slave labour produced vital luxuries for the middle classes, such as sugar and coffee. It made sense, therefore, to focus a boycott campaign on sugar in 1792, backed by pamphlets and petitions. Among the campaigners there was awareness of the rebellion in 1791 in Santo Domingo, which provided a link with both Abolition and revolution.

Arguments in favour of slavery tried to proclaim benefits for the slave. Robert Norris gave evidence to the 1788 inquiry, about slaves on board ship:

The slaves had sufficient room, sufficient air, and sufficient provisions. When upon deck, they made merry and amused themselves with dancing. As to the mortality . . . It was trifling. In short, the voyage from Africa to the West Indies was one of the happiest periods of a Negro's life. (Wilson, 1989)

Clarkson was the researcher. He interviewed 20,000 sailors and collected specimens of the ugly slave-trade ironware. He drew the infamous diagram of the slave ship Brooks, showing spaces for 609 slaves. Thomas Clarkson concentrated on applying pressure for change. He maintained links with like-minded campaigners in

France and the United States, monitoring the political climate in each country. His 1788 "Essay on the Impolicy of the Slave Trade" showed that, of 5,000 sailors on Triangular Route in 1786, 2,320 came home, 1,130 died, 80 were discharged in Africa, and 1,470 were discharged in the West Indies.

The first petition of Parliament against the Transatlantic Slave Trade came from the Quakers in 1783, as the American War of Independence came to an end. The Society for the Abolition of the Slave Trade was formed in 1787, and that started a new era of the mobilisation of public opinion through education, campaigning, mass petitions and boycotts. With revolutionary ferment in France, radicals on the two sides of the Channel tried to learn from each other.

Committee work provided a rallying point for opponents of the Transatlantic Slave Trade. The campaign for Abolition was lengthy and tortuous. It involved the mobilisation of middle class opinion, in advance of the individuals having the right to vote. The campaign had to be outside Parliament, as well as within, using a range of campaigning techniques. In 1792 alone there were 519 petitions, with over 400,000 signatures.

Clarkson saw the Committee as a body,

> made up of a head and of various members, which had different functions to perform. . . . Every one was as necessary in his own office, or dependent, as another. (Wilson, 1989, p. 73)

Clarkson missed many Committee meetings, as he engaged in constant travel, and was the public face of the campaign. He wrote and distributed numerous papers tailored to the needs of particular groups of decision makers and readers. His efforts became obsessive and, worn out, in 1793 he went to the Lake District, to spend time with the Wordsworths, Southeys and Coleridges. In his two volume history of the abolitionist movement, he gave limited coverage of the roles of others such as Zachary Macaulay and James Stephen.

The Parliamentary spokesman was William Wilberforce, who depended on support from William Pitt the Younger and his government, if the law was to be changed. Clarkson prepared briefing material tailored to the concerns of the target audience, and located in the context of current debates. Sir George Stephen on Wilberforce, in "Antislavery", suggests that Wilberforce could have achieved little without support:

> He worked out nothing for himself; he was destitute of system, and desultory in his habits; he depended on others for information, and he required an intellectual walking stick (Wilson, 1989, p. 22)

Wilson, in her biography of Clarkson, argued that:

> Clarkson's chief contribution to abolition was his conception of this new form of extra-parliamentary action (Wilson, 1989, p. 26)

Between 1787 and 1788, the Society issued 51,432 pamphlets or books; 26,526 reports and other papers, as well as 103 petitions.

Thomas Clarkson was the driving force behind the campaign. He was the only one of the 12 founding members of the London Committee for the Abolition of the Slave Trade to live to see the emancipation of slaves in 1838, after a campaign lasting over 50 years, with its public climax coming when the Transatlantic Slave Trade was abolished in 1807. He was the researcher, writer, network builder, strategic planner, for example in relations with the campaign against slavery in France and the French overseas territories. He kept the records of the early committee meetings, and published memoirs to ensure that the battles on Abolition were won, and stayed won. His younger brother John Clarkson was a naval captain who transported freed slaves to supposed safety in Nova Scotia and Sierra Leone in 1791–93.

Thomas Clarkson maintained an uneasy relationship with Wilberforce, whose Parliamentary presence was seen as vital. Thomas Clarkson prepared the tailored briefings for Parliamentarians, building up the information base for the campaign. He worked in what was perhaps the most famous NGO campaign in history. His example was vital in the development of Amnesty International, from a small group in a back room to winning the Nobel Peace Prize in 1977.

Clarkson had explored the alternative avenue of pressing for emancipation with French colleagues through "Les Amis des Noirs". The problem was that the political environment was much less stable and manageable, during the successive phases of the French Revolution. The slaves of Santo Domingo and Guadeloupe responded to the declaration of the abolition of slavery in 1794, but in such a way that generated military conflict in the French West Indies. This polarised opinion, and precipitated warfare with the great powers, eclipsing arguments for emancipation.

From a Machiavellian perspective, we can understand Clarkson's strategy of working through accepted political channels, and not giving pride of place to African faces and voices. The argument was best pursued on the basis of tacit self-interest, in an iterative process of reaching the Parliamentary tipping point.

Thomas Clarkson secured the successive stages of emancipation of slaves in 1787–1838 by engaging those whose voices commanded the attention of target audiences. He understood the stages into which the process could be broken down. He recognised the value of symbols and public perceptions. In particular, he realised that the self-congratulatory tone of Parliamentary debates could help to consolidate each stage of change, albeit at the expense of inflating the egos of those concerned.

We should not neglect the ongoing campaign after 1807, both in Britain and in the West Indies, to ensure that slavery ended, that the law was obeyed in the colonies, and that alternative plans were explored for the relocation of slaves. Clarkson recorded the story to date in his 1808 "History of the Rise, Progress and Accomplishment of the Abolition of the African Slave-Trade by the British Parliament". In 1814 he was chairman of the "Society for the purpose of Encouraging the Black Settlers at Sierra Leone, and the Natives of Africa generally, in the Cultivation of their Soil, by the Sale of their Produce", which traded until 1819.

Pressure was maintained during the 1814 Congress of Vienna, where the slave trade was branded:

> desolation of Africa, the degradation of Europe, and the afflicting scourge of humanity

and then in the 1822 Congress of Verona. With renewed efforts, in 1830–31 the Society established 1,300 new branches, and submitted 5,484 petitions to Parliament.

After the death of Wilberforce in 1833, Clarkson engaged in spirited debates on the respective contributions of the two leaders, for example in the 1838 "Strictures on a Life of William Wilberforce" (with Henry Crabb Robinson). Wilson regarded that life as fatally flawed:

> The Life survived to take from Clarkson both his fame and his good name. It left us with the "simplistic myth of Wilberforce and his evangelical warriors in a holy crusade" (Wilson, 1989, p. 175).

Wordsworth dedicated a poem to his friend Clarkson, who visited the Lake District to relax in the company of romantic poets: "To Thomas Clarkson":

> Clarkson! It was an obstinate hill to climb:
> How toilsome – nay, how dire, it was, by thee
> Is known; by none, perhaps, so feelingly:
> But thou, who, starting in thy fervent prime,
> Didst first lead forth that enterprise sublime,
> Hast heard the constant Voice its charge repeat,
> Which, out of thy young heart's oracular seat,
> First roused thee. – O true yoke-fellow of Time,
> Duty's intrepid liegeman, see, the palm
> Is won, and by all Nations shall be worn!
> The blood-stained Writing is forever torn:
> And thou henceforth wilt have a good man's calm,
> A great man's happiness; they zeal shall find
> Repose at length, firm friend of human kind!

WILLIAM WILBERFORCE

William Wilberforce was the Member of Parliament for his native Hull. Wilberforce was an eloquent speaker, and well connected in Parliament, where he valued his independent status. Having identified key issues, he pursued them remorselessly. An Evangelical Christian, Anglican and member of the Clapham Sect, from 1787 he pursued his God-given vocation – "the abolition of the slave trade and the reformation of manners". Thanks to meeting Clarkson, and with the support of his university friend William Pitt, Wilberforce agitated against the slave trade and took every opportunity in the House of Commons of exposing its evils. He finally saw the Bill through the Commons, and Prime Minister Lord Grenville took the Bill through the House of Lords, in 1807.

Success in achieving abolition would require careful calculation. An abrupt move to emancipation could constitute a serious threat to the property rights of the slave owners in the West Indies, who were also voters and Members of Parliament at home in Britain. Political power and voting rights were based on property, and only a small minority of the population had the vote in Parliamentary elections.

The great campaigner William Wilberforce had purchased his Parliamentary seat in Hull. His political instincts, reinforced by his close links with the government of William Pitt the Younger, were to steer away from conflict. He wanted to see the Committee as part of a broad popular movement. There was a growing network of local committees, in Exeter and Plymouth, Newcastle, Nottingham, Edinburgh, Glasgow, Sheffield, Bristol, Norwich, Birmingham, Rotherham, Durham, etc.

As argued by Oldfield, in "Popular Politics and British Anti-slavery", the prevailing view of the abolitionist petitioners, in 1788, was that their feelings of guilt with regard to the British role in the slave trade could be cleansed through passing new legislation.

We are determined to persevere in our Application to our Representatives, with an additional Fervour, in Hopes that they may finally enact a Law for that most benevolent Purpose, and by so doing, clear the Land from the Guilt of Blood; nor suffer History to record that the Parliament of Great Britain was the Advocate of slavery, at the Time when the Virtue of the People demanded its Annihilation. (Oldfield, 1998)

John Wesley's last letter, written to William Wilberforce, expressed the vehemence of his own convictions:

February 1791

I see not how you can go through your glorious enterprise in opposing that execrable villainy which is the scandal of religion, of England, and of human nature. Unless God has raised you up for this very thing, you will be worn out by the opposition of men and devils. But if God be for you, who can be against you? Are all of them together stronger than God? O be not weary of well doing! Go on, in the name of God and in the power of his might, till even American slavery (the vilest that ever saw the sun) shall vanish away before it.

Reading this morning a tract wrote by a poor African, I was particularly struck by that circumstance that a man who has a black skin, being wronged or outraged by a white man, can have no redress; it being a 'law' in our colonies that the oath of a black against a white goes for nothing. What villainy is this? That He who has guided you from youth up may continue to strengthen you in this and all things, is the prayer of, dear sir,

Your affectionate servant, John Wesley

In 1792 3,865 people signed the Edinburgh petition on the spot, with a total of 10,885. The national total of 400,000 signatures represented 13% of the adult male population.

Wilberforce persisted with his campaign, with numerous publications, such as "Letter on the Abolition of the Slave Trade Addressed to the Freeholders and Other Inhabitants of Yorkshire" (1807), in which he sought to explain his campaign to northern residents. He was of course accused of being a fanatic, a charge he accepted in a speech in Parliament on 19 June 1816:

> They charge me with fanaticism. If to be feelingly alive to the sufferings of my fellow-creatures is to be a fanatic, I am one of the most incurable fanatics ever permitted to be at large.

LEARNING FROM WILBERFORCE

The abolition of the Transatlantic Slave Trade was not achieved overnight, but required an extensive campaign of mobilisation of opinion, both among decision-makers and the wider public. This was despite the fact that the findings from investigations into the slave trade, combined with generally accepted moral and religious principles, seemed overwhelming.

However, once the decision had been made, it was adhered to, and then used as the moral justification for subsequent policies, applying pressure on other countries to comply. Britain could claim the moral high ground, and avoid discussing the extent to which it had been committed to practices it now declared illegal. Once the tipping point had been reached, the world had moved on.

The lead spokesman, William Wilberforce, did not have a lengthy personal background in the specific field, but was an excellent communicator, and commanded respect as a campaigning philanthropist, whose integrity was not in question. He worked with a team of leading experts, with complementary skills and networks, using a set of international contacts. His core arguments were based on human rights, and appeals to moral and religious positions which were widely shared. Crucially, the campaign was carefully paced, and operated with the available procedural mechanisms of current political institutions. The campaign, the details of the arguments and the objectives developed over time.

It was important for Wilberforce to secure backing from government at the highest level where possible, and from influential speakers and opinion formers, giving them centre stage. This required a seat in Parliament, good connections, excellent timing, a capacity for rapid response, and sensitivity to the concerns of others. As a result, there was a series of Parliamentary debates, encouraging the view that the desired reform would come, and that it was simply a matter of time. The debates had an educative function, and were published. In 2006, one of Wilberforce's speeches on the slave trade was included in Melvyn Bragg's "Twelve books which changed the world". Parliament was seen as a place where change could be made.

The international dimension needed to be pursued, looking for parallels, synergies and opportunities for pressure. Close links were maintained with the USA and France, and efforts were synchronised where possible. This meant refining the message so that it was understood across borders. Furthermore, the objective was to secure international agreement with abolition, which meant it was important to build a trans-national movement.

Vested interests from the Transatlantic Slave Trade resisted reform at each stage, so needed to be exposed to a wider audience. The ongoing public relations battle was important, and needed expert writers, with effective networks. Particular objectors could be targeted with tailored arguments. The arguments of key opponents needed to be addressed, with a series of modified proposals if necessary, maintaining momentum. This required mastery of institutional procedures, for example in drafting Parliamentary bills. It also required support from an authoritative research team. The ongoing movement for emancipation has much to learn from Clarkson and Wilberforce.

WHAT WAS ABOLISHED IN 1807?

One major conceptual leap is required. Many of those who celebrate the abolition of the Transatlantic Slave Trade will see this as a landmark event in the history of race relations. More recent revisionist historical accounts have cast doubt on what was achieved in those terms, noting that abolition of the Transatlantic Slave Trade did not in itself mean emancipation of slaves, and that compensation was paid to the former slave owners, not to the former slaves.

Others point out that credit has conventionally been given to abolitionists in England. This has enabled the British to take pride in abolishing the Transatlantic Slave Trade, rather than acknowledging the scale of their involvement in that trade, and the extent to which it benefited the wealth of particular individuals and groups at the time. Instead it is suggested that the achievement of slaves in Santo Domingo, in the French Caribbean, in rebelling against their owners, building an army to defend the island, and defeating both the French and British armies over a prolonged and bloody war, was at least as important. In other words, the slaves won their freedom, despite their brutal repression at the hands of Napoleon for a period, and the political chicaneries and great power politics of the French, Americans and British.

Once the British had abolished their own involvement in the Transatlantic Slave Trade, they took on the role of world policeman, checking that others followed suit. There were of course aberrations. Illegal slave trading continued. There were large slave populations in Brazil, Cuba and the USA after 1838. King Leopold II of Belgium claimed to be ending the slave trade in Congo, while imposing his own régime of slave labour. All was not as it might have seemed.

As for the labour needs of the British West Indies, from 1838 these were met by the provision of Indian indentured labourers. By 1841, 7,000 poor Indians had been imported into the West Indies. By World War I, 250,000 came into Guyana, 134,000 into Trinidad, 33,000 into Jamaica. Very few returned home after their period of indenture.

We have to see Abolition in terms of Control and Participation. Slavery represents an extreme version of the situation where individuals lack Control over their own life and work, and lack the means of Participating in decision making. The key point about the legislation on abolition of the Transatlantic Slave Trade, in 1807, was that it changed the language of the debate. Perhaps it matters less that the vote was carried because it was in the interests of the British government to disadvantage the French colonies in the West Indies, cutting off their supply of new slaves on which their successful sugar production depended.

PRAGMATISM

There was a vital pragmatic aspect to the abolitionist campaign, and its support by the government of William Pitt the Younger. Simon Schama has illuminated this period with his "Rough Crossings". In the American War of Independence the British were prepared to arm freed slaves. For many of the states fighting for independence, slavery was an integral part of their economic and political system. For the British it was different. They had traded in slaves, but not kept them at home.

When the French Revolutionary government declared slavery illegal in 1794, this was regarded by the British as a threat to the order and sustained economic success of plantations in the West Indies and North America. Toussaint L'Ouverture seized on the announcement as supporting his 1791 rebellion in Santo Domingo, and the example was followed in other islands such as Guadeloupe. In an extended and bloody campaign in the French West Indies, British troops intervened to try to re-impose slavery and stability after the rebellion in Santo Domingo, seeking to defeat a black army of freed slaves. The slaves had gone well beyond being docile workers: here they were jeopardising British interests at international level. What was more, they posed a challenge to the military might of the British and French, who had each assumed superiority over a slave army.

The British were then prepared to end the Transatlantic Slave Trade, in order to cut off the supply of slaves to the French sugar plantations in the West Indies. By 1807, the United States was self-sufficient in slaves. The British West Indies were in decline by comparison with the French West Indies. Sugar production was developing in the East Indies, where slavery was not required.

It is hard to mount a sustained and principled campaign based on such considerations. The message needed to be carefully tailored, and phased. At each point it was vital to take into account the self-interest of the decision makers concerned, and to seek changes which could command majority support where it counted at the time.

The campaigners against the Transatlantic Slave Trade, such as William Wilberforce, were not originally arguing for the emancipation of slaves, which would have been seen as an unrealistic and extreme attack on the established order of things. Abolitionists were seeking the end of what we might today call the "extraordinary rendition" of slaves, their forced removal from their homes and delivery into servitude, without any reference to systems of law. It was argued, by Wilberforce, that slaves should be bred rather than traded. This would allow the hierarchical nature of society to continue, rather than chaos breaking out, in an imitation of the French Revolution. It was not suggested that all slaves who reached British shores should automatically be declared free. Indeed, it seemed important to find arrangements which did not result in an influx of freed slaves.

Stories emerged of grotesque abuses and scandals; live slaves being thrown overboard, rape and cruel torture. As such stories became more frequent, and the details were published, reform of some sort became necessary, and more likely. If the Transatlantic Slave Trade could not be made acceptable, following incremental reforms, it should be abolished.

STAGES OF EMANCIPATION

Emancipation, once it began, took place in stages. The ending of the Transatlantic Slave Trade, once enforced, cut off the supply of new slave labour to the New World. This did not necessarily inhibit trading between different colonies in the New World. In fact, the business case for breeding slaves was strengthened, and some plantations took this as a priority.

It was then a matter of managing the existing slave populations, restricting their capacity for rebellion. Knowledge of the slave rebellions in Santo Domingo and Guadeloupe, and of uprisings in the United States, was restricted. In areas where white owners and workers were heavily outnumbered by slaves, a strong local régime of law and order was required. When slaves escaped, it was considered to be important that they should be caught and returned, to maintain the status quo.

When emancipation came in 1833, under British legislation, this still did not mean crowds of free black former slaves on the streets of London. In the first instance, slaves were converted to apprentices until 1838. The practice of forced enlistment into the armed forces continued, involving both former slaves and newly captured Africans from West Africa. It was simple enough to institute forced labour for defined periods.

FROM ABOLITION TO EMANCIPATION

Abolition was not the end of the process, although the spotlight of history has been turned off. Emancipation in both West Africa and the West Indies was linked to the early stages of extending empire. The Slave Trade continued in Sierra Leone, despite abolition, with 1,000 transported in six months in 1813.

The Society for Propagation of the Gospel (SPG) had slaves in Barbados until the 1830s. In 1772 Thomas Thompson (SPG) declared that

> The African trade for Negro slaves is shown to be consistent with the principles of humanity and with the law of revealed religion.

The Church of England had neglected the introduction of Christianity for slaves, by comparison with approaches by the French, Spanish and Portuguese. It had been felt that there were dangers of baptism leading to calls for liberty. The Church owned the Codrington estates, which had been left to SPG in 1710, with 300 slaves. On abolition in 1833, SPG received £8,823 8s 9d in compensation. The work of the Society for Propagation of Christian Knowledge concentrated on education, not emancipation.

However, resistance to slavery increased. In 1823 Thomas Fowell Buxton MP led the campaign against slavery. He took a cautious approach to mitigation and amelioration:

> That the state of slavery is repugnant to the principles of the British Constitution and of the Christian religion; and that it ought to be gradually abolished throughout the British colonies with as much expedition as may be found consistent with due regard to the well-being of the parties concerned.

Away from direct British rule there could be difficult conflicts. The focus of abolitionist campaigning changed, and was often linked to missionary activity. The conflict came to a head in 1823, with the Demerara Uprising, when London Missionary Society missionary John Smith was sentenced to death. This weakened the abolitionist case until the 1830s, and missionaries avoided political involvement. British legislation in 1833 helped change attitudes in the West Indies, and owners received £20 million compensation.

PROPERTY RIGHTS

Straightforward emancipation of slaves would have been a threat to property rights, which were seen as fundamental to the system of law. The right to vote was determined on the basis of property. After a campaign of 20 years, the abolitionists achieved their Parliamentary victory, in a Parliament based on a limited franchise, by not challenging the vested interests of slave owners. Compensation was then offered to slave owners, who were being deprived of their property, not to former slaves, who had been deprived of their liberty.

GLOBAL EMANCIPATION

The campaign for emancipation continued. In 1850 Lord Russell argued:

> It appears to me that if we give up this high and holy work, and proclaim ourselves to be no longer fitted to lead in the championship against the curse and the crime of slavery, we no longer have a right to expect a continuance of those blessings, which by God's favour, we have enjoyed. I think the high, the moral and the Christian character of this nation is the main source and secret of its strength.

The debate raged, as it was argued that slavery provided the motor for African development. Zubayr Pasha was quoted, in Lord Lugard's "The Dual Mandate",

> Slavery you say is bad. I agree that it is bad, but slave labour is to the interior of Africa what steam-power is to your country. In your great factories where steam is used, is all well with the employees? Is there not much misery and suffering? Well, if the Angel of God came and saw the unhappiness of your factories and said: "This must not continue: abolish steam" would you think it a wise decree? (Lugard, 1965, p. 365)

There was a series of international conferences on slavery, beginning with the 1815 Congress of Vienna. The French were reluctant to yield to British pressure. In 1839 the British and Foreign Anti-Slavery Society was founded, with middle class support, fuelled by guilt. The British were opposed to the Islamic Slave Trade, and David Livingstone sought to stop it.

ANTI-SLAVERY AND THE WORKING CLASS

The campaign for which William Wilberforce was the figurehead was created to secure the abolition of the Slave Trade, rather than the emancipation of slaves. Wilberforce believed that slaves should be bred, rather than traded. The campaign was not primarily based on a shared concern for human rights, but driven by a need to feel comfortable with the role of Britain in the world. The campaign involved few slaves or former slaves, but made great use of marketing techniques, such as Wedgwood's medal "Am I not a man and a brother?".

The timing of the British Parliamentary process in 1787–1838 was conditioned by international political and economic realities. As it became clear that the newly independent USA did not need continued imports of new slaves, the economic balance of evidence shifted, and the Triangular Slave Trade took on a new form, servicing the colonies of other European nations. During the period of the French Revolution and Napoleonic Wars, with conflicts in North America and the West Indies as part of a world war between Britain and France, policy on slavery kept changing. The British abolition of the Transatlantic Slave Trade was in essence an attack on France, via the French West Indies, after alternating policies on slavery from the Revolutionary and Napoleonic governments in France.

On this basis, the Anti Slavery Movement could be seen as the mobilisation of middle class citizens from middle England. They succeeded in shifting the centre of gravity of debate. Because of the limited electoral franchise in Britain, the 400,000 petitioners against the slave trade in one year exceeded the national electorate. A tipping point was reached. Unlike France, Britain was not going to re-establish the slave trade or slavery. We need to understand what had changed.

It is illuminating to read E.P. Thompson's classic "The Making of the English Working Class", and to find silence regarding slavery. A similar silence can be heard from Tristram Hunt's "Building Jerusalem", concerning Victorian cities.

The Committee for the Abolition of the Slave Trade were mobilising the middle class, building groups in towns and cities around the country, publishing a flow of material and co-ordinating the preparation of petitions. They were seeking to influence decisions in Westminster, and the publications were tailored to the detailed circumstances. They were working during the period of the French Revolution and the early days of the United States. Thomas Clarkson maintained close international links.

It would be a mistake to be dogmatic about the content of the silences. We can, however, speculate.

The economic benefits of the slave trade, and the trade in the other goods in the Triangular Trade, helped fuel the British industrial revolution. Successful merchants typically preferred to present themselves as civic benefactors, distancing themselves from the slave trade and plantation ownership which had brought their wealth. It was not proper, in polite society, to be associated with practices which were now recognised as barbaric. The campaign for abolition, and its success, gave rise to feelings of self-righteousness, and superiority over those other countries who continued the trade which Britain had dominated. The Parliamentary vote for Abolition in 1807 was seen as a landmark decision in which the British could take pride. That perception is echoed in public sentiments in 2006.

There were few slaves in Britain, so the decision was in some senses symbolic. Slaves were not freed until 1838, after a period of apprenticeship from 1833. The decision did not require the petitioners to change the organisation of their work. They were from the middle classes, employers of workers. Slavery as conducted by others threatened to undercut their own prosperity. Abolishing slavery in the French West Indies would be good for British business. There was no pressure to emancipate slaves in Britain, or to offer asylum to former slaves. Property rights continued to dominate. Slave owners, including the Church of England, benefited from compensation. It was convenient to draw a veil over the past.

Thompson's attention was on the employees, and their formation into a working class. Hunt highlighted the squalor of nineteenth century cities, where the focus had been on private profit rather than on public services.

In many respects, the industrial working class in Britain, and groups such as Welsh quarry workers, enjoyed lives that were little better than those endured by many slaves. They lacked control over their own work. They were unable to participate in decision making. They worked long hours for low pay, and lived in poor conditions. They had no voice in Parliament. However, they were not racially distinct from their employers, and in principle it was possible for a worker to become an employer.

For the growing working class, the campaign for the abolition of the Transatlantic Slave Trade had little practical relevance. If the campaign was understood at all, it was seen as being in the interests of the middle class, who were trying to develop their political influence. The conditions of the workers did not change. Textile workers depended on cotton imports, but these could increasingly come from the East Indies, where slave labour was not used, rather than from the Southern states of the USA.

"The Age of Revolution", as chronicled by Eric Hobsbawm, transformed the political situations in France and the United States.

In Britain, by contrast, slavery and the slave trade can be seen as pawns in an international chess game, in which the British ruling class were able to strengthen their position both overseas and at home. Marx and Engels saw Britain as ripe for revolution, which did not come.

PARALLELS

In today's continuing campaigns in the context of slavery and Citizenship, we can identify a number of compelling parallels.

Child labour

There are International Labour Organisation conventions to be ratified, but then difficult issues of enforcement in an era of deregulation. In many cases parents connive in the underage employment of their children, for financial reasons. At the same time, children working under age are not being educated, as is their right, and may be exposed to risk. This is a successor issue to slavery and the slave trade, and is seen as such by the International Labour Organisation and Anti Slavery International.

Corporate killing

The Blair government in Britain gave repeated assurances in 1997 that legislation was planned to hold company managers responsible for deaths of workers, but there has been a long delay. In the interim, there have been cases, such as rail crashes, where company executives have escaped punishment, although the public view, and that of the judge, has been that they were responsible. Steady pressure, and co-operation on pilot programmes for improved safety and advice to managers, is likely to produce results.

International outsourcing

International outsourcing can enable managers to externalise the costs and risks associated with particular functions, reduce their wage costs, and ignore the health consequences for workers. Improvements have come from pressure group campaigning.

Social gradient

Here we have the most radical challenge. International epidemiological research has shown a consistent correlation between social status and health outcomes, across the world. Where people lack control over their lives and work, and lack the chance to participate in decisions about their own futures, this is reflected in health outcomes, and in measurable levels of stress. The gaps between rich and poor, strong and weak, in most societies, are becoming wider.

Each case requires a distinctive strategy and tactics, with practical intermediate targets. It is a matter of taking the debate forward so that the "tipping point" is reached, enabling change, and paradigm shift. What had previously seemed radical positions need to become seen as mainstream common sense. There need to be sound reference points, reflected in the language used. This process must be carefully handled, so that there can be maximum ownership of the change, which can then be sustained.

Patterns of decision making have not wholly changed over the last 200 years. There is always a public position, expressed in simple terms. The "truth" is more complex. Details tend only to be disclosed on a need to know basis, with tight control over sensitive information.

For the UK, the history of the Slave Trade, slavery and emancipation raises questions of social class, domestic service, forced labour, transportation to the colonies, treatment of the Irish and treatment of the working class. Many of these issues can be addressed through a consideration of Control and Participation.

CHAPTER 5

DIASPORA

We respectfully beg leave to inform your Excellency that we have communicated with our tribe (that is in Trinidad) and have resolved to brave all dangers and run all risks, if the British government will afford us a passage to Sierra Leone. Those dangers and risks we do not apprehend to be either as serious or as numerous as the philanthropic Secretary of State for the Colonial Department in his anxiety for our safety and welfare seems to anticipate, as some of our tribe have already performed the journey from our country to Sierra Leone, overland. On our arrival at that settlement we shall meet with a number of our brethren and we shall then make such arrangements as will ensure us a safe journey across the Country. This of course will be done at our own expense from our own resources. We never thought of taxing the generosity of the British government so far as to require an escort from the Sea Coast.

Jonas Bath, and Mandingo slaves of Trinidad, 1831. de Verteuil, A. (1992) *Seven Slaves and Slavery: Trinidad 1777–1838*. Port of Spain, NP, pp. 266–9.

SUMMARY NARRATIVE

At one level, there is a simple narrative of the African Diaspora associated with the Transatlantic Slave Trade.

In West Africa, centuries of the Transatlantic Slave Trade meant raids, war and the fomentation of factionalism between local tribes and states. It meant an increase in the supply of arms, and a variety of forms of trickery, which could lead previously free citizens being sold as slaves.

⋅ As a result, the West African coastline and inland states were destabilised. The population was greatly reduced, with the removal of able bodied and skilled personnel. Local markets and industries were destroyed.

More radically, slavery brought with it cultural genocide. Whole peoples were uprooted and scattered, with destructive and enduring effects on the African psyche. Continuity of cultural traditions was broken. It may be difficult or impossible to reconstruct the links.

Meanwhile in Europe, the textile industries of cotton and wool grew. Jobs were created in shipbuilding and its attendant industries. Ships needed crews, and often crews were pressed, rather than recruiting volunteers. Sugar refining required both capital and labour. Burgeoning economies needed banking and insurance. European economies, especially in Britain, were booming.

In the Caribbean and Americas, raw labour was a major resource. After emancipation, employment became an acute problem. The infrastructure was not developed. Most people cultivated the land on small plots for a living, and provided a cheap hired labour source for the sugar industry and agriculture.

During the late nineteenth century, slavery was formally abolished around the world, but the legacy of racially based employment relations was continued in European empires, including the British Empire. At the end of the nineteenth century and the early part of the twentieth century, the Scramble for Africa placed new pressure on Africans in their homelands. New borders were set out by the colonial powers, whose main objective was to achieve great power status.

After the First World War, major powers took on Mandates on behalf of the League of Nations, supposedly helping colonial people toward independence.

After the Second World War, European colonial powers like Britain had a labour shortage. They turned to their colonies in the Caribbean in order to address the shortfall. Immigrants to Britain suffered poor housing, racism and physical abuse. A growing British-born generation of black people began to suffer from deprived inner-city blight and racism. They were more likely to be unemployed than their white counterparts, and they suffered more at the hands of the police and criminal system. Increasing racial tensions led eventually to riots in Brixton, Liverpool, Bristol and other urban areas where there was a large black population, at various times from the 1950s through to the 1990s.

There has been an ongoing negative impact of slavery on black people. Slavery is not an event but a process, whose legacy continues. Africans in Europe saw that their original home countries had been destabilised, and did not feel fully at home in Europe. There had been a history of compromises and complicity in the Transatlantic Slave Trade, which is still difficult to discuss, even when the historical facts are known. The psychological trauma involved cannot be underrated. African people felt uprooted. They realised that Africans had been seen as fair game for slavery because they were not generally Christians. They had been dehumanised: their lives had been considered of less value than those of white people. The dehumanisation affected both the slave and the slave owner.

The African experience of slavery, and the African Diaspora experience of Empire and independence, have often been absent from school curricula. Parents have relied on schools to provide balanced education and socialisation, but school students have often failed to find the history of their own people. Teachers themselves have had a limited background. As a result, both the descendants of slaves and of slave owners have been deprived of a balanced picture of the past, and this has had continuing adverse effects on current relationships.

There is a strong case for reparations, in the sense of writing and publishing an honest account of the events of the African Diaspora, which has been a major event in world history. Our picture of the past needs to be repaired, which can be conducted through dialogue in the present, enabling a sustainable future based on mutual healing.

Reparation is also a process of recovery. It requires a supportive space, or an area for dialogue, in which the scope for agreement can be explored. With care, and over time, areas of sensitivity can be revealed. It is a two-way process, as simple "apologies" without acceptance and reciprocation tend to achieve little. Experience of a process of Truth and Reconciliation, as was found in South Africa after Apartheid, can have problematic stages. The outcomes will not be predictable.

Once silence is broken, it cannot be assumed that mutual understanding will automatically follow. It is more likely that there will be an interim period of difficulty and uncertainty, as the dialogue partners gain insights into each other. To take one simple example, members of the majority white population may ask why Africans do not go back to "their own countries", or make reference to practices which continue in "their own countries", without grasping that the Diaspora experience involves not having one's own country.

THE DIASPORA EXPERIENCE

Whole communities in West Africa were uprooted and scattered by the Slave Trade. Young people were transported to locations across the New World, separated from friends and family. During the era of slavery they had no choice regarding where to live, and no opportunity to return to the land of their roots. The Transatlantic Slave Trade was a process of forced globalisation, as slaves, and then their descendants, made their lives in new countries, such as the United States and the West Indies. This distorted economies and societies. Residence did not necessarily feel permanent. Individuals had a yearning for a past about which they knew little, and which did not relate to their present reality.

As Abolition and emancipation began, there were attempts at relocation of freed slaves, for whom there was no welcome in societies which had been dominated by slavery. There were few freed slaves in the United States or the British West Indies. Slaves had been seen as a good way of dealing with a short term transitional labour problem, but there had been no long term plan. It was assumed that somehow slaves would go home, or move elsewhere, once their services were no longer needed. Where slaves died in transit or at work, the problem did not arise. As families developed, and slaves lived into old age, the issue of co-existence in a multi-cultural society began to develop.

Piecemeal attempts at relocation, such as in Nova Scotia and Sierra Leone, met with limited success. Groups from mixed backgrounds had to form new cultures, often in hostile circumstances. In Sierra Leone, former slaves were returning to an area where the slave trade was still active.

The opportunities for the Diaspora populations were then constrained by the policies of host countries. They could not establish their own identities in their own lands. They did not fit neatly into the pattern adopted by other minority groups, who could be "hyphenated", as German-Americans, Italian-Americans, etc, with affiliations and loyalties in two separate countries. To be Afro-American, or African-American, was not as straightforward.

In the United States, a permanent underclass of poor black families developed, located in the Southern States, with no real chance of overall improvement. There was a possibility of social mobility for a select few, but this was exceptional. Former slaves and their descendants had reverted to small scale subsistence farming, and tended not to be active participants in the new industrial society.

As Empire changed to Commonwealth, with self-determination and independence, there could be complications, such as the role of Indians and other Asians in administering the British Empire. Hierarchies developed, based on race. In numerous British colonies, Indian administrators had managed government in the period of indirect rule, and had provided much of the entrepreneurial middle class. In the British West Indies, however, Indian indentured labourers had provided a new labour force once slaves were emancipated.

The process continues, as each generation of young people tries to make sense of their own situation, and their background. There is no single history, and there has been little attention to the African Diaspora experience in the mainstream education system.

There has still been no wholesale international recognition of the prolonged process of genocide which took place, or of the scale of cultural dislocation. Diaspora communities are now active, returning to their roots, though geographically distant. Discussion of reparations is growing. The debate cannot be avoided. There needs to be a way in which the debate can have productive outcomes. Simple demands for financial compensation tend to produce adverse responses, especially from those who feel that their own interests are threatened, and have limited understanding of the events of the past.

Unlike the Holocaust in which 6 million Jews died in the twentieth century, the genocide associated with the Transatlantic Slave Trade had enduring shameful associations. The status of a slave continues to be seen as humiliating. With each phase of discovery of new information, the shame can be complicated. The sexual aspects of slavery cannot be avoided: rape, forced sexual relationships and exploitative behaviour by slave owners have left a literal legacy in genetic form: many African Diaspora members have mixed ancestry, about which they have only partial knowledge. In a world where people like to research their family histories, the African Diaspora is not well served.

DIASPORAS

There are many groups who see themselves as having undergone Diasporas. They trace a history of enslavement by a larger and oppressive imperial power, but seek to retain a distinctive identity. Typically there have been means of escaping to exile overseas, while retaining links to the homeland. Over time, links between home and exile communities have fluctuated.

It may be helpful to compare the African and Jewish diasporas. The Jewish people were united by a common core faith, and focused on scriptures. Wherever they are, across the world, traditions have been observed over the millennia. History has been complex, with the Jews continuing to feel united by persecution. They know who they are.

By contrast, the peoples of West Africa were not part of a single nation, with a single language and an agreed set of borders. Instead, there were numerous states and languages, oriented towards the interior of Africa, and little known in the outside world. There is a long and varied coastline, but this had been of little interest to West Africans. Trade, including the slave trade, had been across the Sahara. There was a strong tradition of culture and learning, but this was not known by, or of interest to, external traders.

The African Diaspora was not occasioned by invasion or political decisions, but driven by commercial motivation. Africans left West Africa, not of their own volition, but because they had been captured and sold, as part of a trade in human beings. They did not know where they were going, and it was rarely possible to maintain any contact with home. In essence, they were regarded, by their own communities, as having died, as if in a Tsunami, swept away in a human tide. The African Diaspora left a trail of damage at home, together with a flow of individuals forced to relocate and rebuild their lives in new continents.

Diaspora peoples face the challenge of whether to try to maintain their distinctive cultural identities, or to integrate with the cultures in the contexts to which they have moved. This implies the existence of some element of choice.

The African Diaspora faced additional difficulties. Individuals were captured and sold, and removed from the groups to which they were accustomed. Their new owners sought to keep them apart from their former colleagues and communities, in order to make them easier to manage.

THE NEW WORLD

In many parts of the New World, slaves formed a majority of the population. There was no pre-existing local organisational culture into which to integrate. Slaves were simply set to work hard, in hostile environments, and with high death rates. They were likely to die before they got old.

The United States were distinctively different, for example as compared with the West Indies and Brazil. Plantations in states which maintained slavery developed stability in relatively healthy conditions, which meant that slaves were able to develop family life and children, reducing reliance on imports of further slaves. A slave culture could thus develop over several generations, but without the support of formal education.

Not only did slaves not share a common language and culture from West Africa. Few Africans were literate. There were few established literatures, but a strong oral tradition.

Individual Africans were plucked from an oral tradition in which they could make sense of life and relationships. They were deposited in an alien setting, where often nobody else spoke the same language, obliging them to use Pidgin English, Pidgin French or Créole.

It is therefore not surprising that the culture of the African Diaspora has been varied and discontinuous. There has been forced syncretism, rather than the maintenance of a common culture.

INTEGRATION

Approaches to integration varied by geographical area. In the United States, political leaders recognised the anomaly of fighting for freedom but maintaining slavery. Thomas Jefferson assumed that if slaves were to be freed, they would have to be moved to another country. He saw no possibility of maintaining a multi-cultural multi-ethnic society after the inevitable end of slavery. State law and plantation practice reinforced the distinctions between black and white, slave and owner. Racially mixed sexual relationships were discouraged.

By contrast, in the West Indies, mortality rates were generally higher, both in transit and at work, so there was a reliance on a continued flow of slaves. Slaves could be the majority of the local population. Sexual relations between owners and slaves were more common, resulting in the development of a mulatto population, with varying shades of skin colour.

There has been research comparing culture and relationships in slave and post slave societies in the United States and Brazil. In both cases, the law distinguished owner and slave, white and black. The cultural contexts became very different. As a result, societies vary greatly, despite the common origins of the slaves, as citizens of Africa.

With the end of the Transatlantic Slave Trade, there was some continuing trade in the Americas, meaning that individual family histories can become very complex.

CULTURES OF DIASPORA

Music and theatre provide a backdrop to Diaspora, with an atmosphere and rhythm, allowing the audience to join in. They can reveal underlying connections.

Negro spirituals, blues and jazz have crossed borders. The themes are familiar and universal. By voicing concerns which are conventionally kept silent, they are made public and articulate. There is tacit knowledge, which can be maintained and shared, expressed but not verbalised. Consciousness has to be raised and updated, ready for implementation of decisions when the time is right.

Slavery and post-slavery life in the USA was made almost bearable for some, through the creation of what became in effect an alternative reality. Life on the plantation was self-contained for the slaves, with limited prospects of any change in a total institution. With emancipation, integration with the white majority population remained limited. Black culture continued to be coherent and different, but with some means of access to non-black participants.

In an oral culture, with a foundation of shared experience, there can be access to tacit knowledge. Paradoxically, cultures based on the written word have come to be dependent on explicit knowledge, to the exclusion of other forms of knowledge. In contrast, the oral culture deals with implicit knowledge of how organisations and societies work, and relies on tacit knowledge, often expressed in non verbal terms.

During the Enlightenment of the eighteenth century, the dominant European cultures from which the slave owners came created an elaborate structure of academic disciplines. They developed accounts of evidence and reasoning in increasingly exact terms. This was presented in the name of science, as if the founders of the new disciplines, and their own cultural contexts, were insignificant. We can praise the achievement of Sir Isaac Newton in laying the foundations for physics, and presenting a view of the world as stable, following the supposed model of the heavens. We need to recall that he suffered personal financial ruin as a result of his investments in the Slave Trade, through the South Sea Company. In practice, the scientific establishment defined the nature of what would pass as science. This depended on a sound foundation of formal education, which was of course denied to slaves. The result was a parallel set of realities. The formal disciplines have then provided ramparts against external attack. The call has been for "evidence based decisions", a call which is perhaps less credible when it emerges that those who issue the call like to determine what is to count as evidence.

Traditionally Afro-American culture has been seen as inferior to the dominant white culture. A deficit model has been used, seeing Afro-American culture as lacking scientific and technological foundations, compared with the ideal represented by White Anglo Saxon Protestant (WASP) culture.

Two hundred years after the abolition of the Transatlantic Slave Trade, we may see the culture of the African Diaspora as having achieved a previously unrecognised level of dominance. In the USA, the claims of science and technology, made by descendants of the fathers of the European Enlightenment, were overstated. This led to the creation of silos of specialists in a society with wide power distance between rich and poor. It has been assumed that technology can provide the answer to a wide range of human problems, ranging from missile defence to environmental emissions. The black perspective has been more human centred. Knowledge is socially constructed, based on networks, rather than vertical hierarchies. This corresponds more to modern popular culture, including the technologies of globalisation.

The black American experience was of chattel slavery. White Americans, all immigrants or descended from immigrants, had experience of wage slavery, in the context of the myth of equality of opportunity in the New World of the USA. In neither case did the individual have control of his own life and work, nor was there an effective opportunity to participate in decision making. The common experience of the working man is of distance from power.

Today the popular culture of the Southern states of the USA reflects the Afro-American past. This may be contrasted with Europe, where the discourse still refers back to the intellectual context of the Enlightenment.

THE ROLE OF LEADERSHIP

It is easier for leaders to subject others to slavery than to facilitate their arrival at citizenship. Leadership tends to focus on the role of the individual. However, the challenge is to provide a way forward for others, in a way that does not depend on the continued position of that particular individual.

Is there advice that can be shared? We can refer back to past experience, but we cannot necessarily transfer that to others who have not shared that experience. From joint experience we can build incremental trust. Building citizenship is about trust and social capital formation. It is culturally situated. It takes time.

Leadership during a Diaspora process is a matter of creating contexts in which citizenship could be created. These contexts have to be linked back to what was familiar, providing an anchor point. Individuals need to recognise how they can draw on their past experience, and apply it to the new situation. They need an opportunity to put this to the test. Arriving at a destination, the leader needs to enable others to realise that they can take on the necessary set of complementary roles. This means incremental experience of decision making, and the possibility of making mistakes.

The Jews were led by a series of prophets, taking them through the Wilderness to the Promised Land. They were together, with recognised structures, and with chroniclers.

For the African Diaspora, this was inherently much more dif-ficult. Individuals had been artificially put together, from many different backgrounds, in contexts that were humiliating to all concerned. There was a lack of opportunities for shared experience and incremental building of trust. Groups were kept separate on plantations. Rebellions often represented the first chance for joint working. The French Diaspora communities, bringing together Francophone communities around the world, are beginning to appreciate the strength of their own tradition.

TOUSSAINT L'OUVERTURE

Toussaint L'Ouverture was unusual among slaves, in that he was highly educated, and able to work with fellow slaves, steering them towards key leadership roles. He persuaded them that they could command slave armies, and they succeeded in defeating a series of European opponents. In so doing, they undermined the central assumption which had been instilled into Europeans: it was obvious, they had thought, that Europeans were inherently superior to Afri-cans. Interestingly, on their return, the surviving defeated forces of Britain, France and Spain said very little about their experience in Santo Domingo and the French West Indies. Their regiments tend to omit details of the campaign from their supposedly glorious his-tories. The silence speaks louder than any words.

The humiliation of Europeans by Africans in the Americas, despite their very different journeys through life, was the key element that determined the need to abolish the Slave Trade, and then slavery. The experience of Santo Domingo showed that there could be no assured security for slave owners in a slave society. It could not be assumed that order could be maintained, or that it could be restored by force once it had broken down.

LESSONS FROM DIASPORA FOR THE UK

There is a need to consider the impact on the UK of the breaking of the silence on the history of the Transatlantic Slave Trade and slavery. The need goes beyond the African Diaspora communities, as there have been deep-seated assumptions regarding the history and legacy of the British Empire. That history must be re-written, and the legacy re-considered. We will not reach definitive conclusions, but we can open up new, and long overdue, dialogue.

The foundation of much British wealth in London, Bristol, Liverpool and the Midlands, was laid through the Transatlantic Slave Trade and the other sections of the Triangular Trade. Slavery provided the products for coffee shop society. Leading businessmen preferred to present themselves as civic benefactors, rather than as slave traders or plantation owners. They were not proud of how they made their money.

When the Slave Trade was abolished in 1807, there was an extended process before slaves were first converted to apprentices in 1833 and freed in 1838.

It is vital to recall that slavery pre-dated the Transatlantic Slave Trade, which added the rigid and visible overlay of race to a form of work organisation based on restricting control and participation for the individual worker. Stereotypical views continued, and racial difference still overlays social class. As in the USA, the view of the white majority was taken as the basis for government, governance and the management of business and society.

If we accept the orthodox view that there is a current transition, from vertical steering to horizontal networking, as the basis for business and society, we are faced with a paradox. The present leaders of British society and business, drawn from the white majority community, have typically reached senior positions through the vertical system. Networking has not formed part of their way of life. They have had a focus on vertical reporting, relying on detailed analysis of explicit quantitative data.

While it has been standard for developed countries such as the UK to lead management and leadership development in Africa, there has, until recently, been less discussion of learning by the UK from this experience.

We can compare the situations of slaves and industrial workers. Slavery was based on an authoritarian approach to work organisation. The individual worker was denied control over his work or an opportunity to participate in decisions. The conditions of the British industrial working class were based on a vast power distance between rich owners and poor workers, typically of the same race. The campaigners against the Slave Trade were not all seeking the emancipation of slaves. Their concerns did not extend to the conditions of the working class, and did not involve practical change at home. There were revolutions in the USA and France, but not, the textbooks have told us, in Britain. We may wish to challenge that view, and conclude that the British establishment did not wish to come to terms with the revolutionary implications of networking.

INDEPENDENCE

Training for former colonies has often carried implications of colonial ways of thinking. Top down management, outsourcing, improving efficiency: colonial administrators would feel at home. Indians have long been administering such processes in the British Empire, and now in the globalised economy.

Arguably the UK, and in particular England, would benefit from lessons on how to achieve and sustain independence. How can the necessary networks be built which enable a transition, from vertical rule by others, to horizontal rule by the community and society?

At the moment England is in a transitional phase, as a side-effect of devolution in the UK. There is a Scottish Parliament and a Welsh Assembly, but an absence of local regional democratically accountable self-government in the English regions. Scotland and Wales had complained of centuries during which they had been ruled as colonies. Devolution has met some of their concerns.

Now the former colonies have been made independent, and joined by Scotland and Wales. Attention has reverted to Northern Ireland, and the restoration of devolved administration.

Where does that leave England? A large number of major employers are now owned overseas. It is easy for jobs to be relocated. There is considerable reliance on immigrant workers, who take on the low paid jobs which the native population seeks to avoid.

The British social class system continues: less visible, but as influential as Apartheid in South Africa. The gap between rich and poor is as wide as ever. There are separate forms of life.

TIME TO LISTEN

Slaves left African villages to serve owners in the New World. Their descendants are the African Diaspora.

The new generation of black African leaders epitomise another set of stories. They speak English or French as part of their imperial heritage. They have often studied internationally. It is time to listen.

Colonial administrators left England to manage outposts of the Empire. Some continued as expatriates, but with continued contacts at home. How can we make sense of that British Diaspora?

The British abroad tend to have taken their cultural baggage and assumptions with them. On the other hand, they expect immigrants to the UK to integrate. The British have assumed that their culture is naturally dominant. This has not equipped them to deal with the USA or the EU.

RECONCILIATION

Lessons can be learned from the experience of the South African Truth and Reconciliation Commission. After the period of Apartheid had come to an end, it was recognised that there was a need to break silences; individuals and organisations needed to be able to acknowledge responsibility for their past actions.

The Bicentenary celebrations in 2007 will place the last two centuries under the microscope. Questions will be asked about a period which has been largely excluded from school history books in recent years. Mature debate depends on access to information. In a field where there are still many areas of silence, the quality of debate can suffer. It is time to listen to the African Diaspora, and to learn.

GLOBAL CITIZENS

It is clear that the history of the African Diaspora has transcended national borders. African Diaspora members can rarely associate themselves with a single country. Their lives, and those of their ancestors, have involved movement, and little stability. In a world now characterised by globalisation, and rapid change in both technologies and organisations, the experience of the African Diaspora could prove vital. As processes of dialogue and networking are developed, we should recall that such skills have been vital for both effective resistance, and for survival.

Africa holds the key to the origins of human civilisation. The African Diaspora may hold the key to its continuation. Reparation for a tragic past may be integrated with preparation for a constructive future.

RENDEZVOUS OF VICTORY

Rendezvous of Victory is a Heritage Learning movement that seeks to continue and advance globally the historical work of Communities of Anti-slavery Abolitionist Resistance. The name was inspired by the vision and words of Aimé Césaire, in his "Notebook of a Return to my Native Land".

CITIZENSHIP EDUCATION IN THE LIGHT OF PAN-AFRIKAN RESISTANCE TO THE MAANGAMIZI

By Kofi Mawuli Klu, Joint Coordinator, *Rendezvous of Victory (ROV)*

I would rather die upon yonder gallows than live in slavery!

Sam Sharpe, 1832

This is a quotation recorded by Henry Bleby during his prison visits to Sam Sharpe, one of the most outstanding Heroes of the Pan-Afrikan Resistance to the Chattel Enslavement of Afrikan people by the European powers. This was just before he was executed by hanging, in the name of the British Crown, on 23rd May 1832, after a kangaroo trial for spearheading the "Anti-Slavery Christmas Emancipation Rebellion" which took place between 28th December 1831 and 5th January 1832 in the so-called West Indies island of Jamaica. It sombrely yet vividly depicts the great indomitable *Sunsum* (Spirit) of Active Citizenship, defending Human and Peoples' Rights, which characterised the Abolitionist Freedom-fighting of the Afrikan people against Chattel and other forms of Enslavement.

This same kind of Active Citizenship is continuously being regenerated by Pan-Afrikan Resistance worldwide, not only to the vestiges of Chattel and Colonial Enslavement from the past, but also to the present-day Neocolonial Enslavement of Afrikan people all over the continent and diaspora of Afrika. It lends the greatest credence to the view we share that true Citizenship cannot be limited to the narrow confines of a single nation-state or even particular union of states (e.g. the European Union or the United States of America). Rather it makes better sense, more so in terms of universal human rights in this World of increasingly faster globalization, in the transnational dimensions within which Afrikan people are compelled to exercise defence of their still globally transgressed Human and Peoples' Rights: hence our preference for the term Global Citizenship. This Global Citizenship, in the Pan-Afrikan perspective, is derived from such indigenous Knowledge and Value Systems of Afrikan Civilization such as *Maat* (Ancient Kemet), *Ubuntu* (South Africa), and *Nunya/Nyansapo* (the Ewe and Akan of West Africa).

The wide diversity of Communities of peoples, to be found in most countries, demands the historical and contemporary concretization of Citizenship Education not only in the United Kingdom but also the rest of Europe and the World. This would enable us to meaningfully ascertain the specifics in the experience of each Community so as to more accurately outline the generalities for all Humankind from the actual realities of Life over the span of all Time for each and every people. There is no way Citizenship Education can make any sense to anybody who is Afrikan or of Afrikan descent anywhere in the World today without it having to truthfully tackle the facts of the real *Safari* of the globe-trekking journey of great discoveries that Afrikan people have had to make from Antiquity. Afrikans were the very first Human Beings and, therefore, the Originators of Human Civilization, throughout all of World History right up to our contemporary era. Such a *Pyramidscan* of the *Safari* of the Black people of Afrikan origin in World History will demonstrate that there really is no Black nor White History. There is only a World History of all Humankind. The Black making of Civilizations, beginning from Afrika and spanning the entirety of our planet Earth, is the longest of *Ourstories*. It is also full of the glories and tragedies in which all of Humanity shares in our common quest for Survival, Development and Progress through Active Citizenship.

Hence we explore the vicissitudes of the Afrikan role in the Black contributions to the making of World History by all the peoples comprising the whole of Humanity. We discover *Ourstory* of thousands upon thousands of years which have seen Afrikan people experience the building and destruction of their own independent polities. These included magnificent communes, chiefdoms, states, federations and empires of all sizes, democratic and otherwise, from the likes of Kush, Nubia, Kemet (Ancient Egypt), Ghana, Mali, Songhai, Benin, Ethiopia, Kongo, Mapungubwe and Zimbabwe on the continent of Afrika.

The process continued through the recurrent genocides of the *Maangamizi* of Chattel, Colonial and Neocolonial Enslavement. Amidst these horrors they still managed to persistently rise up in brilliant feats of Resistance, Pan-Afrikan Community Regeneration and People's Liberation Creativity in all fields of human endeavour, including Global Citizenship. The achievements reached great heights, as evident in their various forms of Anti-Slavery Abolitionist self-organisation, self-defence and self-empowerment, for example the Republic of *Palmares* (1595–1696 in what is now the provincial state of Alagoas in Brazil), *Haiti Dechoukage* and the various *Maroon* havens of refuge and other similar initiatives of the *Pan-Afrikan Community of Resistance* (*PACOR*) throughout the World of the Afrikan Diaspora.

The *Maangamizi* is taken by the worldwide Pan-Afrikan Community of Resistance to mean the Afrikan Holocaust. This covers a continuum of not only Chattel Enslavement and Colonial Enslavement of the past but also the present-day Neocolonial

Enslavement of Afrikan people largely by European Imperialism. This has so stretched the Spirit of Resistance, endurance and perseverance of all Afrikans and Afrikan Descendants that it has drawn some of the best examples of Global Citizenship Activism from their own Anti-Slavery Abolitionist Sheroes and Heroes in order to prolong their very survival for all these five hundred years.

Active Citizenship in the Pan-Afrikan Resistance to Chattel Enslavement was evident in the exemplary Anti-Slavery Abolitionist Freedom-fighting lives of the likes of Zumbi of the *Kilombo* of *Palmares*, Nana Nanny Acheampong of the Maroons, Toussaint L'Ouverture of *Haiti Dechoukage*, Nat Turner, Denmark Vesséy, Harriet Tubman of the *Underground Railroad*, Sojourner Truth, Frederick Douglas, Olaudah Equiano, Attobah Kweku Enu (Ottobah Cuguano), Robert Wedderburn, William Davidson, etc. Active Citizenship in the Pan-Afrikan Resistance to Colonial Enslavement was evident in the exemplary Anti-Slavery Abolitionist Freedom-fighting lives of the likes of Mbuya Nehanda, Nana Yaa Asantewaa, Marcus Garvey, Osagyefo Kwame Nkrumah, W.E.B. DuBois, Antonio Maceo, Frantz Fanon, Ben Bella, Dedan Kimathi, Amilcar Cabral, Paul Robeson, C.L.R. James, Amy Ashwood Garvey, Amy Jacques Garvey, Claudia Jones, Malcolm X, Martin Luther King, George Padmore, Ras Makonnen, Sekou Toure, Patrice Lumumba, Mwalimu Nyerere, Gamal Abdel Nasser, Josina Machel, Eduardo Mondlane, Agostinho Neto, Samora Machel, Steve Biko, Mangaliso Sobukwe, Josiah Tongogara, Funmilayo Kuti, Nelson Mandela, Chris Hani, Solomon Mahlangu, the Soweto Martyrs, etc. Active Citizenship in the Pan-Afrikan Resistance to Neocolonial Enslavement continued and still continues in the Anti-Slavery Abolitionist Freedom-fighting lives of the likes of Felix Moumie, Pierre Mulele, Ben Barka, Walter Rodney, Juan Almeida Bosque, Thomas Sankara, Huey P. Newton, George and Jonathan Jackson, Johnny F.S. Hansen, Abdias do Nascimento, Dennis Brutus, Ngugi Wa Thiong'o, Maina Wa

Kinyatti, Micere Githae Mugo, Kwesi Kwaa Prah, Nuhu Dramani, Niapa Wentum, Dani Wadada Nabudere, Fela Anikulapo Kuti, Chinweizu, Ken Saro-Wiwa, Bob Marley, Mutabaruka, Kwame Adjimah, Delali Yao Klu, Mumia Abu-Jamal, Mutulu Shakur, Sundiata Acoli, Herman Bell, Assata Shakur, Geronimo JiJaga, Angela Davis, Bell Hooks, Omali Yeshitela, Maulana Karenga, Molefi Kete Asante, David Commissiong, Minkah Adofo, Explo Nani-Kofi, Kwame Adofo Sampong, Nana Kwasi Mensah, Esther Ekua Stanford, Chernoh Alpha Muhammad Bah, Issifu Lampo, Viewu Aku Adom, Dorothy Benton-Lewis, Winston Martin, Opeyemi Araromi, etc.

The remarkably amazing story of each and every one of these Sheroes and Heroes is an illustrious testament not only to the indomitable dignity of what Osagyefo Kwame Nkrumah called *the Afrikan Personality* throughout the ages. It also shows the towering heights of "beautyful" Humanity, in the sense which Ayi Kwei Armah means it, to which the Pan-Afrikan "overstanding" of Citizenship can raise even the most "Wretched of the Earth". For we see, in the rich examples of their Freedom-fighting lives, the practice of Global Citizenship Activism in principled defence of their own and other human and peoples' rights by way of engagement in all the fields of Active Citizenship. Trevor Desmoyers-Davis for example specifies: Responsibilities with Rights, the Right to Know, the Citizen and the State, including the Legal System, the Citizen and the Political Process, the Citizen, Society and the Community. In this connection we must note the very important identification Issa G. Shivji makes of the two tendencies, the dominant and the revolutionary, in Human Rights Discourse. Noteworthy also is the crystallization of this revolutionary tendency by Angela Davis into what she aptly terms *Abolition Democracy*.

For it is in recognition, assertion and promotion of the universal Human and Peoples' Rights of the revolutionary tendency at the heartcore of such "Abolition Democracy" that such Sheroes and Heroes courageously faced their Global Citizenship respons-ibilities to fight for their own and other peoples' rights. This was particularly with a view to realising the demands enunciated under the *Pan-Afrikan Reparations for Global Justice* banners of the Repub-lics of Palmares and Haiti, as well as of the polities of the Maroons, and, indeed, also initially of the Republics of modern Ghana, Guinea, Mali, Tanzania, Guinea-Bissau, Cape Verde, Angola, Mozambique etc.

Hence the need for all to comprehend the fact that it is the contemporary praxis of *Pan-Afrikan Reparations for Global Justice*, as it is expounded in accord with Osagyefo Kwame Nkrumah, Chin-weizu and Karenga by the Scholar-Activists of the Pan-Afrikan Reparations Coalition in Europe (PARCOE), which best expresses the principles as well as the holistic programme, strategy and tactics of Global Citizenship Activism. The heroic internationalist examples of the likes of John Brown, Ernesto Che Guevara, Sub-Comandante Marcos of the *Zapatistas*, Basil Davidson, Peter Fryer, Noam Chomsky, Stuart Hodkinson, George Monbiot and Mark Curtis in their practical demonstration of Freedom-fighting iden-tification with the cause of total Afrikan Liberation, help to support their Pan-Afrikan counterparts in illustrating this kind of Global Citizenship Activism. This is what is still being concretised today, within the *Ubuntu* Spirit and paradigm of *Uniting Humanity*, by the worldwide Pan-Afrikan Community of Resistance in its continu-ing *Freedommarch*, in the sense which Ossie Davis means it, along the thorny pathways of the *Maangamizi* towards the *Rendezvous of Victory*.

> . . . For it is not true that
> the work of Man is finished
> that we have nothing more
> to do in the World
> that we are just parasites
> in this World
> that it is enough for us

to walk in step with the World
For the work of Man is only just beginning
and it remains to conquer all the violence
entrenched in the recesses of his passion . . .
And no race holds a monopoly of beauty, of
intelligence, of strength
and there is a place for all at the
Rendezvous of Victory . . .

Aime Cesaire
Notebook of a Return to My Native Land
(*Cahier d'un retour au pays natal*).

·······························

CHAPTER 6

CONTROL AND PARTICIPATION

One third of the population of the South is of the Negro race. No enterprise seeking the material, civil or moral welfare of this section can disregard this element of our population and reach the highest success . . . Nearly sixteen millions of hands will aid you in pulling the load upward, or they will pull against you the load downward. We shall constitute one third and more of the ignorance and crime of the South, or one third its intelligence and progress; we shall contribute one third to the business and industrial prosperity of the South, or we shall prove a veritable body of death, stagnating, depressing, retarding every effort to advance the body politic.

Booker T. Washington. The Atlanta Exposition Address, 18 September 1895.

SLAVERY AS AN EXTREME CASE

Slavery provides a powerful starting point for wider reflections on control and participation at work and in society. Owner and worker are clearly separated, with a gulf between them. Slave workers are seen as property, as factors of production, rather than as autonomous human beings.

Slaves lack control over their own lives and work, and are denied the right to participate in decision making. They are dehumanised, at one extreme of a complex continuum of working relationships. It is now becoming recognised (Karasek, 2006) that such absolute low social control, in socio-economic institutional structures, causes chronic disease. We cannot expect to find an extensive literature on slavery and stress, or the psychosocial factors associated with, for example, chattel slavery or child labour. Where phenomena are either illegal or denied, it is hard to conduct scientific research. We are obliged instead to extrapolate from other relevant data and theories. Stress has achieved notoriety in the twenty-first century. Can the account help us with the eighteenth century?

The Transatlantic Slave Trade was complicated by the overlay of racial difference: control was applied by whites against blacks on a systematic basis, which went well beyond the workplace. The starting point was the need for labour, and the absence of voluntary sources of supply. Forced labour was the chosen solution, with colour coding, indefinite terms of service and status inherited between generations.

American plantation owners tried to break down the power of slaves, by dividing those who came from the same village or family. It was easier for them to control individuals, and it seemed prudent to restrict their rights of association. This broke down the networks on which individual slaves had depended. Building new networks with unfamiliar people, often speaking different languages, was difficult.

In a modern society, individual workers can strengthen their bargaining position by joining a trade union. This is a characteristic of a free society, and is enshrined in ILO Conventions. Such options were, and are, denied to slaves.

More generally, lack of control and participation are associated with inequality and poor health. Countries with wide income and power gaps between rich and poor tend to have associated health problems, compared with countries with more equal distributions. It is not simply a matter of master and slave, but of subtler gradations in relative status.

Epidemiological evidence provides an overall picture (Marmot, 2004), but does not provide causal proof. Typically there is limited information available regarding problems of the poor. However, as we assemble data from many populations, and analyse it in terms of relative status, the picture seems clear.

HUMAN RIGHTS AND WORK ORGANISATION

There is remarkable agreement regarding the explicit evidence, both for the historical past of slavery (Thomas, 1997), and for current debates on productivity and innovation (Fricke & Totterdill, 2004). However, this does not mean that what we might regard as the appropriate practical inferences (von Wright, 1974) have been drawn, resulting in action.

The problem is that the explicit evidence constitutes only the tip of the iceberg. We will also need to come to terms with both implicit knowledge and tacit knowledge (Göranzon et al., 2005). This applies both to our understanding of the historical past, and our engagement in current business and management. The modern business world was shaped by the past, including the slave trade (Williams, 1964). There are many unresolved questions, many silences. The history of slavery tends to have been written by the owners, or the descendants of owners, rather than by the slaves.

On slavery, for example, it is now recognised that some 11 million Africans were taken to the New World, and that during the century before the abolition of the Transatlantic Slave Trade some 6 million were transported, of which 2.5 million were taken by British slave ships. (We can find agreement between Williams 1964, Blackburn 1988, 1997; and Thomas 1997.)

There is similar agreement regarding relative wage levels in the modern globalised economy, in which international outsourcing is increasingly common. There are numerous sources of data on wage levels, but less systematic reporting of living and working conditions (Ennals, 1999, 2000, 2001; Rantanen et al., 2001).

In both cases, strategic decisions have been made by executives whose primary concern has been to maximise shareholder value, considered in the short term. There is scope for debate on stakeholder involvement. The Transatlantic Slave Trade was seen as making good business sense for a period, when the requirement was for unskilled muscle power, and then the change was made to operate factories in industrialising countries, with efficiency increased by scientific management. Today new factories, and call centres, are being operated in developing countries. Organisational changes can take place almost overnight, with radical implications for workers.

Information Economics

Neoclassical economics has been based on the assumption that decisions are made on the basis of full information, with all participants having equal access. In practice, this is not the case. Decisions are made on partial information, and are affected by the exercise of power, which is unevenly distributed. This was the basis of Stiglitz's Nobel prize in economics, and of his critiques of the International Monetary Fund and the Presidency of George W. Bush (Stiglitz, 2001, 2002).

In order to make sense of the history of slavery, and the continued inequalities in terms of control and participation which characterise modern working life, we need to develop a model of who knew what, and when. It is no good assuming that all actors in the particular situations had access to the same explicit knowledge that we have today. We have to test our assumptions by making our own interventions, either acting in the present, or asking questions about the past. We need to explore the different belief systems, and identify their foundations. We are not going to obtain complete information to support our decisions. Instead, we need enough to enable us to know how to go on (Wittgenstein, 1954).

Silence

> When there is much that cannot be said, we have to learn to listen to silences (Pålshaugen, 2004).

Silence can be made easier by distance

The British played a leading role in the Slave Trade, but it was conducted off shore, in the notorious "Middle Passage". Ships left Liverpool and Bristol for West Africa, full of British manufactured goods, including textiles and guns. They returned from North America with cotton, timber, maize and sugar. In between, safely out of sight, they carried slaves from West Africa to North America. Few slaves were brought to England. A comfortable fictional account could be presented of slaves singing and dancing on the Atlantic crossing, and of their happy lives with new masters. Many of those who owned plantations in the West Indies never visited. They enjoyed the income from their investments, and had no wish to know the sordid details of how the profit was obtained.

International outsourcing is made easier by virtue of being conducted away from the glare of publicity. Leading companies, for whom corporate social responsibility is an important marketing tool, tend to see corporate social responsibility as primarily an issue for the home market, and for the home investors. It is rarely applied in global terms. The British have yet to join the European debate, in which corporate social responsibility includes obligations by employers to their employees, and former employees.

Silence can be assisted by the choice of language

Trading companies were seeking to maximise profits, and judgements such as how many slaves to transport in one voyage were made in that context. Shareholders wanted reports of success, if they were to be persuaded to invest again. They did not need to know details, merely that the company was being managed in such a way as to further their interests.

Finance directors today are concerned to analyse hard data, and are resistant to arguments based on soft factors, such as health and learning. It is notoriously difficult today to make the business case for investing in people, even when the rhetoric declares that people are the most important resource. We have no agreed ways of valuing human capital, or of measuring the impact of investments in the health and learning of the workforce. Thus any such expenditure tends to be seen as a cost to be cut in the short term, rather than an investment in the longer term.

Silence is helped by silos

In organisations and societies where specialist knowledge is handled by experts, and where there is little communication between disciplines, the implications of developments in one field, for life in another field, can be overlooked. Where the discourse is conducted in technical language, the status quo is all the more likely to be preserved. In a traditional steering society, with vertical reporting and top-down control, boundaries can be enforced.

Slaves would have few opportunities to consult doctors, and there were no arrangements for inspecting their working and living conditions, or for setting standards with regard to their occupational health. Slaves were property, and could be insured, with any compensation paid to their owners.

THE EPIDEMIOLOGY OF CONTROL AND PARTICIPATION

There has been a mass of recent epidemiological research, which may provide the basis from which to penetrate some of the silence concerning the modern workplace, with implications for our understanding of the past. The most accessible account has been Marmot's "Status Syndrome" (2004), in which he shows that social standing directly affects health and life expectancy. In simple terms, building on earlier work with Wilkinson (1996), he shows that accounts could be drawn up, for organisations and for countries, considering evidence of health outcomes rather than simply financial results. Research suggests that those organisations and countries with the greatest in-equalities in terms of income and social status experience the worst health problems and the greatest differences in terms of life expectancy.

Looking for a possible explanation of this widespread phenomenon, Marmot cites the work of Karasek and Theorell (1990), and discusses control and participation. He argues that where individuals lack control over their life and work, and where they have no chance of participating in decisions regarding their own future, they can be seen to experience a range of illnesses which can be explained in terms of their work.

Two interesting points can be made at this stage. Firstly, as Levi (1981) and Cooper (2005) have argued, the strength of the research evidence has not been reflected in changes in policy, and where policies have been developed they have rarely been implemented. Although it might be obvious to us what is going on, current practices continue. Decision makers choose which evidence they are to regard as relevant. This is policy-driven evidence, not evidence-based policy.

Secondly, this modern mystery may help to cast some light on the past. Slavery represents an extreme case of the individual being denied control and participation. Our apparent inability to make changes today may provide clues about the continued existence of slavery into the nineteenth century. Indeed, it also helps explain the continuation of modern forms of slavery, including child and female labour.

We may then wish to consider the economic system which followed slavery. Slaves worked on plantations, with overseers. As industrialisation developed, it became more economically viable to organise manufacturing production in factories, where workers were to be deployed as factors of production. Early factories were reminiscent of slave ships, in terms of design, and the attitudes of management. Slaves could typically be identified by skin colour. In factories, and more generally in industrial society, social class was important. Skin colour has often come to be correlated with assumed social class.

Discussion of health effects of industrialisation has often been in terms of a concept derived from the study of machines, which deteriorate through use. Stress has been applied to the description of human consequences of work, where workers have been seen as part of the machine (Selye, 1956). One problem has been that the pain experienced by individuals cannot be directly measured. Accordingly, a surrogate is used: measurements are made of cortisol levels. In the context of large studies, this indicator can be correlated with others to show patterns of association.

SOCIETY AND INDIVIDUALS

One problem which we have to address is how conclusions at a society level should be translated into the actions of individuals. This raises questions of ethics.

It was very hard for individuals who were familiar with the nature of the slave trade to argue that it was defensible. Arguments had to take the form that in some sense slaves were less than fully human, and that the condition of slavery in the New World should be seen as preferable to life in Africa. Nobody argued that they would like to be a slave. Europeans might be taken as indentured workers, but not slaves, other than by Barbary pirates. The Roman Catholic Church opposed enslaving native Americans, but tolerated African slavery.

TIPPING POINT

Conventional analysis fails to explain the rapidity with which slavery shifted from being an accepted part of many societies, and of international trade, to being prohibited. We encounter the concept of the tipping point, the point at which the situation can be transformed.

William Wilberforce's campaign for the Abolition of the Transatlantic Slave Trade, aided by Thomas Clarkson, and supported by William Pitt the Younger, may be presented in popular myth as an outcome of a campaign of mass mobilisation, driven by religious conviction. Close scrutiny of the events gives a different, much more complex, picture. Clearly there was moral fervour among many of the campaigners, but until the late eighteenth century the major religious groups had paid little attention. There had been a series of annual votes in Parliament, which had made little progress. Plantation owners often had seats in the

House of Commons, and only a small minority of the population had the right to vote. There were more signatories to anti slavery petitions than there were Parliamentary voters. However, most of the signatories had no involvement in slavery. They were expressing their abhorrence, based on the information which had reached them.

Debate continues about the economics of slavery, and the links between abolition of slavery and the pursuit of British overseas naval policy (Schama, 2005). Clearly Bristol, Liverpool and London had been beneficiaries of the slave trade, meaning that there were powerful vested interests. Once it was clear that the economics of the Slave Trade was changing, and a majority could be achieved, the votes were gathered to make the result secure. Once Abolition had become law, it became attractive for the British to enforce compliance on other countries. Anti slavery became a powerful component of foreign policy, enhancing British control, to the detriment of international commercial competitors.

It has been hard to operationalise human rights in a sustainable manner. The task has been complicated by the strength of legal traditions of property rights. Both in court cases over slavery prior to abolition of the Transatlantic Slave Trade, and in the US Supreme Court's treatment of constitutional amendments on civil rights, we can see the problem. Property rights tend to have prevailed as a controlling factor, and human rights, leading to broader participation, continue to be problematic.

DIALOGUE

Dialogue has been invoked as an appropriate way forward, from a number of different perspectives, enabling an extension of participation and social capital formation, beyond formal political structures.

Gustavsen (1992) introduced principles of democratic dialogue, and dialogue conferences have a central role in enterprise development programmes and regional development programmes in Norway. A number of cases are reported (Ennals & Gustavsen, 1999; Ennals, 2002; Ennals, 2005; Gustavsen et al., 2007). Emphasis is placed on learning from differences. Göranzon (1995) and Göranzon et al. (2005) have concentrated on dialogue across disciplinary boundaries, and on addressing the problem that explicit knowledge represents only the tip of the iceberg. The case is made for analogical thinking, which provided the starting point for the current research.

This work has explored what is possible in a network society, where control is not monopolised by those at the top of hierarchical systems. However, the diverse patterns of thinking, and alternative modes of social organisation, highlight the extent to which crossing borders of country and discipline can continue to be seen as deviant. We should not underestimate the importance of power, as studied by Foucault (1970, 1972, 1977, 1989, 2001) in his histories of the period. When studying knowledge in particular disciplines, we need to understand power relationships in the institutions concerned.

In the eighteenth century, we have suggested, the Lunar Society was able to operate in this manner, laying the foundations for a new industrial society with foundations in science, technology, art and design. As Dissenters, they operated outside establishment structures, and took control of their own lives and decisions.

By contrast, the limit that was possible for slave societies was to organise to overthrow the slave owners. Efforts were then concentrated on resisting attacks by European armies. Networking was vital for Toussaint L'Ouverture, but it was not sufficient of itself to make the new society sustainable.

Dialogue, social capital, and networking could all be regarded as ingredients in work organisation, which we could present as the missing link in making sense of the past and the present.

SELF-DETERMINATION: CONTROL, PARTICIPATION AND THE WORKPLACE

As we reflect on the past and present issues surrounding slavery and Citizenship, we encounter a number of challenges, and key unifying concepts, such as self-determination. Under slavery, individuals are denied control over their own life and work, together with denial of participation in decisions about their own futures.

It is not just a matter of making sense of the historical past, but of acting in the context of the present workplace. Kingston University Centre for Working Life Research has worked with the UK Work Organisation Network since 1998, building a bottom-up network based national institutional structure to address key issues of work organisation. The objectives are to increase individual autonomy and self-determination; and facilitate teamworking, networking and coalition building; resulting in healthier work, improved work life balance and a more equitable distribution of power and resources.

On this basis, self-determination is a unifying theme at individual, group and political levels. The issues are international. Slavery dates from antiquity, continuing in various forms to the present day. In Ancient Greece, as in the newly independent United States of America, the rhetoric of democracy coexisted with the reality of slavery. Human rights were subordinated to property rights. Not everything changes.

When considering Corporate Social Responsibility and Human Rights, for example, should we work at the level of individuals, or of groups? Should we operate at national or international level? Through networks and NGOs, we can work at many levels at once. This has long been the basis of trade union activity. We can learn from long standing debates involving organisations such as UNESCO, Amnesty International and International Alert, who have tackled restrictive approaches taken by governments. The mere existence of international conventions, such as from ILO, is not enough. Action is required.

Status Syndrome

The same key issues of control and participation, explored by Michael Marmot in "Status Syndrome" (2004) can be seen as vital in the spheres of politics and work. In both cases, social standing directly affects health and life chances. People typically seek various forms of autonomy, and a chance to participate in decisions about their own futures. As the dividing lines between work and the rest of life become blurred, concepts such as self-determination find new application, reviving discussion of democracy in the work-place. There are added pressures from globalisation, technological transformation, new forms of work organisation and demographic change. It is not just a matter of analysis, but of creating actionable knowledge.

Self-Determination

"Self-Determination: International Perspectives" (Clark & Williamson, 1996) was based on a symposium planned by Martin Ennals, Professor of Human Rights at the University of Saskatch-ewan, and Secretary-General of Amnesty International when they won the Nobel Peace Prize in 1977. The symposium addressed the resolution of claims to self-determination on the part of different peoples throughout the world, seeking to develop a framework for the evaluation and settlement of these claims in a peaceful manner.

Martin Ennals died 18 months before the conference. His brother David, who died before the book was published, noted the impact of the symposium on the World Conference on Human

Rights, in Vienna in 1993. He reported on the Assembly of Unrepresented Nations and Peoples Organisations at the Hague; the International Lawyers Conference in London, on Tibet's claims to self-determination and independence; and the International Year of Inter-Religious Understanding and Co-operation, also 1993. David Ennals argued that both the United Nations Charter and the International Covenant on Human Rights state, in Article 1, that all peoples have a right to self-determination. By virtue of that right they are free to determine, without external interference, their political status and to pursue their economic, social and cultural development. However, there is no agreement on the content, applicability and implementation of the right to self-determination. The right to self-determination presupposes the free and genuine expression of the will of the peoples in question. Democratic processes are required. They may need support.

Archbishop Desmond Tutu wrote in the foreword: "Martin Ennals himself recognized that claims to self-determination and resistance to those claims have become an increasing source of conflict and violence in our world, and consequently, of the gross abuses of human rights which accompany violence. He also recognised that effective mechanisms are urgently needed peacefully to mediate such claims and to ensure that justice prevails."

The continuing challenges

The political challenges of self-determination continue, and lessons can be learned from different experiences around the world. The Dalai Lama continues to seek a peaceful way forward for Tibet. His example influenced the campaigns for self-determination and independence in the Baltic States, and in particular Lithuania. Legal arguments developed for Tibet were applied in the Lithuanian case. Lithuania, Latvia and Estonia are now members of the European Union.

Self-determination in the workplace remains a complex and pressing issue, but the concept may be valuable in combating the less pleasant implications of globalisation. As we see major corporations outsourcing and offshoring, lines of responsibility and accountability can become blurred. Sometimes it seems that Corporate Social Responsibility is seen as applying only in one country, and to be invoked only as a tool for public relations and marketing.

Self-determination does not offer straightforward solutions for the workplace. In the world of politics, there has been a similar problem. Martin Ennals argued in 1991, speaking at a UNESCO Forum on Culture and Democracy, in Prague: "The present dilemma is multi-disciplinary and cross-cultural. On the one hand, the right to self-determination is clearly established in international law; on the other, it is so hedged around by escape clauses that it is virtually meaningless as a basis for legal or political debate".

Rodolfo Stavenhagen, in the opening chapter of "Self Determination", argues that "what is needed now is a thoroughgoing collective effort to spell out the universal, rigorous criteria by which the defining characteristics of the claimants to self-determination will be accepted as widely as possible". This will need to be followed up with networking support. Indeed, networking has a pivotal role in the facilitation of sustainable change. The key elements need to be manoeuvred into position, and then tested to ensure that they can bear the necessary weight.

EMPOWERMENT

Peter Totterdill

Professor Peter Totterdill is Joint Chief Executive of the UK Work Organisation Network

The extreme nature of slavery, representing the complete denial of self-determination and individual agency, induces a reluctance to use the word even rhetorically to describe aspects of work anywhere in contemporary Europe. It is also very clear that "control by individuals over their own lives, and the right to participate in decisions about their futures" is not a characteristic of contemporary working life for the great majority of employees. Public policy measures such as the European *Information and Consultation Directive* (European Commission, 2002) represent an important statement of intent about self determination and citizenship. Evidence that employee empowerment "works" in terms of innovation, business performance and competitiveness is compelling. Yet little can be inferred about the common experience of work. What we do know is that there is a persistent gap between progressive practice and common practice in the workplace: a long tail of organisations whose employees are, to varying degrees, disengaged and disempowered.

Is this slavery? Not in any meaningful sense of the word: people in the labour market can still make conscious choices and trade-offs between income, time and quality of working life even if the consequences associated with those choices are much more severe for some than for others. The enslavement of working time and *working consciousness* to practices and codes which appear beyond question or scrutiny remains palpable.

RECALLING WORK

Work can be the most significant way in which people engage with, and construct, the world. This axiom recurs in philosophy and research throughout the modern era: in Marx, in Ruskin's attack on the degradation of creative work by machines, in Hannah Arendt's theories of self-actualisation, in the Human Relations School and its successors, and in banal HR clichés. People at work are rarely treated as if this was the case. Constructing work as a developmental activity would, as the above schools suggest, place a premium on trust, autonomy, tacit knowledge, reflection and creativity. As several studies have found, such workplaces do exist, but in small numbers, often having experienced a process of gestation which is hesitant, incomplete and under pressure. Even evidence of demand for self-determination amongst employees is scarce and contradictory. Why then should it be the case that evidence-based practice remains so unknown and untried in many workplaces? Why is the voice of the emancipatory interest (in Habermasian terms) so weak in the discourse of the wider labour market and society?

Empirical observation can provide only a part (and in our view a very small part) of the answer. Command and control has become a very unfashionable idea; even "heroic" models of leadership advocate the need for some measure of consensual agreement and compliance within the workforce. Bullying by managers is notionally punishable; employee engagement is the new orthodoxy.

WELSH QUARRIES

As Steven Lukes (2004) argues in his view of power, we need to look at levels of explanation that are less readily observable, including the counterfactual. History reveals a few important and bitterly fought struggles against the enslavement of working practices and culture.

In 1979 David Gillingwater and Peter Totterdill began a study which sought to explain the lack of an alternative political discourse in North Wales on the future of the area's economy, and the apparently consensual subservience to external economic interests notably in the form of the Central Electricity Generating Board they discovered in the work of the labour historian Merfyn Jones (1981) that a possible part of the answer lay in a devastating and critical event. The North Wales slate quarrymen's strike at the beginning of the 20th century was an emblematic struggle of Welsh speaking, rural, chapel-going Liberal workers against the English, urban, Anglican, Tory quarry owners. Beneath the symbolism, the conflict was fundamentally driven by the defence of deeply-embedded practices grounded in tacit knowledge and self determination. The English quarry owners sought as a block to impose a "factory system" of production based on hourly pay and regulated working time. The quarrymen were defending a system based on quarterly auctions, in which consortia of individual workers and their and families bid for the right to exploit a specific pitch on the quarry face. The price was determined by a process of bargaining in which the ability of the quarrymen to anticipate a "good" pitch, one which would yield a high proportion of quality slate, with limited need to remove low grade rock, was critical, since this would determine the level of payment received from the owners. Their tacit knowledge, an ancestral understanding of the mountain, defined the job itself:

Get Welshmen to Break the Stone
(Dafydd Jones)

Os bydd eisiau cael swyddogion,
Danfon ffwrdd a wneir yn union,
Un ai Gwyddel, Sais neu Scotsman,
Sydd mewn swyddau braidd ymhobman.

Mewn gweithfeydd sydd yma'n Nghymru,
Gwelir Saeson yn busnesu;
Rhaid cael Cymry i dorri'r garreg,
Nid yw'r graig yn deall Saesneg.

(If officials are needed,
They are at once sent for from afar,
Either Irishmen, English or Scots,
Are in jobs almost everywhere.

In works here in Wales,
Englishmen can be seen interfering;
You must get Welshmen to break the stone,
For the rock does not understand English).

From a collection in the British Museum called "Welsh Songs etc 1767–1870"
http://sniff.numachi.com/~rickheit/dtrad/pages/tiBREAKSTN.html

Once the pitch had been allocated, there was little or no surveillance by the owners until the next reckoning day. Women in the family worked on the dressing floor, cleaning and preparing the slate extracted by the quarrymen, a dimension which must have contributed to the sense of collective enterprise. Work was inherently flexible and self determined, allowing for changing economic and social circumstances. For example many families possessed smallholdings, and working time in the quarry could be balanced with the needs of harvesting and lambing.

Introducing the factory system, with its regulation of time and its supervision of work processes, into this environment represented a massive assault on the self-determination of workers, and on the wider political, social and economic culture. The strike lasted three years, such was the significance of the issues at stake for the quarrymen and their families. Their eventual defeat, Gillingwater and Totterdill argued, must have left its mark on deeper structures of political consciousness and dialogue, constraining the possibility of collective choices not predicated on English economic dependency or managerial surveillance. While language revival and even political independence were vibrant issues, economic self determination remained beyond the scope of political inquiry, even where the alternative led to the domination of large parts of the post-slate economy by a single employer and the domination of large parts of the Welsh landscape by the hum of nuclear power generation.

The intensity of the research fieldwork, with its exploration of the dramatic quarried landscapes of Snowdonia, and the interviews with trade unionists, politicians and other actors for whom the slate industry lay at the heart of the area's culture, made a deep personal impact on the researchers. Critically though, it led to a realisation of how our current possibilities for action might be defined by the defeats and successes of long ago: sometimes even those that are forgotten (Williams, 1991). It also highlighted the possibility of research practice capable of exposing the hidden constraints.

TAYLOR AND THE CODIFICATION OF WORKING KNOWLEDGE

The persistence of Taylorism (see Taylor, 1911) in the workplace is a recurrent topic of discussion amongst researchers. Taylorism persists, both at the level of conscious design, and as an implicit set of assumptions in management and shop floor practice

(Totterdill & Hague, 2004). Work with sewing machinists, supervisors and managers during the early 1990s explored the meanings and assumptions that each group brought to the workplace. In a system largely determined by piecework the setting of "standard minutes" became the dominant narrative in the relationship between machinists and the company. Managers employed work study techniques to maximise the performance of operatives and reduce the cost per garment by tightening "loose rates": in other words raising performance targets that were "too easy" to meet. Machinists likewise continually used their tacit knowledge to increase individual earnings in ways concealed from managers, so supervisors were recruited from the lines to put such knowledge at the disposal of the company. Both sides saw the setting of the rate as a continuous "war of attrition" in which poor quality, injury, stress and high labour turnover were merely collateral damage. Yet it was unusual for either managers or employees to perceive the possibility of an alternative. Job quality was rarely raised as an issue in group discussions even with machinists: a "good" piece of work was one where you could earn your money fast if you kept your head down: short cycle times and no problems to solve. Nor was it seen as an issue for managers struggling to recruit and retain skilled machinists: "girls (sic) just come here to earn their money: that's the only quality of working life they care about". Sometimes Taylorist job design was even invoked as an aid to recruitment, albeit not always a successful one. "I've simplified the job so much that any moron could do it, but I still can't get anyone to come and work for me" was the memorable response of one manager to an interview on the state of the local labour market.

In this industry the enslavement of ideas and working practices was deeply codified in the form of the Taylorist principles that constituted the "common sense" of almost everyone in the industry. Yet merely describing these relationships and practices does little to enhance our understanding of the potential for change. The starting point lay with the counterfactual, or at least the exceptional. A small number of companies were identified which had, to a substantial degree, abandoned Taylorism, replacing production lines with semi-autonomous teams. Working with David Middleton of Loughborough University, Peter Totterdill invited teams of machinists to take part in a process of collective remembering, in which "then" (the production line) was compared with "now" (teamworking). Most participants spoke with pride and often surprise when they considered the distance they had personally travelled between their lives as piece-rate line workers and those as multi-skilled team workers. They had developed a range of personal competencies at work that often carried into their personal lives. A "good" piece of work was one where you could take pride in the quality of the garment, in having worked well as a team. Most said that they would leave the industry rather than go back to line working. Critically it was the contrast which they drew between the "then" and the "now" which exposed the "natural order" of Taylorism as a myth (Middleton & Totterdill, 1992).

Exposing the enslaving properties of codified systems of practice has been a recurrent theme in subsequent action and research. UKWON work in the National Health Service points to the weakness of a regulatory regime, which by measuring hospital performance against some 400 separate indicators, manages to detach quality assurance from quality improvement. Management and staff effort becomes so focused on compliance with regulatory standards that the ability to use tacit knowledge and creativity in improving patient care, minimising risk or enhancing organisational performance finds little place in the working lives of most NHS employees. Even staff employed by the regulatory agencies point to the ways in which the codification of quality assessment processes prevents them from using their "soft" skills and knowledge to work with staff in NHS Trusts to secure real innovation and improvement.

The denial of self determination is in nobody's interests, in the complex and fast moving environment of the twenty-first century. In the clothing industry it imposed rigidities that prevented successful adaptation to less price-sensitive market. In the NHS it continues to deny patients, management and government access to the understanding, experience, and eventually the goodwill, of frontline staff that could play such a key role in real improvement.

Research alone cannot change this. But, with Habermas, we would argue that participative research can animate and inform dialogue capable of revealing both the emancipatory interest and the codified structures which constrain it.

SPICE OF LIFE OR KISS OF DEATH?

Lennart Levi

Lennart Levi is Emeritus Professor at the Karolinska Institute in Stockholm, and was Chairman of the Occupational Psychiatry Section of the World Psychiatric Association

Cooper, C.L. (ed.) (2005) *Handbook of Stress Medicine and Health*, Second Edition. Boca Raton: CRC Press, (Introduction)

The Swedish Government chose to use the new opportunities offered by advanced technologies to analyse the tangle of issues, and to try to shape a better society and working life. It appointed a Swedish Commission on the Work Environment, against a background of the government's concern about recent trends in work-related morbidity, long-term absence due to sickness, and premature retirement.

The resulting Swedish Work Environment Act now states the following concerning the characteristics of the work environment:

• Working conditions shall be adapted to people's differing physical and psychological circumstances.

- The employee shall be enabled to participate in the arrangement of his own job situation, as well as in work on changes and developments that affect his own job.
- Technology, work organisation, and job content shall be arranged so that the employee is not exposed to physical or mental loads that can cause ill health or accidents.
- The matters to be considered in this context shall include forms of remuneration and the scheduling of working hours.
- Rigorously controlled or "tied" work, where the worker may not leave his post for a phone call or even a bathroom break, shall be avoided or restricted.
- It shall be the aim for work to afford opportunities for variety, social contacts, and co-operation, as well as continuity between individual tasks.
- It shall be the aim for working conditions to afford opportunities for personal and occupational development as well as for self-determination and occupational responsibility.

These objectives can be promoted using a stick (liability to penalty) or a carrot (financial incentives to management). Sweden has chosen to give priority to the latter approach.

The Swedish Work Environment Act was also based on the EU Framework Directive, according to which employers "have a duty to ensure the health and safety of workers in every aspect related to the work." The directive's principles of prevention include "avoiding risks", "combating the risks at source", and "adapting the work to the individual". In addition, the directive indicates employers' duty to develop "a coherent overall prevention policy". The European Commission's Guidance (Levi, 2000; Levi & Levi, 2002) aims at providing a basis for such endeavours.

Based on surveillance at individual workplaces and monitoring at national and regional levels, work-related stress should be prevented or counteracted by job redesign (e.g. by empowering the employees, by avoiding both over- and underload), by improving social support, and by providing reasonable reward for the effort invested by workers, as integral parts of the overall management system. And, of course, it should also be prevented or counteracted by adjusting occupational physical, chemical and psychosocial settings to the workers' abilities, needs and reasonable expectations.

The British government (Secretary of State for Health 1998, 1999) developed similar ideas several steps further in its Green Paper "Our Healthier Nation: A Contract for Health", and its White Paper "Saving Lives: Our Healthier Nation". Four years later, the Swedish government (Ministry of Social Affairs, 2003) presented its Public Health Objectives Bill. It is based on an intersectional structure approach, comprising 11 major goal areas to promote coherence in public health work.

The overall approach of the EU guidance on work-related stress was further endorsed in the Swedish EU Presidency conclusions (2001) which said that "employment not only involves focusing on more jobs, but also on better jobs. Increased efforts should be made to promote a good working environment for all, including equal opportunities for the disabled, gender equality, good and flexible work organization permitting better reconciliation of working and personal life, lifelong learning, health and safety at work, employee involvement and diversity in working life".

In its report "Mental Health in Europe", the World Health Organization (2001) similarly emphasized that "mental health problems and stress-related disorders are the biggest cause of early death in Europe. Finding ways to reduce this burden is a priority. And, soon after, the executive board of WHO resolved (2002) that "mental health problems are of major importance to all societies and to all age groups and are significant contributors to the burden of disease and the loss of quality of life; they are common to all countries, cause human suffering and disability, increase risk of social exclusion, increase mortality, and have huge economic and social costs".

ENABLING

Norman Sartorius

Norman Sartorius was Director of Mental Health at the World Health Organisation, and President of the World Psychiatric Association

Sartorius, N. (2002) *Fighting for Mental Health*. Cambridge: Cambridge University Press, Chapter 8

Goals of rehabilitation of people who have had a mental illness are changing, and so are the principles that govern them. Quality of life and the capacity to contribute to social capital of society are, for example, replacing the preoccupation with re-employment. It is likely that, in the future, rehabilitation will no longer be the task of health and social services: it has to become a joint enterprise of these services and people who have mental impairments and their families.

Some of the principles that will have to govern the shift are known and others are emerging. They are relevant to the rehabilitation of people who have had mental illness, but also to the rehabilitation of psychiatry as a discipline. They are particularly relevant to countries in which the investments into rehabilitation services are beginning to grow; they are, however, also of importance for countries in which such services are already well funded and for those countries in which no funds whatsoever have been foreseen to help the people with mental illness and their families overcome their illness and its consequences.

First, the goal of rehabilitation must become the improvement of quality of life of those with mental illness and of their immediate family. Employment or integration into a community could be important in this respect: but they must be seen as subsidiary and included as goals if they contribute to the overall quality of life as perceived by the individuals most concerned.

In most countries of the world the concept of employment has no real meaning. In agricultural communities members of the family or a clan are working on their land and have no salaries, no syndicates, no contracts, no insurance in case of accidents or pensions for old age. When they are sick, they are given shelter in the family compound and fed for a long time, provided that they are not too aggressive or otherwise disturbing. The number of criticisms about their behaviour, or about the fact that they are not participating in the work of the family, is often low. In countries marked by a high level of technological development, on the other hand, it is becoming obvious that it is not necessary or possible to employ everyone. In some instances those seeking jobs are not driven by the need to earn enough to maintain themselves and their family alive: rather, the search for a job is fuelled by the wish to meet people, gain some money in order to buy luxuries, to be more independent. The number of those who are opting for part-time temporary jobs is growing in many countries. Why should we then insist that full-time employment is the goal of rehabilitation and the main proof of its success?

Finding a job and becoming employed is still considered to be the confirmation of the person's worth, even if it produces less money than the unemployment benefits and might mean additional financial losses due to the need to hire a person who will do chores around the home. Social productivity, help to others, upbringing of children, creative or artistic production, for the fun of it and for a small circle's consumption only, and many other activities that have made our society distinguishable from herds of animals are given incomparably less attention and reward than traditionally structured jobs.

And yet, the acceptance of the principle of recognition of unpaid work as any other employment and at least in terms of paying for it of insurance, recognition of advancement and respect, is of vast importance for rehabilitation of people with mental illness and of many others suffering from similar disadvantages. A change from the current disregard and debasing attitudes for useful activities that are not paid would not only recognize the work that carers do for people who are disabled: it would also make it possible to recognize the contribution that people with impairments are making to the maintenance of the society and to the enhancement of its social capital.

Related to the change of attitudes and consequent legal action concerning work is also the attitude to leisure. Schools, media and the population at large consider leisure and work as two opposite states rather than as two interchangeable modes of spending our time. From childhood on, all have to learn that leisure is pleasure, that it has to be earned; that work is hard and that it should be made easier, shorter, less demanding.

So, when a person cannot find a job or stops working – for example because of an illness – he or she suddenly stands before an abyss of non-organized, non-structured time that does not offer any opportunities for self-affirmation nor chances to regain self-respect that is so often lost in the course of a prolonged illness.

THE INGRATITUDE OF IT ALL: A MEMORY

Tee L. Guidotti

Professor Tee L. Guidotti is Chair of the Department of Environmental and Occupational Medicine at George Washington University, Washington DC

Many years ago, I worked with a wonderfully competent surgeon. He was generous, refined in manner and proud of his achievements. After retiring from his hospital position in search of a less stressful life, he had taken a job in an "industrial medicine" clinic providing care for injured workers. He hated it, because he intensely disliked his patients. Over and over he would climb the stairs to sit in my office and complain about the arrogance, presumptive attitude and hygiene of the people he was there to help. Fortunately, I was only in that office two days a week.

In his defense, in his day he had volunteered time to work for charity and forgave bills when the patient could not pay. It was working people who could pay who bothered him.

My generation was taught to respect patients, whatever their habits or beliefs, and to be blind to class. So was his. Something went wrong along the way. It took me many years, and rereading one very old book, to figure it all out, but I think I understand now.

The book is a well-known nineteenth-century guide to physician etiquette and practice management, Cathell's *The Book on the Physician Himself and the Things that Concern His Reputation and Success*. It speaks to how physicians should comport themselves, collect debts and deal with different social classes. As in the gender of the pronouns, there is a deep assumption in the book that goes unstated, one that I missed on reading it the first time. The book assumes that anybody who succeeded in the (then not so arduous) task of becoming a physician had automatically changed class identification. The author, who may perhaps be excused as the product of his time, apparently assumes that physicians are of a homogenous upper middle class. Whatever their social origins (and the very upper class in the United States did not generally go to medical school in those days, since they had inherited wealth), physicians had arrived and need not look back. Unless they were "society doctors," they were counted among the great and the good and by definition clearly better than their patients.

My colleague's ungenerous attitudes were a "class thing." He had no problem volunteering his time for charity but could not stand blue-collar workers who were not needy.

Work attaches to social class in most modern cultures and social class in turn is a powerful determinant of health. Work associated with lower social class tends to involve culturally negative features (such as the caste association of tanning hides in India), high risk (dirty jobs are always low paying and have low status) or unpleasantness (such as garbage pickers). Lower socioeconomic status is also associated with adverse health risk factors associated with lifestyle, such as cigarette smoking and, in developed societies, obesity. It is obvious that a worker's social class is associated with occupational and lifestyle health risk. There was greater social distance between physicians and working class or lower middle-class workers in those days although the gap was beginning to close. Any physician practicing occupational medicine still had to negotiate the distance.

In the United States, the role of class in occupational health has been thrown into confusion by the increasing affluence of the working class and by confusion with other work-related factors such as immigration and education. There is essentially no sociological literature on this, in part because America has always denied the significance of social class, preferring to think of itself as socially mobile. The reality is that social class in America is fixed enough by heritage and education to be as rigid (at least by adulthood) as in most societies.

Social class has the additional dimension in the United States of being associated with health insurance. The uninsured worker is uniquely vulnerable financially in a society without universal health care. Although some independent contractors trade off high fees for forgone insurance benefits, workers are usually uninsured because the employer does not provide insurance coverage for low-paying or temporary jobs.

Attitudes toward workers' social class cannot help but come into play when they seek care, even when health care providers try to maintain a studied neutrality. The health insurance problems of low-paid workers are a great obstacle in providing health care and significantly compromise compliance when necessary treatments and medications must be paid out of pocket. Any physician who has had the experience of treating patients in both an inner-city emergency room and a comfortable suburban office knows that there is a world of difference between the two in practice, no matter how the physician tries to maintain objectivity and detachment. (This is also a uniquely American situation, since in most other countries the city center is where the affluent live and the suburbs have lower average incomes.)

Physicians in the United States, on the whole, are well-paid and politically conservative but socially liberal. There are many exceptions but it is a point of professional pride and an ethical imperative for physicians to be tolerant, objective and neutral. For many, this takes an effort.

Traditionally, physicians have provided care for which they did not expect compensation. This charitable work was possible because the physician's income from other patients allowed a measure of largesse in supporting the indigent and the desperate. It made the physician feel good to be needed and to provide care on the basis of generosity and humanitarian impulse. Physicians, like all people, wish their good works to be appreciated as springing from noble motives, not obligation. Everybody, almost, want to be recognized for humanitarian spirit. Altruism is for saints, who may yet demonstrate the sin of pride manifested through prideful self-abnegation.

Early on, injured workers were poor and needed the generosity. The treating physician provided the working poor with health care free or on favourable terms, until they "got back on their feet." There was great satisfaction in helping members of the lower orders. Then came workers' compensation, health insurance benefits (introduced during the Second World War as a device to retain employees) and rising wages. Now workers could pay, by and large, and expected decent medical services. The culmination of all this coincided with one of America's periodic but perpetually unresolved crises in health care. This time around, in the 1950's, American medicine (led by general practitioners who dominated the American Medical Association) was battling the consolidation of the medical profession into group practices. Occupational medicine, as it was then practiced within companies, was seen as a threat to private practice and was vociferously denounced as unprofessional and unethical. The mood toward injured workers also soured.

In past generations, physicians who treated injured workers experienced satisfaction in helping poor people. Now, workers were appearing in waiting rooms with good insurance, expecting to be treated as equals. Class lines were crossed. Workers with dirt under their fingernails were expecting to be treated like middle-class patients and had no reason to be grateful to their physician as benefactors.

Throughout this period, as doctors started working for managed care organizations and patients began feeling empowered, some of the aura and mystery of being a physician was lost. Now the class distinction was disappearing as well. Many older physician, especially this one, did not like this development one little bit.

Occupational medicine has been locked into low status in the United States, at least until very recently. One contributing reason, hidden from memory, may be this class distinction. Perceptions of the field are now improving. The social history of occupational medicine speaks to class relationships and inequities in medicine that are better off left to history.

CURRENT PERSPECTIVES ON OCCUPATIONAL STRESS IN BRAZIL

Ana Maria Rossi

Ana Maria Rossi is a Committee Member of the Occupational Psychiatry Section of the World Psychiatric Association

Today, Brazil is considered one of the most important countries in setting the course of the world's economy, along with Russia, India and China. In the past few years, Brazilian companies have grown, but with the growth came mergers, downsizing and privatisation processes. Unemployment permanently haunts the economically active population and the amount of informal work is growing, particularly for the low-income population. In view of this scenario, Brazilian workers are currently presenting high levels of occupational stress. 70% of economically active Brazilians suffer the consequences of excessive stress in their daily life. 30% out of those are already experiencing burnout symptoms. The data are from a study undertaken by the Brazilian branch of the International Stress Management Association (ISMA-BR), a non-profit international association that studies stress and ways to prevent it.

It is estimated that Brazil spends approximately US$ 20 billion annually (approximately 3.5% of the GDP in 2004) on problems related to high levels of occupational stress. This value includes worker turnover rates, absenteeism, presenteism, work-related injuries and sick leaves. It is also known that Brazilians work an average of 50 to 52 hours per week, excepting labourers and public servants. This has been generating high levels of anxiety (81% complain of the problem), distress (78%), irritability (71%) and anger (52%). The consequences of stress also are shown in physical symptoms. And data show that 86% of workers suffer from muscle pain, including headaches, 69% suffer from tiredness, 35% insomnia and 23% from gastro-intestinal disorders. Furthermore, 66% state that stress affects their quality of life.

Brazilian data show that people are still trying to deal with stress efficiently. Brazilian companies have been active on different fronts: developing life quality program at work, stimulating employees to exercise, establishing more flexible working hours, stimulating activities related to the third sector. However, many companies are currently going through mergers and acquisitions, changes in the management and in the internal structures. This situation contributes to increase anxiety and worsen fears of imminent unemployment. The Brazilian Institute of Geography and Statistics (IBGE) has found an unemployment rate of 9.2%, in January 2006 affecting approximately 2.04 million workers.

Outside the corporate environment, there is also the social situation of the country, which has direct influence on stress levels. Unemployment associated with poverty increases levels of violence. This factor was cited by 71% of Brazilians as the greatest cause of stress, followed by unemployment, which was cited by 57% of people, according to a survey carried out by the International Stress Management Association in Brazil, in 2005. Results of that survey indicate that, while men (91%) are more worried about their position in the company and their chances of promotion, women (94%) focus their attention on carrying out daily chores because they believe that they need to work twice as hard to get similar recognition as their male counterparts.

Another issue known in the country is that there is no national, institutional, policy to train people to deal more effectively with the demands and pressures of their daily life. Initiatives to implement stress management programmes are still isolated actions, but it is increasingly evident that people are concerned with finding ways to alleviate the consequences of distress. That is particularly true of those active in the labour market, who are aware of the impact of negative stress on their quality of life; and entrepreneurs, who suffer losses due to low productivity. Anyway, it seems that Brazilian professionals have a long way to go before they are able to reduce the effects of stress on their physical, mental and emotional health, learning to distinguish between the situations that they have control over and are thus able to change, and those where they must have the courage to decide between fight or flight.

THE CENTRAL-EASTERN EUROPEAN HEALTH PARADOX – WHY ARE MEN MORE VULNERABLE IN A CHANGING SOCIETY?

Mária S. Kopp

Mária S. Kopp is a Committee Member of the Occupational Psychiatry Section of the World Psychiatric Association

Up to the end of the 1970s mortality rates in Hungary had been actually lower than in Britain or Austria. Subsequently, mortality rates continued to decline in Western Europe, whereas in Hungary and in other Central East European (CEE) countries this tendency reversed, especially among middle-aged men. (Black et al., 1992, Marmot and Wilkinson, 1999) In the late 1980s, the mortality rates among 45–64 year old men in Hungary rose to higher levels than they were in the 1930s. (Cornia & Panicia, 2000, Kopp et al., 1998, 2000; Kopp, 2000; Skrabski et al., 2003, 2004).

What is the explanation for the vulnerability of middle aged men during this period of rapid economic change? This deterioration cannot be ascribed to deficiencies in health care, because during these years there was a significant decrease in infant and old age mortality and improvements in other dimensions of health care. Furthermore, between 1960 and 1989 there was a constant increase in the gross domestic product in Hungary. Thus the worsening health status of the Hungarian male population cannot be explained by a worsening material situation.

A growing polarisation of the socio-economic situation occurred in the CEE countries, especially in Hungary between 1960 and 1990. The vast majority of the population lived at similarly low level in 1960, with practically no income inequality, and there were no mortality differences between socio-economic strata. Since that time increasing disparities in socio-economic conditions have been accompanied by a widening socio-economic gradient in mortality, especially among men.

One of the most interesting features of the so-called "Central-Eastern-European health paradox" is the gender difference in worsening mortality, in spite of the fact that men and women share the same socio-economic and political circumstances. In Hungary the male/female differences in life expectancy in 2001 was 8.3 years, which is considerably higher than the average difference found in countries of Western Europe, for example 5.8 years in the neighboring Austria, 4.8 years in Denmark and Great Britain. The mortality ratio comparing the lowest to highest educational stratum is 1.8 for Hungarian males, while 1.2 for females.

Based on the data of national representative surveys conducted in the Hungarian population (Kopp et al., 2000, 2005; Kopp & Réthelyi, 2004; Skrabski et al., 2003, 2004, 2005), we found that a worse socioeconomic situation is linked to higher morbidity and mortality rates in Hungary as well. According to multi-variate analyses, however, higher morbidity rates are connected to relatively poor socioeconomic situations mainly through the mediation of depressive symptoms.

A self-destructive circle develops from the enduring relatively disadvantageous socioeconomic situation and depressive symptoms. This circle resulting in chronic stress, plays a significant role in the increase of morbidity and mortality rates in the lower socioeconomic groups of the population. Until the 1970s with the uniformly low living standards, Hungarian health statistics showed more favourable data, than in several Western countries. During rapid socioeconomic changes the disadvantaged continuously blame themselves or their environment, consider their future hopeless, experience permanent loss of control and helplessness, because they cannot afford a car, better living conditions, higher income, while others around them are able to achieve these. They constantly rate their own situation negatively, feel helplessness, and a loss of control. This experience becomes widespread when society becomes rapidly polarised and social cohesion, trust, reciprocity and social support decrease dramatically.

Men were found to be more susceptible to the effects of relative income inequality and GDP deprivation, but the pathway of this relationship is yet to be explained. Two possible explanations can be hypothesised. One is that the income inequality is much higher among men. The other possible explanation might be, that men are more susceptible to loss of status than women. Animal experiments have shown males to be more sensitive than females to loss of dominance position, that is loss of position in hierarchy. (Sapolsky et al., 1990) Most animal studies on social rank examine males, where social rank is the best predictor of quality of life and health. The relationship between social inequality and health applies to women as well as to men in several respects according to several studies, although the income and occupation of women are not as powerful predictors of mortality as they are for men.

In comparison to women, among men socio-economic factors are nearly four times more important predictors of middle-aged mortality differences among regions. Social distrust and the rival attitude are important predictors of middle aged mortality differences among men (Skrabski et al., 2003, 2004, 2005). This indicates that in a suddenly changing socio-economic situation relative economic deprivation, rival attitude and social distrust are all more important risk factors for men while the strong collective efficacy could be a protective factor, even in the case of men. Rival attitude was in highly significant negative association with participation in civic organisations, consequently the protective effect of participation in civic associations might influence health through a lower rival, competitive attitude in members of civic networks among men.

The existing and broad socio-economic differences seem to be less important regarding the middle aged female mortality differences. Neighbourhood cohesion, religious involvement, trust, reciprocity and meaning in life were not so much influenced by sudden socio-economic changes in the last decades, therefore the protective network of women remained relatively unchanged (Skrabski et al., 2004, 2005).

In a traditional society such as in Hungary middle aged men are affected not only by their own social situation but by the subjective evaluation of social status of women as well. The sociopolitical changes may have different consequences for men and women. The feeling of relative socioeconomic deprivation among women in the relatively deprived regions results in a vicious cycle of relative deprivation among men as well, because they feel responsible for the financial situation of their families. (Kopp et al., 2005) The improvement of higher education of women seems to be beneficial both for male and female longevity. Educated women accept more the responsibility for the socio-economic situation of their family. Consequently in preventing the high male premature mortality in Central-Eastern Europe women might play an important role.

FROM MARGINALIZATION TO PARTICIPATION AND EMPOWERMENT; THE BLACK AND MINORITY ETHNIC MENTAL HEALTH WORKFORCE IN THE UK

Annie Lau

Annie Lau is a Committee Member of the Occupational Psychiatry Section of the World Psychiatric Association

In the UK, a number of Government initiatives have come together to address the needs of black and minority ethnic (BME) communities in a systematic way. Under the Race Relations (Amendment) Act 2000, all statutory bodies are required to publish race equality schemes to show how they will:

- Assess whether their functions and policies are relevant to race equality
- Monitor their policies for impact on race equality
- Assess and consult (with BME communities) on new policies they propose to introduce
- Publish the results of their monitoring, assessments and consultations

- Ensure public access to services and information, and
- Train staff in new duties

In February 2004 Sir Nigel Crisp, Chief Executive of the National Health Service, launched a ten point race equality action plan to promote better access and outcomes for BME communities. Five of these action points relate to developing leadership for BME staff. This includes mentoring programmes; expanding training, development and career opportunities; tracking the career progression of staff, and celebrating achievements.

All these developments have been welcomed by BME staff, many of whom have long felt marginalised and relegated to second class status. In my own health care organisation, North East London Mental Health Trust, a mentoring programme was directed at middle grade nursing staff. Mentors were a combination of Executive Management Team members and Non Executive Directors. I interviewed a number of mentors and mentees. Everyone who took part felt the experience had been worthwhile. All the nurses, after a year's participation in the development programme, have either applied for more senior jobs or are well on their way to improving their job prospects, or been promoted. They told me they were helped to overcome perceptions of limits to their ambitions. The mentors also told me the nurses had not considered wider dimensions, and the task was to raise their own aspirations. As well as one to one sessions, there were also group sessions with inspirational leaders from the Royal College of Nursing. They were confronted by a challenge to raise their game, and many responded positively.

The "colour-blind, culture-blind" attitude one finds on mental health acute inpatient environments must undoubtedly also have an impact on BME staff. A recent one day census by the Audit Commission of inpatients admitted to acute adult psychiatric Inpatient Units in March 2005, showed that the pathway to care of Black and Asian patients, in particular, is still significantly different compared to the indigenous White UK population. Few of them received care in the Primary Care sector, and the majority were admitted via the courts or the police. They were significantly more likely to be admitted under mental health legislation, and to receive more control and restraint.

I have conducted a number of staff workshops in race and cultural awareness for staff from both inpatient and community teams, in the NHS, Social Services, as well as for the voluntary sector. Invariably I have found BME staff report that they had been reluctant to contribute insights from their own lived ethnocultural experiences from either family or culture of origin, until facilitated via a training workshop. They felt their views would be marginalised, or discounted, so have often remained silent, and went along with the view of the dominant White UK majority. The opportunity to utilise their experience to inform an ethnically sensitive approach was therefore missed in many cases.

The influence of ethnic professionals needs to be harnessed more effectively, and the learning generated should be collected and disseminated. In my experience many BME professionals have believed that to succeed they need to be "mainstream" and not be too closely associated with peripheral issues eg ethnic issues. The present NHS political climate is however, one that may provide fresh opportunities for new narratives to be heard. It is time for stories to emerge, of good practice in engagement of ethnic communities in the care of patients, and the role of BME staff, and others, in making these connections, and helping others to see, and to use them.

CHAPTER 7

HUMAN RIGHTS

We are Americans, and as Americans, we would speak to Americans. We address you not as aliens nor as exiles, humbly asking to be permitted to dwell among you in peace; but we address you as American citizens asserting their rights on their own native sod . . . We would not lay our burden upon other men's shoulders, but we do ask, in the name of all that is just and magnanimous among men, to be freed from all unnatural burdens and impediments with which American customs and American legislation have hindered our progress and improvement . . . We ask that, speaking the same language and being of the same religion, worshipping the same God, owing our redemption to the same Saviour, and learning our duties from the same Bible, we shall not be treated as barbarians.

Frederick Douglass: On Citizenship, Nationhood and Identity.
Stuckey, S. (1987) *Slave Culture: Nationalist Theory and the Foundations of Black America*. Oxford, Oxford University Press, pp. 224.

SLAVES AS HUMAN BEINGS

Once it was accepted that African slaves were human beings, and deserved to be treated as such, the worst excesses of the Transatlantic Slave Trade and slavery could not be tolerated. Whether or not the arguments for abolition were based on moral considerations, or on separate undiscussed economic or geo-political arguments, the "tipping point" had been reached. Arguments had been aired. Horrendous cases, such as the throwing of slaves overboard from the slave ship Zong, in order to received insurance payments, had been made public. It became harder to maintain silence, or to pretend that one was unaware of what has been going on.

There was clearly a difficult transition period. Slavery and the Transatlantic Slave Trade were well established, and integral to business life in Liverpool, Bristol and London. It represented a major change to declare that this apparent business success, part of the foundation of the British Industrial Revolution and the British Empire, was based on maltreatment of fellow human beings.

The abolition of the Transatlantic Slave Trade was clearly a landmark event in the history of race relations. More recent revisionist historical accounts have cast doubt on what was achieved, noting that abolition of the Transatlantic Slave Trade did not mean emancipation of African slaves, which required later legislation, and that compensation was then paid to the former slave owners, not to the former slaves.

Others point out that credit has conventionally been given to abolitionists in England. This has enabled the British to take pride in abolishing the Transatlantic Slave Trade, rather than acknowledging the scale of their involvement in that trade, and the extent to which it benefited the wealth of particular individuals and groups at the time, as well as the British economy and society.

We have argued that the achievement of slaves in Santo Domingo, in the French Caribbean, in rebelling against their owners, building an army to defend the island and defeating both the French and British armies over a prolonged and bloody war, was at least as important. In other words, the African slaves won their freedom, despite their brutal repression at the hands of Napoleon for a period, and the political chicaneries and great power politics of the French, Americans and British.

Once the British had abolished their own involvement in the Transatlantic Slave Trade, they took on the role of world police-man, checking that others followed suit, and enforcing the obser-vance of human rights. There were of course aberrations. Illegal slave trading continued. There were large slave populations in Brazil, Cuba and the USA after 1838. King Leopold of Belgium claimed to be ending the slave trade in Congo, while imposing his own régime of slave labour. All was not as it might have seemed.

TOWARDS HUMAN RIGHTS

The key point about the legislation on abolition of the Transat-lantic Slave Trade, in 1807, was that it changed the language of the debate. Perhaps it matters less that the vote was carried because it was in the interests of the British government to disadvantage the French colonies in the West Indies, cutting off their supply of new slaves on which their successful sugar production depended.

The transition from the Transatlantic Slave Trade and slavery involved compensation payments to the owners, and a gradual change of status for the African slaves, who went through a period of apprenticeship from 1833 before being declared free in 1838. There were difficult problems of enforcement during this tran-sitional period, especially in the British West Indies, where eman-cipation threatened financial vested interests.

It was in many ways easier to change the focus, and praise the British for leading the world in abolishing the Transatlantic Slave Trade and slavery. There had been an unprecedented campaign by the middle class across the country, which could be turned to national advantage. The Royal Navy was attributed with a new moral mission.

We could now paint a picture of slavery as an historic phenomenon, and to contrast it with a modern enlightened citizenship. That would be comfortable and convenient, but false. The tensions between property rights and human rights, which have been discussed since the Ancient Greeks, continue today. Globalisation means that international law now has to rise to meet the challenge of reconciling different traditions. It is not clear that the transition has been fully completed in the UK, as in other countries. Whenever governments emphasise their support for business as a priority, this may be interpreted as possibly implying further adverse consequences for other human beings. There are still silences to be broken.

HUMAN RIGHTS AND PROPERTY RIGHTS

This declared recognition of human rights, as a consequence of abolition and emancipation, was at the expense of property rights and economic freedom for employers. Capitalists could emphasise profit over human rights, and demanded a laissez faire approach to regulation and legislation.

Can one human being own another, or must they find ways of working together as fellow citizens? Working together requires some kind of mutual recognition as fellow human beings and citizens, on the basis of acceptance of parity of esteem. In turn this assumes some degree of acquaintance and familiarity, meaning that people need experience of more than their own immediate social group. Rigid systems of social class represent obstacles. There is such a thing as society. It is not just a matter of individuals and their families. We need to deal with a wider range of relationships. In addition, we need to recognise the diversity of relationships which can be considered under the same headings.

At work, where there are employers and employees, it is hard to envisage a model of citizenship based on full equality. Clearly the power is not equally distributed. In a capitalist society, property rights of the owners have implications for the workers.

Adam Smith pointed out the distinction between owners and managers, and complained that the latter group, who are simply one category of employees, can tend to act as if they were the owners. He lamented the consequences of joint stock companies, and the ease with which managers could act against the interests of the workers and of the public.

Under slavery, the slave owners regarded other human beings as their property. The prime task of the owners was to ensure the financial success of their businesses. This was easier if the costs of labour could be minimised. They felt able to disregard matters which did not appear in their accounts. These attitudes could also be applied to the conditions of workers, working in factories and living in industrial towns. Typically such workers did not have the right to vote. Through limited access to education, it was difficult for them to make their voices heard.

This tension continues, with debates in Europe about the responsibilities of employers with regard to workplace health and safety, and information and consultation at times of change.

Whenever people in the industrialised North assume that they are entitled to maintain their current lifestyles, which can be contrasted with relative poverty in developing countries in the North, this can be regarded as an assertion of their own property rights as against universal human rights. It is perhaps natural for people to wish to retain what they have, but once it is understood that we are interdependent, the property rights of one group can be seen as at the expense of the human rights of another group. In an increasingly small world, with globalised communications and economic activities, new questions are being asked, and asked to more people. Those whose lives have been adversely affected by the claims of property rights by others are increasingly demanding their human rights.

The themes of slavery and citizenship are universal, and demand a holistic approach. They concern fundamental relationships between human beings. Behind the major competing concepts of rights, we find the need for dialogue. Partners in dialogue recognise each other as fellow human beings.

PAST AND PRESENT

There is a clear framework of obligations on governments around the world, as set out in the ILO Declaration on Fundamental Principles and Rights at Work, 1998.

> All members, even if they have not ratified the Conventions in question, have an obligation arising from the very fact of membership in the Organisation, to respect, to promote and to realize, in good faith and in accordance with the Constitution, the principles concerning the fundamental rights which are the subjects of those Conventions, namely:
>
> 1. Freedom of association and the effective recognition of the right to collective bargaining;
> 2. The elimination of all forms of forced or compulsory labour;
> 3. The effective abolition of child labour;
> 4. The elimination of discrimination in respect of employment and occupation.

The Declaration refers to a battery of detailed Conventions:

No 29 on Forced Labour
No 87 on Freedom of Association and Protection of the Right to Organise
No 89 on Right to Organise and Collective Bargaining
No 105 on Abolition of Forced Labour
No 131 on Minimum Wage Fixing

No 138 on Minimum Age

No 155 on Occupational Health and Safety

No 169 on Indigenous and Tribal Peoples

No 182 on The Worst Forms of Child Labour; and
Recom mendation No 190

Despite all the efforts which have been devoted to building such a framework, problems continue. Mary Robinson, UN High Commissioner for Human Rights, reported in Davos, in February 2000:

> One of the greatest ironies of this period of history is that, just as technology remakes our world, the need to maintain the human dimension of our work, and a company's sense of its social responsibility, is growing at an equally rapid pace. Harmonising economic growth with the protection of human rights is one of the greatest challenges we face today.

Although the Transatlantic Slave Trade, and the institution of slavery, was declared illegal by the international community over a century ago, aspects of current working life suggest that the same issues continue, sometimes in new forms.

- It is rare to find parity of esteem between employer and employee, as is implied by the principles of social dialogue.
- Property rights tend to be given priority over human rights. This tends to preserve the status quo.
- Labour is regarded as a commodity, and a cost to be cut when delivering various business functions.
- Managers are encouraged to develop detachment and objectivity, separating themselves from the details of the functions for which they are responsible.
- Workers tend to lack control over their own work, and have limited opportunities to participate in decision making.
- Changes in working life can place workers under additional stress.

- Gaps in communication between specialists mean that injustice and deprivation may not be addressed.
- Corporate social responsibility is honoured in the breach, rather than the observance.
- A voluntarist approach to regulation favours management rather than workers.
- Doctors treating patients still rarely take account of work-related factors.

MODERN SLAVERY

Edited by David Harrison, written and adapted by Birendra Raj Giri

David Harrison, of Birmingham University, is Founder of the Academic Network on Child Labour

Whilst there is some sketchy current public awareness of the activities of the abolitionists, there is little understanding of the continuing consequences of the slave trade and the continuing and increasing exploitation of people's labour around the world. There are now more people enslaved or involved in slavery-like practices than ever before. In a report to the UN High Commissioner for Human Rights, *Abolishing slavery and its Contemporary Forms* (a paper prepared by David Weissbrodt and Anti-slavery International 2002) it was stated that:

> Despite a widely held belief to the contrary, slavery in its various forms remains prevalent as the world enters a new millennium. The concept of slavery has remained quite static during the close on two centuries in which Governments and Non-governmental organisations have attempted to seek its abolition. Nonetheless . . . a number of slavery like practices have evolved.

Present day slavery, although not primarily the traditional form of Chattel slavery practised in previous centuries, is greater than ever. The definition of slavery has been codified in ILO conventions (see Past and Present Section above) on Forced Labour, the 1956 *UN Supplementary Convention on the Abolition of slavery, the Slave Trade and Institutions and Practices Similar to slavery* and slavery is prohibited by the 1948 *Universal Declaration of Human Rights*. The worst forms of child labour are defined in ILO 182. There is no shortage of international law ratified by most countries in the world. The continuing widespread existence of slavery and slavery-like practices however suggest a shortage of will and resources to enforce that law against vested interests.

Anti Slavery International identify four characteristics of a slave:

• forced to work — through mental or physical threat;
• owned or controlled by an "employer", usually through mental or physical abuse or threatened abuse;
• dehumanised, treated as a commodity or bought and sold as "property";
• physically constrained or has restrictions placed on his/her freedom of movement.

Modern forms of slavery include: early and forced marriage (this is not the same as arranged marriages), forced labour, bonded labour, slavery by descent, trafficking and the worst forms of child labour. Child labour has been receiving some media interest in recent years, the worst forms of which include slavery, child soldiers and other exploitative practices. ILO in a recent report, "The end of Child Labour within reach" estimates for 2004 that 126 million work in the worst forms of child labour, **one in every 12 of the world's children (5–17 years old)**; 111 million children under 15 are in hazardous work and should be "immediately withdrawn from this work"; 8.4 million children are in slavery, trafficking, debt bondage and other forms of forced labour, forced recruitment for armed conflict, prostitution, pornography and other illicit activities. However positive the outlook of ILO in suggesting that numbers are decreasing, this remains a major human rights issue of global proportions.

Bonded labour, or debt bondage, is one of the least known forms of slavery but remains one of the most prevalent methods to enslave people. A person becomes a bonded labourer when his or her labour is demanded as a means of repayment for a loan. The person is then tricked or trapped into working for very little or no pay, often for seven days a week. The value of their work is invariably greater than the original sum of money borrowed. Debt bondage can last a lifetime and even cross generations, as debts are inherited.

CASE STUDY – HALIYA AND KAMAIYA BONDED LABOURERS OF NEPAL

In Nepal, agricultural and manual labourers, working on the basis of annual contract or sharecropping agreements, are known most commonly as *haliya* and *kamaiya*. Estimates of numbers involved range between 300,000 to 2 million individuals.

The term *haliya* is derived from the word *halo*, which means plough in the Nepali language. But *haliya* has the broader sense of an agricultural labourer, who works on another person's land on the basis of daily or short-term fixed wages. A *haliya* only gets paid work during the farming season, which is often insufficient to meet the family needs. They may resort to loans to cover living costs and the landlords are often the nearest people willing to offer credit in return for cheap labour. Those who temporarily migrate to the cities or to India during the off-farm period are able to pay back the loans, and avoid becoming bonded labourers. Others who do not leave their villages carry out all forms of agricultural work. This may involve bringing their family to work for the same employer for very little payment. In these circumstances there is a risk of falling further into debt and becoming a bonded labourer. If a *haliya* fails to return the loans through the wages he may fall into the debt trap, and subsequently loses his short-term labour contract and freedom to go elsewhere for higher wages. Failure to find an alternative job often accelerates debt bondage.

In the mid-1990s, an Anti-Slavery International supported survey claimed that as many as 260,000 bonded and non-bonded people may be found under *haliya* practice. In contrast, the Internet bulletin of Nepal's National Dalit Commission estimates 150,771 *haliya* individuals in western hill districts of Darchula, Baitadi, Doti, Achham, Bajhang and Bajura alone.[1] Up to 75% of them belong to the so-called *dalit* (socially disadvantaged) communities[2] while only 12% hold citizenship certificates.

In the ethnic Tharu[3] language, a *kamaiya* means a hard-worker, but in Nepali it means a hired worker, who is given some remuneration for his labour. The *kamaiya* practice in Nepal revolves around a yearly contract made between a poor farmer and a landlord. Every *Maghe Sankranti* (mid-January), a man looking for a *jamindar* (an employer) comes out with a cloth encircling his head and carrying a stick on his shoulder – as a way to identify himself as a potential candidate. If the person has already worked as a *kamaiya* and taken a loan, he may have to find a *jamindar* who is

---

[1] These districts have the most *haliya* workers, but *haliya* people may also be found in other districts ranging from Parbat to Udaypur.

[2] The 2001 Census of Nepal puts the number of *dalit* people at 3,030,067 (or 13.09 per cent) out of the total population of 23,151,423.1, and *kami* (blacksmith) is the largest group with 29.57 per cent and *halkhor* (sweeper) is the smallest group with 0.12 per cent of the total inhabitants.

[3] Tharu people predominantly occupy western Tarai districts of Dang, Banke, Bardiya, Kailali and Kanchanpur, also known as Naya Muluk (new frontier), and their total population stands at 1.2 million or 6.5 per cent of the total inhabitants of Nepal.

willing to go to his former *jamindar* to pay off any outstanding loans and then take him on as a *kamaiya*.

Kamaiya families may need to take out a *saunki* – a sum of money borrowed from a *jamindar* to pay for their family's subsistence. If they fail to pay this back they may become entrapped in debt bondage for years. In many cases, the debt leads to not just men working as *kamaiya*, but women become *bukhrani* (or helper) and children are used as *kamlari* (maid or domestic worker) until they are old enough to take-over their parents' work. In 2001, ILO estimated some 110,000 Tharu individuals working as bonded labourers in five Naya Muluk districts.[4]

Nepal has ratified both slavery Conventions of 1924 and 1956, and also its own National Code of 1965 prohibits any forms of slavery. On this basis, the government of Nepal did not recognise the existence of debt bondage or bonded labour. The formation of a United Nations Working Group on Contemporary Forms of slavery in 1988, and its subsequent claim that South Asia has as many as 20 million "modern slaves" (about 27 million worldwide) alerted Nepali human rights activists and various non-Governmental organisations to initiate a campaign against bonded labour. Eventually, the government of Nepal officially prohibited the practice of *kamaiya* system in 2000 (but not yet the *haliya* issue), and introduced the Kamaiya System (Prohibition) Act in 2002 in an attempt to rehabilitate a large number of ethnic Tharu people from the problem of debt bondage. However, laws were enacted without considering or preparing for the consequences of releasing *kamaiya* and many people are now left in the temporary camps set up to accommodate them. This has led some families to return to their former masters, and others to send their children to work for landlords/moneylenders or the urban middle classes.

[4] This is where around 98 per cent of *kamaiya* workers are found, but other districts extent from Nawalparasi to Jhapa.

CHILD LABOUR

The "Worst forms of child labour" ILO (Convention 182) refers to children who work in exploitative or dangerous conditions. Activities include: commercial sexual exploitation of children, child soldiers, trafficking and child domestic work. There may be a strong element of discrimination (gender, race or religion) as part in why some children work.

> We have no time for study and education, no time to play and rest, we are exposed to unsafe working conditions and we are not protected. (Children's Forum Against the Most Intolerable Forms of Child Labour, Bangkok, 1997)

Not all child work is necessarily harmful, when properly controlled it may present development, learning and important earning opportunities. Most children work because their families are poor and their income is necessary for their survival.

> Child labour has serious consequences that stay with the individual and with society for far longer than the years of childhood. Young workers not only face dangerous working conditions. They face long term physical, intellectual and emotional stress. They face an adulthood of unemployment and illiteracy.

> United Nations Secretary-General Kofi Annan

CASE STUDY – CHILD DOMESTIC WORKERS

Child domestic workers (i.e. children in domestic labour) are children (under 18) who work in households of people other than their closest family, doing domestic chores, caring for children, running errands and sometimes helping their employers run small businesses from home. This includes children who are paid for their work, those who are not paid, and those who or receive "in-kind" benefits, such as food and shelter.

Children as young as seven years old are routinely pressed into domestic service. Despite some children entering domestic labour in the hope of continuing their schooling, most are deprived of opportunities for education and are working in conditions that can be considered amongst the worst forms of child labour. World-wide, the majority of child domestic workers are girls, and many have been trafficked, or are in debt bondage. Child domestic workers are isolated from their families and from opportunities to make friends, and are under the total control of employers whose primary concern is often not in their best interests as children.

As figures from the International Labour Organization demon-strate,[5] child domestic workers are large in numbers, yet they remain invisible and marginalized both economically and socially because of the myths still surrounding their employment. While it is conventional to regard domestic work as a "safe" form of employment, in reality a wide range of abuses, including physical, verbal and sexual violence, routinely accompanies this type of work.

In general terms, concern about the impact of work on the health of children has tended to focus on aspects of the child's physi-cal health from exposure to physical and environmental hazards rather than their psychosocial well-being,[6] and this is a significant gap in child labour research which needs to be filled. However,

[5] The ILO estimates that more girls under 16 are in domestic service than in any other category of work. Recent statistics from a number of countries show the numbers to be in the millions worldwide. In addition, significant numbers of pre-pubescent boys are also engaged as domestic workers in many countries. See *Helping hands or shackled lives?: Understanding child domestic labour and responses to it*, ILO, Geneva, 2004.

[6] Using the understanding of psychosocial well-being as discussed in Woodhead, M., *Psychosocial impacts of child work: a framework for research, monitoring and intervention*, for Understanding Children's Work (World Bank, ILO, UNICEF), 2004.

when it comes to certain types of child labour, where the *circumstances* in which the child is working is at least as much of concern as the work itself, this research gap is even more problematic.

Despite the absence of data, key features of child domestic work intuitively give cause for concern, in terms of the potential for short and long term psychosocial impacts:

- separation from the child's own family: the child is living as well as working away from home;
- the child's complete dependence on the employer;
- isolation within the employers home;
- discrimination and treatment as an inferior;
- little or no time off and few opportunities to make friends;
- lack of freedom to leave the house;
- denial of opportunities for education;
- vulnerability to verbal, physical and sexual violence;
- the child's feelings of obligation to parents/family to stay with the employer and to make the best of the "opportunity", or to keep sending money home, regardless of the exploitative and/or abusive circumstances.

The following paragraphs, taken from "Child Domestic Work" (UNICEF, 1999)[7] sum up the concerns relating to the psychosocial well-being of child domestic workers:

> The daily experience of discrimination and the isolation endured by child domestic workers in the employer's household have been reported as the most difficult part of the child domestic worker's burden.[8] Even if they have affective relations with members of the

[7] Black, M. and Blagbrough, J., *Child Domestic Work*, Innocenti Digest No. 5, UNICEF ICDC 1999.

[8] Camacho, A.Z.V., Flores-Oebanda, C., Montano, V., Pacis, R.R. and Robidillo, R. *The Phenomenon of Child Domestic Work: Issues, Responses and Research Findings* Unpublished paper presented by Visayan Forum Foundation at the ILO-IPEC supported Asian Regional Consultation on Child Domestic Workers, Manila, 19–23 November 1997.

household, these are not on equal terms. The capacity to resist sexual advances or negotiate fair treatment will be non-existent, emotionally as well as practically. There will be little or no experience of expressing desires and opinions with a right to respect for them. Children of the employer are also affected.

Recreation and play may be non-existent, except when minding the employer's own children. The only experience may be to watch television, under carefully prescribed circumstances. Many children are reported to fantasise and develop a distorted view of the world.[9]

Confinement to the house leaves them with no opportunity to make friends or enjoy interaction with peers who share their cultural background and language.[10] A 1987 study[11] to collect quantitative health data using psychological tests and control groups, conducted in Kenya, found that child domestic workers experienced significantly more psychological problems than other children (working and non-working). Bedwetting, insomnia, withdrawal, regressive behaviour, premature ageing, depression and phobic reactions to their employers were common. Depression has also been reported in Bangladesh[12] and in various Latin American countries.[13]

A RESPONSE?

It is easy to feel helpless in the face of continuing massive injustice of this sort on a global scale. Experience of recent global campaigns relating to indebtedness, fair trade and others demonstrate some

[9] Rahman, H., *Child domestic workers: Is servitude the only option?* Shoishab Bangladesh, Dhaka, 1995.
[10] UN Economic and Social Council, Commission on Human Rights. "Report of the Special Rapporteur on violence against women, its causes and consequences, Ms Radhika Coomaraswamy", E/CN.4/1997/47, 12 February 1997.
[11] Bwibo, N.O. and Onyango, P., *"Final report of the child labour and health research"*, University of Nairobi, Nairobi, 1987.
[12] Rahman, H. *op cit.*
[13] Salazar, M.C., *Child Work and Education in Latin America* in Salazar and Glasinovich, UNICEF ICDC and Ashgate Publishing Ltd, 1998.

impact can be achieved from concerted and co-ordinated campaigns. Lessons from the abolitionists being commemorated in 2007 are that you have to produce credible evidence (data) to make a credible case in support of the ethical human rights approach. Law alone is not enough, the ethical argument has not prevailed but, if combined with credible evidence of economic and social consequences, an unanswerable case can be made.

In the UK an academic network has been established to look at links between health and child labour. This network has an interest in the psychosocial and developmental consequences of the worst forms of child labour as well as broader health issues. For example, how does demeaning treatment, deprivation of education and normal family contact affect the psychosocial development of children? What will the impact be of these children in later life as parents and workers? The network believes that academics have a contribution to make to the ending of exploitative and hazardous child labour by promoting teaching, research and advocacy. A significant benefit of academic involvement is the application of academic rigour and hence international credibility to research through identifying and filling knowledge gaps and analysis of existing knowledge. There is very little credible or rigorous research in this area. The inclusion of child labour in teaching is a further important support in Higher Education, informing future leaders and disseminating knowledge to an international audience. By research, teaching and advocacy academics can assist and influence decision makers and policy makers who have an impact on child labour.

Slavery has been with humanity for as long as records exist. It remains one of the major global abuses of human rights and yet is generally not known about. It is not just a product of recent globalisation (itself far from a new phenomenon) or current world trade systems. Where there is poverty and there are vulnerable people, history shows that there is no shortage of people to exploit and oppress them.

TRAFFICKING IN PERSONS

The United States government has faced major controversy regarding illegal immigrants, who have settled in the USA and contribute to the economy. Given that the USA has always been based on immigrants, offering the dream of a better future to those who have chosen to come, sensitivities are strong. This has become a major political issue.

Condoleezza Rice, Secretary of State, wrote the preface to the 2005 report by the US State Department, which was concerned with the problem of trafficking:

> President Bush, the Congress and the American people are united in efforts to eradicate trafficking in persons internationally and within national borders because this global crime opposes the universal value of freedom.

The report provided a context of slavery and civil war in the USA, at the end of which the 13th Amendment to the US Constitution banned slavery.

> More than 140 years ago, the United States fought a devastating war to rid our country of slavery, and to prevent those who supported it from dividing the nation. Although the vast majority of nations succeeded in eliminating the state-sanctioned practice, a modern form of human slavery has emerged as a growing global threat to the lives and freedom of millions of men, women and children. Today, slavery is rarely state sponsored. Instead, human trafficking often involves organized crime groups who make huge sums of money at the expense of trafficking victims. (State Department, 2005, p. 6)

The International Labour Organisation estimate that there are currently 12.3 million slaves in the world: forced, bonded, child, sex, involuntary servitude. The report breaks down the figures of those trafficked across borders:

> Of the estimated 600,000 to 800,000 men, women and children trafficked across international borders each year, approximately

> 80% are women and girls, and up to 50% are minors . . . the majority are trafficked into commercial sexual exploitation. (State Department, 2005, p. 6)

Using data from 9 countries, it is argued that 89% of prostitutes want to escape, 60–75% have been raped, 70–95% physically assaulted, 68% suffer from Post Traumatic Stress Disorder.

The consequences go beyond individuals:

> The loss of family and community support networks makes trafficking victims vulnerable to traffickers' demands and threats, and contributes in several ways to the breakdown of social structures. Trafficking tears children from their parents and extended family. The profits from trafficking allow the practice to take root in a particular community, which is then repeatedly exploited as a ready source of victims. (State Department, 2005, p. 13)

It can have a dramatic impact on prospects for development:

> When forced or bonded labour involves a significant part of a country's population, this form of trafficking retards the country's development, as generation after generation of these victims remain mired in poverty. (State Department, 2005, p. 14)

There have been detailed studies on Child Sex Tourism, and on the link between trafficking and HIV/AIDS. Detailed country studies show international trading routes. For example, the United Kingdom, though praised in the report, is clearly deeply involved:

> The United Kingdom is primarily a country of destination for trafficked women, children and men from Eastern Europe, East Asia and West Africa. Women are trafficked primarily for the purposes of sexual exploitation and involuntary domestic servitude, while men are trafficked for the purpose of forced labour in agriculture and sweatshop industries. The United Kingdom may also play a role as a transit country for foreign victims trafficked to other Western European countries. (State Department, 2005, p. 221)

Poorer countries, such as Zimbabwe, can be trading partners:

> Zimbabwe is a source and transit country for small numbers of women and children trafficked for the purposes of forced labour and sexual exploitation. Women and children were reportedly sexually exploited in towns on the Zimbabwe border with South Africa. There were also reports of Zimbabweans being lured by false job promises to other countries, particularly the UK, where, upon arrival, they were debt bonded, had their passports confiscated and movement restricted, and were exploited in sweatshops or brothels. (State Department, 2005, p. 229)

The report tabulates ILO Conventions signed and ratified around the world, but does not include the USA.

SLAVERY IN BRAZIL

In 1831 the first Brazilian legislation against slavery was passed, but was not implemented. In 1871 children of slaves were declared to be born free, but were obliged to work as slaves until the age of 21. In 1885 slaves over 65 were freed. In 1888 slavery was abolished in Brazil. 3.6 million slaves had been transported. 600,000 were freed. On emancipation, former slaves were offered neither land nor credit.

The problem of slavery continues today. It is estimated that there were 90,000 agricultural slaves in 1970–94. This is in direct contravention of the Universal Declaration of Human Rights 1948, Article 4:

> No one shall be held in slavery or servitude; slavery and the slave trade shall be prohibited in all its forms.

One of the common forms of slavery is enslavement through debt. This is covered by the UN Supplementary Convention on the Abolition of slavery, the Slave Trade and Institutions and Practices similar to slavery 1956, Article 1(a):

> Debt bondage, that is to say, the status or condition arising from a
> pledge by a debtor of his personal services or those of a person under
> his control as security for a debt, if the value of those services as
> reasonable assessed is not applied towards the liquidation of the debt
> or the length and nature of those services are not respectively
> limited and defined.

Linked to this there can be forced labour, which is also proscribed
in ILO Convention No 29, on Forced Labour (1930):

> No concession granted to private individuals, companies or associa-
> tions shall involve any form of forced or compulsory labour for the
> production or collection of products which such individuals, com-
> panies or associations utilize or in which they trade.

Particularly at remote plantations, slavery can be maintained
through methods of payment. This is also covered in ILO Convention No 95 on Payment of Wages (1949):

> Wages payable in money shall be paid only in legal tender, and
> payment in the form of promissory notes, vouchers or coupons, or
> in any other form alleged to represent legal tender, shall be
> prohibited.

The end of the slave trade meant a change, as argued by Father
Ricardo Rezende:

> Black slaves are no longer brought to Brazil from Africa; the modern
> badge of slavery is not colour, but poverty and unemployment.
> (Sutton, 1994, p. 15)

The problem was particularly acute for rubber tappers, as reported
by Euclides da Cunha in Purus, Western Acre, 1905:

> The remoteness, aggravated by poor communications, reduces the
> rubber tappers in the most remote places to being almost a serf, at
> the mercy and discretionary dominion of the bosses. Justice is natu-
> rally circumscribed if not non-existent. (Sutton, 1994, p. 75)

The Comissao Pastoral da Terra, in Araguia-Tocantins, reported
that the problem continued in 1980:

The prolonged isolation of their work, the high turnover, and the lack of roots in the local village, the social marginalization to which they are subject, and other factors appear to obstruct their search for forms of organization to defend their interests. Nevertheless there have been forms of resistance by individuals and groups. (Sutton, 1994, p. 128)

Trade unions have been critical of the role of banks. Sao Paulo Bank Workers Union wrote to the Banco Real Group:

There is a great antagonism: on the one side the bank opens a branch that is totally automated, and on the other it submits rural workers to a regime of semi slavery. (Sutton, 1994, p. 137)

In the 1960s and 70s there were reports of employment practices by major multinationals such as Volkswagen, Nixdorf, Liquigas, some of whom kept poor records. In 1992 it was reported that 9.2 million workers were paid below the minimum wage. They faced violence at estate level, and were obliged to work for food.

In 1993 the Brazilian government acknowledged the issue. They accepted the 1991 report from the World Bank, which showed that Brazil was the third most unequal economy in the world. Workers were in forms of slavery, with low life expectancy, and need for modernization programmes. Economic reform brought mixed blessings, as was argued by the National Movement for Street Boys and Girls:

On the one hand the disorientation of the population and lack of information laid the new frontiers open to the brutal form of pen-etration of capital in its most primitive form. On the other hand government fiscal incentives and financing of programmes such as colonization, cattle-ranching, industrialization, solely strengthened monopolistic economic groups, without responding in any way to social requirements linked to the region's identity. (Sutton, 1994, p. 25)

The government accepted that the issue was citizenship for all, not just an élite. The challenge was great, as revealed in research in

1992 for Anti Slavery International, on recruitment and slavery conditions in different sectors: banks, car manufacture, car rental, charcoal, rubber, prostitution, tea, tanning, cotton. All too often the employment relationship was close to slavery, as contractors held the labour cards of workers. Prof de Souza Martins described this as:

> A kind of symbolic execution of the principles of civil equality and of contract. From this moment the worker is dead as a citizen: and a slave is born (Sutton, 1994, p. 34)

BUSINESS AND HUMAN RIGHTS

In principle, if the arguments set out above are as strong as their proponents claim, there should be a constructive response from business. Gören Lindahl (2000) President and CEO, ABB, has conceded that there is a central role for major companies in supporting the advance of human rights:

> Big companies need to step into the breach to ensure that globalization delivers more than a litany of dashed hopes. We must now act as co-guarantors of human rights.

He noted that this is also in the self-interest of the companies concerned:

> Companies that are good local citizens will find it easier to hire and keep talent, obtain good financing and gain societal approval, political support and regulatory consent.

A similar view has been expressed by former European Commissioner Peter Sutherland (2000), Chairman of BP Amoco:

> Getting it right is not only a matter of ethical behaviour and moral choice. Enlightened business people have realized that good business is good for business. Good business is sustainable, is part of global society, not at odds with it, and reflects values which are shared across the world.

Sophon Suphaphong (2000), President of Bangchak Petroleum, Thailand has added a global perspective:

> The world's markets just won't buy products if they are manufactured by countries that exploit child labour, that are dictatorial, and that destroy the environment. Eventually business people will have no choice but to take part in the process of solving our social problems.

Reebok (2000) has emphasised Human Rights Production Standards, partly influenced by adverse publicity for its rival Nike:

> Reebok's experience is that the incorporation of internationally recognized human rights standards into its business practice improves worker morale and results in a higher quality working environment and higher quality products.

Sir Geoffrey Chandler (2000), Chair, Amnesty International UK Business Group, placed the issue on the agenda for strategic management:

> Inaction is not an option. The choice is between the exercise of corporate leadership in developing appropriate company policies, or being forced by public opinion to bring corporate practice into line with the values of society.

Pierre Sané, Amnesty International Secretary General, argued in 1998:

> It is a company's responsibility to anticipate and provide for human rights problems at any point in its operations, in the same way that it has learnt to anticipate environmental problems. Policies need to be explicit and open. Mistakes may still be made, but secretiveness leads to the suspicion that these are at best carelessness, at worst collusion.

The Norwegian Confederation of Business and Industry expressed a strong collective view, 1998:

> Both companies and individual business people can get involved in defending those whose human rights have been violated, regardless of whether they are victims of torture, random arrests, illegal imprisonment or miscarriages of justice.

The 1948 UN Universal Declaration of Human Rights offers a basis for developing the framework of company policy. This arises in revenue allocation and corruption; problems of operating in conflict zones; the use of security forces, for example by Shell in Nigeria; and indigenous peoples' rights. Company cases can be considered in labour rights, such as freedom of association, with Reebok in Indonesia; child labour, with Pentland in Pakistan; working conditions, with B&Q in India; and bonded and forced labour, in India, Pakistan, Nepal, Myanmar and China.

There are many UN Conventions, such as on the Rights of the Child, which have yet to be made fully effective. Somalia has not signed or ratified; USA has signed but not ratified.

Shareholder pressure can be important: there have been resolutions to AGMs on social responsibility at Boeing, Exxon, General Motors, Lucent and Morgan Stanley.

It is now almost commonplace for major corporations to make public declarations of their commitments. BT. In "The Way We Work . . . Getting it right" (1999), declared:

- We are committed to protecting and enhancing the human dignity of all those engaged with our company. To this end we have based our policies and procedures on the principles set out in the UN Universal Declaration of Human Rights.
- As the global influence of multinational companies widens, many of the principles enshrined in the Universal Declaration of Human Rights are relevant to the way they conduct themselves.
- We in BT will continue to take human rights seriously. We shall seek to apply our commitment to human dignity in whatever part of the world we operate.

The Shell Report (1998) was similarly robust:

- We support the Universal Declaration of Human Rights.
- We speak out in defence of human rights when we feel it is justified to do so.
- We are setting up Social Responsibility Management Systems designed to help in the implementation of our Business Principles and therefore our stated support for human rights.

- We are developing awareness training and management procedures to help resolve human rights dilemmas when they arise.
This includes a guide to human rights for managers.

A further link has been made with the Universal Declaration of
Human Rights, in the Norwegian Confederation of Business and
Industry checklist:

> Article 4: No one shall be held in slavery or servitude; slavery and
> the slave trade shall be prohibited in all their forms;

> - Does the company have procedures that prevent slavery, forced
>   child labour or hard labour performed by prisoners?
> - Does the company have guidelines that prevent collaboration, trade
>   or partnership with or deliveries from enterprises that
>   use slaves, forced child labour or hard labour performed by
>   prisoners?
> - Does the company fulfil the standards set out in UN CRC and
>   ILO Conventions Nos 29 and 138?

The leading capitalist guru, George Soros (Avery, 2000, p. 11),
argues:

> The doctrine of laissez-faire capitalism holds that the common good
> is best served by the uninhibited pursuit of self-interest. Unless it is
> tempered by the recognition of a common interest, (our democratic
> open society) is liable to break down.

On the basis of such a consensus of enlightenment, we might
expect to find a transformed future. Sir Anthony Cleaver, in
"Tomorrow's Company" (1995), wrote:

> The companies which will sustain competitive success in the future
> are those which focus less exclusively on financial measures of
> success – and instead include all their stakeholder relationships, and
> a broader range of measurements, in the way they think and talk
> about their purpose and performance.

The Nobel Prize winning economist Amartya Sen (1999), has
made the connection between human rights and development:

> The substantive freedoms of political participation and dissent are among the constituent components of development . . . Freedom is not only the primary end of development, it is also one of its principal means.

Nelson Mandela broadened the political and economic agenda, at the World Economic Forum (1997):

> Development can no longer be regarded as the responsibility of government alone. It requires a partnership of government with its social partners: private sector, labour and non-governmental organizations.

Juan Somavia, Director-General of the ILO, in 1999, noted the additional complications of globalisation:

> Globalisation has brought both prosperity and inequalities, which are testing the limits of collective social responsibility. If we are to avoid a serious backlash against the process of globalization, concerted action is needed.

Kofi Annan, at the World Economic Forum in 2001, took a similar view: (p. 22):

> If we cannot make globalization work for all, in the end it will work for none. The unequal distribution of benefits and the imbalances in global rule making will produce backlash and protectionism. And that, in turn, threatens to undermine and ultimately unravel the open world economy.

James Wolfensohn, President of the World Bank, argued in 2000 (pp. 19–20):

> As business looks to expand over the next 25 years, it finds that the most rapidly growing markets are, in fact, in the developing world. By 2025, the world's population will have increased by 2 billion people, all but 3% of whom will live in developing countries. So executives perceive poverty reduction to be in their own interest.

The pressure is now on business. Jennifer Woodward, of PricewaterhouseCoopers, acknowledged in 1999:

Gradually we will see a shift from managing reputation crises following a media expose, to companies gaining positive competitive advantage for their good record on human rights.

Those companies that insist their social record is irreproachable and resist independent monitoring are inviting the very criticism they seek to avoid. (p. 59)

OCCUPATIONAL HEALTH AS A HUMAN RIGHTS ISSUE

When there is such apparent agreement among business and world leaders regarding the importance of human rights and corporate social responsibility, why do we see the continuation of practices in the workplace which are damaging to human health?

This book has concentrated on relationships in the workplace, and on approaches to work organisation. Apart from explicit regimes of control and participation, there are clearly issues of knowledge and responsibility. Explicit slavery is not seen as acceptable in the industrialised world, where employment relations have replaced ownership and feudal obligations. The rhetoric has been of a free market. Increasingly responsibilities have been devolved to individuals. National agreements have been replaced by individual negotiations and individual contracts.

Controversy arises when we consider implicit relationships, based on implicit knowledge, and rarely expressed in formal explicit documents. In this debate, knowledge is closely linked to power. Power can include control over the disclosure of information, meaning that decisions and negotiations are based on unequal foundations. Conventionally we have assumed that decisions are based on full information and equal access, but this is clearly not the case.

Attempts to deal with slavery around the world in the early twentieth century have provided examples of this phenomenon.

Indirect rule, the pragmatic basis of the British Empire, Mandates and Protectorates, was concerned with control of, and through, information. British governors such as Lord Lugard believed that for slaves to leave their owners without good reason could have adverse effects in political and economic terms. It was rational therefore to avoid disclosure of the rights of individuals, in contexts where they might otherwise remain ignorant.

In the UK, and other colonial powers, we may note continuity between the methods of colonial rule and approaches to management of organisations. This is particularly the case when there is an enduring system of social class, in which managers and workers operate separately, and adopt adversarial relationships. In this context, human resource management is a continuation of indirect rule.

In countries without rigid systems of social class, it is more possible to talk of working life, as an experience shared by most adults. This means recognising and respecting the tacit knowledge of the experienced worker. If the manager has never engaged in the kind of work undertaken by those for whom he has responsibility, mutual recognition and respect may be harder. This will restrict the extent to which industrial democracy is possible.

We are accustomed to considering the workplace and employment relations in financial terms. When we plan for the future, we undertake cost benefit analysis, hoping to demonstrate a likely return on investment. In such exercises, we will give primacy to quantitative data. With both social and environmental accounting, and reports to stakeholders, there have been efforts to broaden the perspective. To date this has been regarded as an optional extra.

The work of Marmot and colleagues (discussed in Chapter 6), analysing health outcomes of relative social status, provides a starting point. Public health arguments have been based on epidemiology. Occupational health arguments can be linked to work organisation. The workplace is a context where interventions are possible, and their effects can be evaluated.

POWER

In an economy and society based on social class, the employer may fail to disclose to his employees details of their work environment, and their rights. Trade unions increasingly see it as their task to address such issues, but many employers prefer not to recognise trade unions. British law still enshrines this inequality, in contravention of European law, by stating that the obligations of employers should be exercised "in so far as is reasonably practicable". This covers risk assessment and the provision of specialist occupational health and safety services. Unless tested in court cases, the judgements are those of the employer, and are typically made on the basis of cost, an approach which is explicitly ruled out in the preamble to Framework Directive 89/391.

Power inequality characterises the framework in which occupational health is addressed. The traditional system has been for companies to retain the services of company physicians, with a relationship to corporate management. Control over processes of diagnosis and treatment may be open to abuse. Managers do not want health problems to be linked to their actions or the work environment. This may affect the acceptable options for diagnosis: a diagnosis of Repetitive Strain Injury (RSI) may seem to pre-empt the process of seeking causes for individual medical problems.

Medical science is supposedly universal. However, occupational medicine is culturally situated. There are health impacts of actions by agents, who operate within complex contexts. It makes little sense to leave power in the exclusive hands of occupational physicians. There is a further implication of this argument. Despite the attractiveness of the call, from ICOH, for Basic Occupational Health Services for all, once we move beyond the medical sub-set of issues, there can be no one best way. A range of interventions will be needed, preferably seen as integral to the local culture.

It seems odd to rely on doctors to deal with problems which have, at least in part, been caused by work, the work environment, management decisions, and work organisation. Unhealthy work practices need to be identified and addressed. For managers to pretend ignorance may mean that avoidable harm results for workers. It may become implicit policy. Information may be developed on the basis of what the managers regards as the need to know.

In principle, the worker is free to negotiate on an individual basis. In practice, the management may have decided to own the knowledge of the health dimensions of work, leaving the workers as slaves of their ignorance. On this basis, a large proportion of workers may be seen as slaves to ignorance. This does not simply refer to their individual levels of knowledge. It deals with the restricted information on the basis of which they are obliged to make decisions. In addition, the economic pressures, which mean that the employee needs to retain income from employment, inhibit full debate.

PEOPLE AND MACHINES

If workers are not partners with whom managers share knowledge, then they are less likely to be sources of knowledge. It has been traditional to regard older workers as if they were machines, no longer operating as smoothly as the more recent models, and subject to control. They are deficient by comparison with younger workers. Some employers are now recognising the benefits to be derived from regarding older workers as having gained experience and tacit knowledge, which represent valuable resources for the organisation.

Chattel slavery was the extreme case. The slave worker was not considered to be a full human being, equivalent to the owner. There was no progression route from slave to owner. There was no investment in education and training for slaves. There was no outlet for their wisdom and experience. Most slaves would die before they got old.

Current demographic change poses the question: is the worker to be regarded as a slave or a citizen? What will citizenship mean in practical terms? Does this require changes in management? There will not be a consistent process of transition from slavery to citizenship, even in the context of workplace health. In each setting, there is a reference back to perceived local history. There are ongoing relationships and power structures. If the focus is purely on occupational medicine, there are likely to be problems.

If we take a specific issue such as child labour, we begin to encounter complexities. If we wish to eradicate harmful child labour, we need to understand impacts, not just in terms of individual health, but also in terms of educational, social, financial and political dimensions.

Human rights are an individual entitlement, but they are socially constituted. Occupational health is discussed in terms of the health of the individual, concentrating on what is associated with the context of work.

FREEING MINDS

Concerns for human rights can face obstacles from the conventional perspectives of specialists, who work in their own distinct fields, and do not engage in wider debate. For example, psychiatrists emphasise the important of practice, by which they mean individual cases.

- They find it hard to derive actionable knowledge from epidemiology, beyond guidelines for good practice.
- They tend to be sceptical about the utility of general frameworks and strategies, such as can emerge from workplace health promotion.

- They are better able to engage in discourse with other medical practitioners, with what they assume is a shared professional reference point.
- Frequently a number of different specialisms can contribute to the understanding of a new problem with hybrid characteristics.
- Insights often arise from conversations on the fringe of international conferences. It can be difficult to translate the insights into action.

This book is intended to provide a means by which complementary insights, from the different disciplines, can be brought to a wider audience.

AN NGO FOR HEALTHY WORK

Non Governmental Organisations exist in order to promote and implement agendas which cannot simply be left to governments or the private sector. Occupational health is often given little priority, and treated as of marginal importance. Within government, responsibilities can be unclear, as between health and employment. In private sector organisations, finance directors can find it difficult to recognise the case for investment.

The terms of debates vary between countries, according to the focus of economic activity. Legislative and institutional histories are important, together with the relations between the different specialist groups. In short, there is no one single discourse on healthy work. Doctors can find it hard to talk to business strategists. Within the set of occupational health professionals, there can be tensions between occupational physicians, hygienists, nurses, safety officers, advisers and consultants, and there are many models for joint working.

The International Commission on Occupational Health has been addressing the field for a century. The world of work has changed. Research has been conducted, and many of the conclusions are not reflected in policy or practice. It is not obvious that simply conducting more research will bring about change in the quality of working life and improvements in the work environment.

Epidemiological research has highlighted the correlation between relative social status and health outcomes, based on numerous studies across the world, with data on diverse health problems. However, epidemiology does not yield causal explanations, and provide actionable knowledge. There have been highly publicised conclusions in terms of stress, but accounts of stress are not straightforwardly translated into conventional medical diagnoses at the individual level.

In this book, rather than starting with a medical focus, we argue that the central issues concern human rights, operationalised in terms of control and participation. This changes the context in which plans can be discussed, and suggests that lessons may be learned from experience of other NGOs in the area of human rights. This debate has not been part of the standard curriculum for medical or business professionals, who develop their careers within established structures and conventions. Perhaps this is not entirely surprising, as the professions are artificial constructs, in which power is exercised by senior members. Seniority is achieved through sustained conformity with norms.

The terms of public debate do not remain the same. We can identify particular "tipping points", where the balance shifts, and new paradigms can gain ascendancy. This is the territory of social constructivists, and even of "spin doctors". The history of NGO activities suggests that the work of individual engaged researchers can have an impact that changes history. This role includes communication and dialogue as central elements.

OCCUPATIONAL HEALTH AND EQUITY

In 2000, at the ICOH Congress in Singapore, I argued that occupational health should be seen as a human rights issue, for which a proactive international NGO is required. ICOH has typically operated on the basis of 35 Scientific Committees, conducting their own programmes over the triennial periods between congresses, with varying levels of activity, and a collective impact that may not be more than the sum of the parts. It is primarily a scientific organisation, with conferences and seminars, which may link separate Scientific Committees.

The ICOH Board appointed me to co-ordinate an ICOH network on occupational health education and training in developing countries. An initial project was developed and implemented in South Africa, with occupational health nurses, supported by the Swedish National Institute for Working Life. The new ICOH network lacked resources, manpower, and an institutional base, so little could be achieved beyond adding to initiatives of the Southern African Development Community (SADC), WHO and ILO. Efforts to secure the engagement of major providers of new technologies, such as digital satellite communications and low-cost receivers and personal computers, arrived at prototypes, but support for sustained implementation was not achieved.

In 2003 in Iguassu the ICOH Congress took the theme "The Challenge of Equity in Health and Safety at Work". This posed problems to some conventional occupational physicians, who felt that they were being asked to go beyond the medical field in which they felt professionally competent and secure, in order to address issues which they saw as primarily political. They felt insecure at the boundaries between science and politics. The plenary presentations were spirited and controversial. Some representatives of the United States government experienced discomfort, as economic and foreign policies of their government were linked with discussions of occupational health.

I was elected as a member of the ICOH Board, with responsibilities in areas which were seen as not requiring specialist medical expertise: age, unemployment and health, and sickness absence. I have developed links with ICOH members in the UK, where there is considerable expertise, but occupational health has, until recently, been given relatively low priority by government. At the mid-term meeting of the Board, the ICOH President presented a vision of "Basic Occupational Health Services for All", while noting that around the world 70% of workers have no access to occupational health services at all. Research has shown us where the major dangers arise from exposures. However, research is not being translated into policy, and policy is not being translated into practice.

In 2006 in Milan the ICOH Congress celebrated 100 years of occupational medicine, with an agenda based on reflections on historical achievements, and challenges expressed in primarily medical terms. Where there was discussion of child labour, for example, it was simply in terms of analysis of particular exposures, not with an agenda for change.

In 2009 in Cape Town the ICOH Congress will address "Occupational Health: A Basic Right at Work – An Asset to Society", building on a legacy of work by the Scientific Committee on Occupational Health and Development, and considerable expertise in Southern Africa. A major problem for developing countries, especially in Africa, is that their expensively trained medical professionals, in fields including occupational health, are being recruited to work in industrialised countries, from which they rarely return.

THE FUTURE AGENDA

Most societies have had systems of slavery in the past. The emancipation process is incomplete. General awareness of human rights has increased, but it is not always obvious what has to be changed in order to achieve citizenship in the workplace.

The different ICOH Scientific Committees should be invited to provide briefing papers for a policy development process. This would emphasise the international and cross-disciplinary nature of OH. The focus on slavery and citizenship, set out in this book, can be linked to specialist research fields, where the practical aspects of the transition are under study. An ICOH Network could address child labour.

Sustainable economic development requires attention to occupational health. This is not simply a matter of medicine, but requires fresh insights into work organisation, providing a context for implementing healthy work. This could be expressed in terms of a move from slavery to citizenship.

The proposal for hosting ICOH 2012 in Glasgow located occupational health in the context of the working lives of ordinary people, the policies which governments need to develop, and enlightened and sustainable approaches to business and society. Glasgow workers have often felt by-passed by decision makers, and then victims of poor working conditions.

John Harrison (2006), as the UK national secretary for ICOH, set the scene:

> The wealth of a country derives from its use of resources. People are its greatest resource. Throughout history people have exploited the natural resources of the environment, but at a cost. Occupational health is concerned with the health and well being of people at work. Its focus has been the identification and prevention of occupational diseases, although the changing demographics of working populations in the so-called developed world has led to new roles in the promotion of health and work ability and the rehabilitation of workers.

> The Industrial Revolution was a time of great social change in the United Kingdom. Developments in manufacturing and engineering, driven by the use of water and coal to produce energy, led to

the creation of many large cities. Scotland has a rich occupational heritage linked to innovation, entrepreneurial spirit and hard work. People living and working in and around Glasgow have benefited from the wealth created by its industry, but some became ill or were injured because of it. Pneumoconiosis, noise-induced hearing loss and hand-arm vibration syndrome are all too familiar occupational diseases that affected the working population of Glasgow, resulting from work in the mines, factories or ship yards. Perhaps because of this, Glasgow and Scotland has a strong medical tradition and it has become a leader in the UK for occupational health initiatives.

The world of work is changing. Large manufacturing companies are disappearing to be replaced by a multitude of small companies. These companies, with limited resources for health or welfare provision for their workers, often have had no occupational health expertise. Healthy Working Lives[14] in Scotland is an initiative from the Scottish Assembly to have an integrated occupational health approach that will give access to people working in small companies, free of charge. This is not currently available elsewhere in the UK. It is an example of partnership working: Government, Trades Unions, Employers and occupational health professionals working together for mutual benefit. This project can be an exemplar for the UK and for the rest of the world. The promotion of health and well being in populations must recognise that work is an important part of life: People should not be made ill by their work and the work environment has the potential to promote well being and positive health behaviour.

This summary goes beyond classical scientific medicine. It emphasises the importance of work, and argues that work should not make us ill, but "promote well-being and positive health behaviour". It is fully consistent with the ICOH President Jorma Rantanen's call for "Basic Occupational Health Services for All".

[14] http://www.scotland.gov.uk/library5/health/hwls-00.asp (Accessed 15/2/06).

WHAT IS TO BE DONE?

In taking forward a campaign for occupational health based on human rights, we have much to learn from the experience of the campaign to end the Transatlantic Slave Trade, for which William Wilberforce was the leading public spokesman. He was a Parliamentarian, not a researcher. Abolishing the Transatlantic Slave Trade was important to him, but he did not argue for emancipation. He opposed the continued transportation of slaves, but did not object to new generations being born into slavery. His focus increasingly shifted to the challenge of converting Hindus in India. Wilberforce, together with his successors in Anti Slavery International, has inspired many of those now working on campaigns within ICOH, such as on child labour.

ICOH is potentially well placed to reach a new "tipping point" in the field of occupational health, seen within the context of human rights. Study of the campaign against the Transatlantic Slave Trade, whose success is commemorated in 2007, suggests that there was a marked difference between the myth which has been preserved and celebrated, and the practical reality at the time. This is the territory of engaged researchers and NGOs.

Thomas Clarkson was the driving force behind the campaign for the abolition of the Transatlantic Slave Trade. He was the only one of the 12 founding members of the London Committee for the Abolition of the Slave Trade to live to see the emancipation of slaves in 1838, after a campaign lasting over 50 years, with the public climax when the Transatlantic Slave Trade was abolished in 1807. He was the researcher, writer, network builder, strategic planner, for example in relations with the campaign against slavery in France and the French overseas territories. He kept the records of the early committee meetings, and published memoirs to ensure that the battles on Abolition were won, and stayed won. Thomas Clarkson prepared the tailored briefings for Parliamentarians, building up the information base for the campaign. He was a master of the technique of developing the business case to persuade particular audiences. He maintained an uneasy relationship with Wilberforce, whose Parliamentary presence was vital.

Clarkson's example was vital in the development of Amnesty International, from a small group in a back room, to winning the Nobel Peace Prize in 1977. His work could also have lessons for ICOH as a proactive NGO, over the coming years, as it enters its second century. We have had two centuries since the abolition of the Transatlantic Slave Trade. It is perhaps now time to promote healthy work.

CHAPTER 8

UNITING NATIONS

Haiti is the first Black republic in the world and the second independent state in the Americas and the Caribbean . . . We celebrate our African heroes who, in a single-minded struggle for their liberation, made us understand that none but ourselves can defeat those who subject us to tyranny and oppression . . . Haitian independence represents their defeat . . . Today we are engaged in an historic struggle for the victory of the African renaissance because we are inspired by the Haitian revolution.

Thabo Mbeki. President of the Republic of South Africa, 1 January 2004.

BEYOND THE WORKPLACE

The move from slavery to citizenship has been complicated by the political context. There had been no long-term plans for slavery to end, and for slaves to be freed, acquiring rights that were equal to those of their former owners. This meant that there would be a painful intermediate period, characterised by empires.

Political history to date has always been a matter of competition between nations, and between their rulers, for power. There has typically been little participation in key decisions from ordinary people.

For centuries these contests were fought out largely at a regional level, within the confines of particular continents. This changed in the fifteenth century, with the voyages of discovery, initiated by the Portuguese, but emulated by other seafaring nations. Triumphant explorers would return home with their prizes, intended to reflect glory on the monarch. Trophies taken from ancient civilisations implied some superiority for the modern conqueror.

Northern Europeans were well situated to explore the Atlantic, and to take advantage of systems of ocean currents, which corresponded to potential trade routes. Thus, for example, the Triangular Trade between Europe, West Africa and the Americas simply meant using prevailing winds and currents. Sailors were rarely volunteers, but were often forced into dangerous voyages, with high mortality rates. The appeal of prize money, and lucrative contracts to supply slaves, proved effective drivers.

The development of major naval capabilities, rather than traditional reliance on land forces, meant that ambitions could become global. As long as sea power was in place, and not vulnerable to over frequent attack, nations at a distance from each other could be united, through trade and colonial relationships. What was more, details of overseas activities would not be known at home. The realities of the treatment of slaves would not be reported. Benign myths could be maintained.

National histories tend to depict their own sailors as heroic adventurers, while other countries may recall the same individuals as pirates, murderers and slave traders. By conducting their escapades at sea, and at a great distance from home, it was often possible to present an account which appealed to public opinion. William and John Hawkins, and Francis Drake, attract extremes of description: British national heroes, who also commanded navies in times of war, slave traders and murdering pirates.

COMPETITION IN THE SLAVE TRADE

The Transatlantic Slave Trade had been one expression of international competition, and the preparedness to treat non-Europeans as inferior. The British, for example, were not content with supplying slaves to their own colonies, but valued the Asiento monopoly contract to supply the Spanish empire.

Policies on slavery could be changed at will, if this offered a means of gaining advantage over traditional rivals. While the United States became able to breed its own population of slaves, not requiring transatlantic imports, the West Indies, with a less hospitable environment, continued to need imports. Thus, once the British had reduced their engagement in North America, and had started to take more interest in the East Indies, where slave labour was not used, it was economically and politically convenient to abolish the Transatlantic Slave Trade, causing inconvenience to the French West Indies.

World wars were fought predominantly between European countries, but involving overseas colonies, both as the battlefields and the providers of many of the troops. There were sensitive issues when it came to arming slaves, as they would then become more difficult to control. In the long run, forced recruits could become reliable soldiers, but only if there were sustained moves towards citizenship.

Once the British had abolished the Transatlantic Slave Trade, they felt able to occupy the moral high ground, and enforce compliance by other nations. Arthur Herman (2005) is typical in praising the British contribution to liberty:

The world system that emerged after 1815 would be one increasingly reliant on the Royal Navy as international policeman. The sea routes on which the British Empire depended were made accessible to other nations, as an expression of the British principle of free trade. The peace and security the navy brought to Britain's shores increasingly extended to other parts of the world. The personal liberty Englishmen enjoyed became a basic human right, as the navy wiped out the slave trade. British naval vessels regularly intervened to protect Briton and non-Briton alike from tyranny and violence. An empire, originally born out of ruthless ambition and brutality, had become the basis for a new progressive world order. (Herman, 2005, p. xix)

FROM SLAVERY: COLONISATION AND THE SCRAMBLE FOR AFRICA

It is important to come to terms with the past, and to go beyond simple comfortable myths. The past informs the present.

The Hogarth Press was run by the Bloomsbury Set in London, with family links back to the abolitionists. James Stephen, brother in law of William Wilberforce, was great uncle of Virginia Woolf. In books such as "White Capital and Coloured Labour", by Lord Olivier, the enterprise of colonisation was stripped of its imperial rhetoric. The underlying economic assumptions were revealed:

> Practically the whole of our recent colonization of Africa . . . has been essentially capitalist colonization . . . financed by European syndicates and investors, and the active directing of it done by men who go out as landowners or farmers and employers and organizers of labour, the labour which they expect to employ being not now specifically chattel slave labour, but the labour of native black men. (Olivier, 1929, p. 14)

Slavery was generalised into the exploitation of Africans. The story for domestic consumption in Britain was that the Empire was a civilising mission. Underpinning this were assumptions about European superiority, and the economic benefits available:

Tropical countries are not suited for settled habitation by whites. Europeans cannot work in their climate or rear their children there. The native can prosper and labour under good government, but is incapable of developing his country's resources. He is barbarian, benighted and unprogressive. One of the principal reasons for this arrested development is that his livelihood has been made so easy for him by natural conditions that he has not been obliged to work, at any rate not to work steadily and in a proper and workmanlike manner. The European therefore must, in the interests of human progress, make arrangements to enable and to induce the black man to work productively under his direction and training. To him the economic profit, which the black cannot either create or wisely use; to the black man peace and protection, relief from disease and famine, moral and social improvement and elevation and the blessings of European culture in general. (Olivier, 1929, p. 20)

Amid the competition to annex new colonial territories, the rhetoric had been of philanthropy and humanitarian motives. The public commitment to oppose slavery was not accompanied by the practical implementation of equal human rights.

Historically, the Partition of Africa was not engaged in to take up the White Man's Burden or for any philanthropic or humanitarian motive, but in order to ensure that the productive resources and the consuming markets of the distributed territories should be kept open to the several national powers that appropriated them, or, in some cases, to guarantee from encroachment the boundaries of previous appropriations. (Olivier, 1929, p. 27)

Because of the number of European nations engaging in the new competition, there were considerable public relations battles. In practice, when considering colonisation and conquest, moral or philosophical justifications follow later, and are secondary in importance to the interests of the imperial power.

THE BELGIAN CONGO

This pattern was repeated in the "Scramble for Africa" which preceded the First World War. European powers were competing to gain colonies, which they saw as a source of political and economic strength. Britain and France had prospered: Germany, Italy and even Belgium wanted to emulate their great power status.

King Leopold II of Belgium wanted greatness, but felt no need to actually visit the Congo in person. He regarded the country as his own personal possession, and the basis of his own splendid self-image. Africa was a board on which games were played, and deals were struck with domestic political audiences in mind. Those domestic audiences were poorly informed, and often easily gratified with news of victories and displays of trophies. The Congo rubber trade proved lucrative, but very demanding on local workers.

Stanley was an adventurer, a journalist who had made his name by finding David Livingstone. He was always happy to give a selective account of the truth when reporting to the public. He was a pragmatic ally of King Leopold II, who knew what he wanted to be said about the Congo, and paid well.

By contrast, the independent journalist Morel studied the emerging financial information from Congo, and tried to make sense of it, based on his knowledge of both Belgium and the Congo. The story was simple. There was a two way trading pattern, which only made sense on the basis of slave labour, which incurred no labour costs. This contrasted with the public position that the Belgians were concerned to eradicate the Slave Trade in Congo, and indeed were deploying large quantities of weapons for that purpose. Morel unearthed conclusive evidence for genocide in the Congo, conducted under the pretext of humanitarian intervention. It is estimated that some 10 million died (Hochschild, 2005).

The three way and two way patterns of trade, with associated compilation of figures, are worthy of wider study, as they exemplify a wider problem. Accounts are prepared for the relevant business audiences, who may tend not to ask questions if their requirements appear to have been met. Silence may seem financially prudent, and thereafter it becomes ever harder to break the silence, or even concede that a silence had existed.

Morel traced the historic origins of the atrocities in the Belgian Congo to the first encounters between Europeans and Africans, in the days of Prince Henry the Navigator. He described the path from exploration, to slave trading, to colonial rule, and then genocide.

Morel's conclusions from the Belgian Congo raise obvious questions for the other European empires in Africa. Other countries in the region, such as Uganda, Zimbabwe and Kenya, have had complex histories, during empire and commonwealth periods, with numerous allegations of atrocities. It is hard to understand the present without understanding the past. Some of the key documents are still secret.

Despite the years of exploration, and trading for slaves and other goods around the coast, knowledge of the continent of Africa continued to be limited. Thus the maps which were drawn up by Europeans, and the administrative units which they established, bore little relationship to natural boundaries or loyalties of local people. This has complicated subsequent processes of development, for example in Nigeria, where the boundaries of the Federal State cut across former tribal kingdoms.

DENIAL

No modern nation likes to acknowledge past engagement in slavery and the Slave Trade, which contradicts shared official standards of human rights. It is therefore easier to be able to blame the problems of the past on others. For recently independent nations, there is an obvious case for blaming slavery on the colonial powers. Similarly, the colonial powers regard their charges as backward and immature, justifying continued tutorial supervision.

A thorough process of Truth and Reconciliation would reveal many pots calling kettles black. The British adoption of the moral high ground over slavery and the Slave Trade, with the abolition of the Transatlantic Slave Trade in 1807, was a sophisticated policy ploy, used to justify control of the seas and the right to search foreign vessels. This greatly enhanced the global role of the British Navy. However, there was also a continuing basis in reality.

The problem was that subsequent evidence revealed the extent of continued slavery across Africa and Asia. The typical level of control provided by indirect rule did not make eradication of slavery an easy option. Civil service instincts were to deny inconvenient facts, and to resist helpful briefings from NGOs. The survival of empires depended on being economical with the truth, which is not quite the same as lying. However, allowing silences to continue meant that what we may now see as atrocities were continued.

The Transatlantic Slave Trade did not initiate slavery or the Slave Trade. It meant internationalisation and globalisation: national solutions could not be adequate. In the age of globalisation, it is important that new generations of citizens should not be misled. Slavery will emerge in the histories of most countries. Denial of such histories makes holocausts more likely.

A focus on the human rights of the individual, monitored by external bodies, may prove inconvenient to governments, who are concerned to maintain stability and the status quo. To address the rights of individuals may be seen as causing disproportionate disturbance. This means continued creative tensions.

LEAGUE OF NATIONS

Following the First World War, the newly established League of Nations established a system of mandates and protectorates, covering a large part of the world. The leading world powers were

Britain and France, who thus took on greatly enhanced official international commitments. The British had maintained their position of determination to eradicate slavery. It had been one thing to declare slavery illegal at home. It was difficult to enforce the eradication of slavery in large colonies which were governed on the basis of indirect rule. It was even harder to ensure that such well-intentioned policies were applied in countries where the culture of the people was not familiar to the international administrators.

The British commitment to end slavery was tested, with the establishment of mandates, and the foundation of the International Labour Organisation. Measures against slavery were developed incrementally. At first the colonial powers argued that measures against slavery should not be applied in the colonies, as they were not yet sufficiently mature for such critical scrutiny. This argument was unimpressive, and was not sustained. The Anti Slavery Society were a consistent campaigning group in the Temporary Slavery Commission, and their evidence increasingly had to be considered.

Given the vast geographical area for which the British had taken responsibility, while continuing to occupy the moral high ground of the commitment to end slavery, it is fascinating to explore how principle was reconciled with practical reality (Miers, 2003). Britain was represented by Lugard on the Temporary Slavery Commission. He was a formidably experienced colonial governor, with an approach based on understanding the art of the possible. A small number of colonial administrators was enabled to apply a light touch of colonial rule, using a system of collecting specified information, to be reported back to the Colonial Office in London. Schools and universities today could see modern inspection methods, based on tick boxes and league tables, as descendants of Lugard's methods.

The architect of British indirect rule in Hong Kong, India and West Africa was able to claim unrivalled knowledge of the realities of slavery having encountered slavery in different manifestations around the world. It was indeed possible for a system of colonial administration to be presented as uniformly consistent while allowing for local flexibility. In particular, simply declining to announce a policy, such as the abolition of slavery and the enfranchisement of current slaves, could reduce the effectiveness of its application. The law could declare that people born after a certain date were free, but as long as the law remained unannounced, little would change, and the individuals would continue to act as if their slavery continued. Lugard's rationale for this approach was that it was important to maintain economic and political stability, which would be jeopardised by wholesale freeing of slaves. We await histories of the colonial period which take account of the management of information. Spin doctors are not a new phenomenon.

Lugard was concerned with stable government and the defence of the status quo. Encouraging slaves to leave their owners without good cause could disrupt the smooth running of the economy, which depended on unpleasant jobs, such as construction of basic infrastructure for a modern economy, being carried out.

There are many ways in which labour may not be provided on a voluntary basis. Many of these do not involve chattel slavery, where the slave is owned, and has a potential resale value. Within chattel slavery there is not always racial difference between owner and slave. It is not necessarily on the basis of European owners and African slaves.

It is clear that in many areas which became part of the British Empire, in Africa and Asia, slavery was long established and evolving on a local basis. It was not introduced by the Transatlantic Slave Trade, whose enduring contribution was the African Diaspora.

The international battle against slavery has not been predominantly glamorous and in the public eye. It has been a matter of sustained detailed work by what is now Anti Slavery International, engaging with the emerging system of international organisations, and making intricate procedural moves to build a sustainable set of mechanisms. There were particular problems with the mandates in the Middle East, such as Saudi Arabia and Aden, as well as in Ethiopia. There were conflicting pressures on decision makers, regarding economic development and political advantage.

Britain was the world's policeman on slavery for over two centuries. There is a detailed track record, which shows evidence of principled commitment to declarations, but a lack of means of implementation. The British public could be fed the good news about the moral high ground, and spared the details of failures. Not everything has changed.

The British Empire was a powerful brand, with a mystique that has been sustained by a constitutional monarchy, operating in a time warp. The message of "Britishness" has been presented as simple, in a complex world.

TO CITIZENSHIP: UNITED NATIONS

In the years since the Second World War, the former great powers have often acted as if they were not subject to international law, and as if the descendants of slaves lack legal human rights. It has been important for individuals to have protection for their rights as citizens.

Between the wars, the British did not consider decolonisation. After 1945, and Indian independence in 1947, it was a race against time. The myth of European superiority had been damaged by experience of the Second World War.

Council for Education in World Citizenship

CEWC had been founded in the UK just as the Second World War was breaking out in 1939. After the war, amidst the wreckage of Europe, CEWC then contributed to the practical process of reconstruction, as young people participated in international work camps, meeting the needs of refugees and displaced people for accommodation and resettlement.

The United Nations General Assembly first met at Central Hall Westminster in January 1946. The same venue hosted annual CEWC Christmas Holiday Lectures, bringing together 3,000 young people to debate the future of their world. Each year, students had the opportunity to debate a major theme with the leading politicians and public figures of the day.

The twentieth century had been dominated by the competing claims of nation states and rival colonial empires. CEWC, together with United Nations agencies, was concerned to unite nations, and to see beyond nationalism. UNESCO, founded in 1946, was based on the assumption that wars begin in the minds of men. Education, and building a culture of peace, were seen as central to a survivable future. UNESCO was left on the sidelines during the Cold War, and a number of UNESCO staff faced investigation in the United States by Senator Joseph McCarthy, accused of communist sympathies due to their internationalism.

CEWC had a formative impact. Generations of aspiring politicians gained their first experience of public debate with national figures at Christmas Holiday Lectures, where the students were recognised as citizens and leaders of tomorrow.

Uniting a country

The issue of uniting nations has to be addressed at national and international levels. Even for those who have always lived in the country, and know no loyalties to other countries or ancestries, it is far from straightforward. It is not just a matter of requiring individuals to subscribe to common values underpinning citizenship.

Each country seeks to develop some common feeling of nation-hood, making it easier to define what citizenship means in prac-tical terms. Ideally people will feel part of the same form of life, and be happy to follow the same rules. This would avoid the danger of dissident groups demanding their own rights to self determination. However, it can be difficult to provide a definitive account of that common nationhood. There will not be a simple catechism to recite. Citizenship is rather a process, in which indi-viduals engage in dialogues with understood procedures.

Education plays an integral part in this process, especially where there is universal education at primary and secondary levels. A complication arises where the system is split between state and private sector, establishing or reinforcing social divisions along the lines of income, social class and racial background.

Developing this common feeling is more straightforward when, as in the case of Lithuania today, the population is relatively homo-geneous. The people speak a common language, and refer back to a common history and culture, a shared experience which has moulded the people. There is also an international Lithuanian Diaspora community to whom they can relate.

Diversity

The challenge is greater in countries with diverse populations. Compared with Lithuania, developing citizenship following the regaining of independence from the Soviet Union, has been more difficult in neighbouring Latvia, where there is a sizeable ethnic minority Russian population. They may have different views on the recent changes which brought Latvia and the other Baltic States renewed independence from Russia.

In South Africa, for example, there are numerous different peoples, aware of their own cultures and traditions, and there are several official languages, one of them English. There are competing histories of the settlement and development of the country. For many decades, the country operated on the basis of separate development of the different communities, Apartheid. The process of change was difficult, but eventually peaceful, with a transition from Apartheid in 1948 to the first free elections in 1994. The legacy of inequality has continued through varied educational provision.

In the United States, there is a growing realisation that after over 200 years of basing their constitution and political culture on their previous background as a set of British colonies, there is a need to deal with what are in effect several countries within the same borders. Native Americans, African Americans and Hispanic Americans have distinct histories and cultures. The situation is further complicated by the fact that, apart from the Native Americans, the United States is a nation of immigrants and their descendants. Apart from the African Americans, the immigrants had chosen to become Americans.

COLONIAL RULE

Perhaps the most complex situations are found in those countries where there has been a long transition from slavery to citizenship. In the British and French empires, peoples who had been enslaved, and their descendants, were transformed into residents of overseas colonies, under the control of European administrators.

The process of moving to independence was protracted and difficult. The status of slave had first been imposed by the slave owner, whether local or from overseas, and was then inherited by successive generations. The status of colonial resident was assigned unilaterally by the imperial power.

The colonial boundaries had been defined by the imperial power, and often bore little relationship to natural borders as seen by the people concerned. Thus modern Nigeria has been burdened with borders which brought together three major tribal groups,

Hausa, Yoruba and Ibo, with traditions of rivalry dating back many centuries.

How were the people in the colonies to relate to the government and people of the European "home country"? An attempt was made through colonial systems of education, which could result in bizarre classroom assignments: students in West Africa, hundreds of miles from the sea, being required to write about "A day at the seaside".

In the French Empire, the tradition was that the laws of metropolitan France applied in the colonies. Colonial residents had French passports. French colonies in North Africa were only a short distance from France. Across North and West Africa the francophone community has continued to operate, reflecting shared approaches to education and culture, developed during the colonial period.

In the British Empire there was typically greater distance between the home country and the colony. Administration was conducted largely by colonial civil servants, often recruited from India. The rhetoric was of the white man's burden to bring civilisation to dark continents and backward cultures. It was argued that a period of tuition and apprenticeship was required before self-government and independence.

When it came to war, the residents of the colonies were expected to fight in the armies of their respective empires. In business, they were expected to engage in trading activities with companies from the imperial country. Their education systems, and approaches to government, would follow the patterns of the imperial power.

GAINING FREEDOM

As with the abolition of the Transatlantic Slave Trade, we encounter different accounts of the movement to colonial freedom.

From the perspective of the imperial powers, the story is of Britain and France assisting immature countries to gain the competence and confidence to run their own affairs, and then putting in place arrangements for ongoing collaboration. Both Britain and France have created informal networks linking the former colonies.

From the former colonial residents we can hear a different account of events. There are narratives of struggle against colonial oppression. There are horror stories concerning particular incidents, such as massacres in Algeria or Kenya. Political leaders of the independence movements often spent many years in prison. In some cases they emerged, in a managed process, to take over the leadership of the country for whose freedom they had fought. The facts of these past events are available to those equipped to conduct the research. The wider population need to be able to understand the implications. It is not adequate to present a whitewashed picture of the past.

We cannot change the past. We need to come to terms with the fact that others have different perceptions of the past, which colour their attitudes to the present. In countries characterised by diversity, especially where there has been a history of colonial rule and independence struggles, sustainable citizenship involves a capacity to respect different opinions. Crucially, it requires parity of esteem, each side recognising the integrity of the other.

A PASSAGE TO INDIA

There is a different context for discussions of India. Once slavery and the slave trade ceased to be profitable, the process of abolition was accelerated, and presented in moral terms. However, when the British and French turned their attention to the East Indies, they took with them the attitudes of racial superiority which they had developed through the Transatlantic Slave Trade and slavery in the Americas. In both Egypt and India, the British and French competed for influence. There was competition in collecting cultural objects from the ancient civilisations which were supposedly coming under European rule. The European monarchies basked in reflected glory.

The British were proud of their empire over which the sun never set. It was successful in economic terms, but the extent of imperial rule was rarely more than superficial. The Indian people were not formally enslaved, but were expected to remain docile and subservient. The British had long argued that the Africans required a long period of apprenticeship before they could cope with self-government and independence. The argument was different in India, where many of the functions of government were taken on by Indian administrators, who also became colonial civil servants around the world. All the same, it was assumed by the British that Indians as a whole were ill prepared for democracy.

Visiting India today, with E.M. Forster's "A Passage to India" as a guide, is illuminating. It provides a mesmerising introduction to the abiding atmosphere of India. The novel deals with two visitors from England, staying with Anglo-Indians, but yearning for contact with "the real India". The Anglo Indians have now gone, though the post-Independence constitution continues to protect their interests. The real India, which evaded most of the Anglo-Indians, lives on.

In the most technologically sophisticated manner, but working with partners who missed out on the benefits of industrial society, India has charted a route to international citizenship. Challenges remain. In India, social class arrangements, continued since the days of Empire, were overlaid on social caste, dating back centuries, and still much in evidence today. If we judge a society by its treatment of its weakest members, there is more to do.

EUROPEAN HISTORY

There could be no one agreed history of Europe, after so many centuries when borders have changed.

The European Union exists because of that realisation, and the pragmatic judgement that it makes more sense to talk to people who had been traditional enemies, rather than engaging in constant war. Having had two world wars based in Europe, there was a strong case for not having a third. There are now 25 member countries of the European Union, each proud of their distinctive national traditions, and more countries are preparing to join. The growing infrastructure of collaborative projects is intended to make it harder for hostilities to be resumed.

There are however problems. How are we to deal with situations where decisions at European level, in which all member countries will have been involved, conflict with policies and practices at national level? To what extent do people in Europe now see themselves as citizens of the European Union? How strong are continuing feelings of nationalism?

AMERICAN HISTORY

The history of the United States has involved successive compromises regarding the levels at which citizenship is exercised.

At the time of Independence, the rhetoric favoured "life, liberty and the pursuit of happiness", but many Southern states retained slavery. Their engagement was important for the new United States.

By the time of the American Civil War, there was a schism which could be described in two different ways. In simple terms there were states in the South which favoured the continuation of slavery, and states in the North for whom slavery was inappropriate, and seen as abhorrent. Put another way, there were issues

on which individual states felt entitled to make their own decisions, even when the resulting inconsistencies had effects on all
the states. President Abraham Lincoln's main concern was to save
the Union. His judgement was that this could not be done if the
country was half slave and half free. It was necessary to abolish
slavery. He therefore proposed the 13th Amendment to the American Constitution in 1865.

It is one thing to make a legislative change regarding the abolition of slavery. It is quite another to implement a form of society
that provides equal treatment for all. The period of Reconstruction
after the American Civil War highlighted the depths of divisions
between racial groups. The Civil Rights Movement of the 1960s
continued the process of campaigning for freedom and equality.
Hurricane Katrina in 2005, and the devastation of New Orleans,
showed how far there is to go.

AFRICAN HISTORY

The history of Africa requires radical reappraisal. Clearly the
Transatlantic Slave Trade brought a fault line between a rich
African cultural past, which included slavery and slave trading, and
a more subservient externally driven period. The oral tradition was
broken, and memories of states before the coming of Europeans
and international slave traders faded.

Histories of the slave trade and slavery have typically been
written by Europeans and Americans, from the perspectives of the
countries trading or receiving slaves. Little was recorded about the
countries from which they had come.

The African Diaspora then meant the dispersal of peoples from
particular areas of West Africa, across a vast area of North, Central
and South America, and the Caribbean. African history has globalised. 2007 provides an opportunity for that Diaspora to find a
voice, or a multiplicity of voices. There is wisdom to be distilled.

INTERNATIONAL INSTITUTIONS

History cannot be changed, but need not be repeated. Nation states continue to dominate the political landscape. Sustainable peace depends on the creation of new relationships and institutions. Thus we have seen the efforts of the League of Nations, and now the United Nations. The United Nations is now led by a Ghanaian Secretary-General, Kofi Annan.

In each continent there have been efforts to unite nations, with the building of alliances and common agendas. This process has been more complex for former colonies, which have had to retrieve their own identities and priorities. The challenge has been to move from vision to reality.

LINGERING LEGACIES

There are many examples of the impact of the past on the present. The French had operated coconut plantations on the Indian Ocean island of Diego Garcia, using slaves taken from Mozambique and Madagascar. After the defeat of Napoleon, the islands passed to British rule, and slavery was abolished in 1838. The islands became attractive to the United States, as an air base giving convenient access to areas including Afghanistan and Iraq. Under a complex secret deal, the British were offered nuclear weapons at a discount price if they could evict the population, and make the islands available as uninhabited. This was agreed by Conservative and Labour governments, using a device of granting independence for Mauritius while retaining control of Diego Garcia. The people were forcibly evicted to Mauritius. Diego Garcia has been busy with bombing attacks on Afghanistan and Iraq. In 2006 the residents of Diego Garcia won their case in the British High Courts, demanding the right to return to their homeland. There is no indication that the US or UK governments have any intention of accepting the ruling.

CULTURE OF PEACE OR WAR

Neither the United States nor the United Kingdom have been disposed to give way to international pressures which might restrict their freedom of action in international policy. They have retained permanent seats on the United Nations Security Council, enabling them to veto resolutions they find unacceptable.

They have felt able to disregard treaty obligations and the rights of individuals. In 1983, under President Ronald Reagan, the United States launched their Strategic Defense Initiative, in defiance of the Anti Ballistic Missile Treaty. In 1985 the UK signed a secret Memorandum of Understanding, agreeing to participate. In 2001 President George W. Bush came to office after a contested election, and launched National Missile Defense, again with British agreement to participate. Missile Defense is now being prepared to protect the USA from potential attack by Iran, with the Fylingdales base in North Yorkshire playing a key role.

In 1985 both the USA and the UK withdrew from UNESCO. In the UK this was followed by the withdrawal of core government funding for CEWC. The two countries returned to membership in 1997, but with an intervening lost generation who had been familiar with the culture of war, but not the culture of peace. The tension between the two cultures continues.

RACE AGAINST TIME

Race relations have been a recurrent theme of the work of the Council for Education in World Citizenship. In the years following the Second World War, the European colonial powers sought ways of enabling smooth transitions to independence for their colonies.

The underlying complication was that historic relationships had been influenced by the slave trade, which had left a legacy of racial difference. The experience of fighting in a world war had shown many Africans, West Indians and Indians that they were the equals of their European colonial masters. Although it is possible to argue that slavery itself was not inherently based on race prejudice, but was primarily an approach to work organisation, this argument does not help us to explain relationships after the end of slavery.

"Race Against Time" was a theme chosen by CEWC on a number of occasions, in the 1960s and 1990s, for conferences to discuss race relations. The overall context has been a commitment by the United Nations to eradicate slavery and move towards world citizenship.

In 1960 the winds of change were blowing through Africa, and this meant radical transformations in individual countries. Importantly, histories had to be re-written, so that those who had been depicted as terrorists could be respected as freedom fighters who were now to lead their nations. The CEWC conference on "Race Against Time" brought together 3,000 sixth formers, the academic élite of the time. Speakers came from a spectrum of opinions, and were prepared to face questions. Students, of which I was one, encountered coherent presentations of unpopular views. For example, there were speakers both for and against Apartheid in South Africa.

In the 1970s, I was teaching about race relations in a secondary school, and living in Lambeth. I served on the Education Committee of the Council for Community Relations in Lambeth, and on the Executive Committee. We were tackling issues of integration and mutual respect between the ethnic minority communities. There were some splendidly innovative examples of community development, such as St Matthew's Church in Brixton, converted for community use. The officer servicing the Education

Committee was Herman Ouseley. In 1981 he was the first to be arrested in the Brixton riots. The police had misinterpreted the situation, and arrested a mediator who later became Chairman of the Commission for Racial Equality, and a member of the House of Lords.

In the 1990s, the world had changed. The former colonies were now almost all independent. The former colonial powers had large immigrant populations from the former colonies. There were causes for disquiet, as the immigrants did not experience equal treatment. The legacy of Empire seemed to linger on. Immigrants felt more like former slaves than citizens.

In Britain there have been a series of riots in areas with large ethnic minority communities, including in Bristol (St Paul's), Liverpool (Toxteth) and London (Brixton), the cities most affected by slavery. Areas of urban deprivation continue.

There have been corresponding experiences in France, following independence for their colonies in North Africa and the West Indies. Immigrants from those colonies are concentrated in the poorer areas of cities.

It is one thing to change working relationships, establishing proper employment contracts. It is another to remove the layers of racial prejudice which can accumulate as a legacy of slavery. There is still a further phase of re-writing to come, as the colonial powers acknowledge the details of their actions. Now, with the bicentenary of the abolition of the Transatlantic Slave Trade, there are still truths to be addressed. The colonial powers may have moved on. The citizens of the former colonies feel unable to move on until they have gained their self respect. For the history of slavery to be neglected is thus profoundly insulting.

UNITING THE AFRICAN DIASPORA

Around the world, as we have seen in our brief tour, there have been journeys to citizenship. Countries divided by race, class and income have found ways of evolving democratic institutions.

For the African Diaspora, the process remains incomplete, a legacy of original forced removal, through the slave trade over 200 years ago. Africans were denied citizenship both of their home countries and of their adopted countries, as slavery was followed by institutionalised racial discrimination.

For new generations of the African Diaspora, there needs to be a reference point for the loyalties and commitment that are a natural feature of adolescence and adulthood.

Although some Africans have settled in their adopted countries, for others the emotional ties are to the ancestral homeland, from which they have long been separated. Indeed, in many cases, Africans have not visited the countries which they continue to regard as home.

In a country such as the UK, it is legitimate for African Diaspora young people to have confused and mixed loyalties. If their own abilities have been underestimated in the country where they live, there has been unrecognised potential. It has taken a long time for black faces to appear in Parliament. For a while they seemed confined to the fringe, but now they are centre stage.

A world of nation states does not provide the whole answer. The African Diaspora obliges us to think in international terms. The descendants of African slaves need to be recognised as world citizens. This requires us to build a robust United Nations within which this citizenship can be expressed.

CHAPTER 9

GLOBALISATION AND EDUCATION

The history of the slave trade and slavery are part of universal history and challenge us all ... Despite the fact that ten million Blacks, men and women from Africa and elsewhere, were subjected for over 400 years to a shameful trade, we must remain clear-sighted about the present and look to the future.

Michael Omolewa, Permanent Delegate of Nigeria to UNESCO.

GLOBAL INFORMATION TECHNOLOGY

Education does not have to follow national boundaries. Mobility of labour can be accompanied by mobility of ideas, freeing minds. Typically education is subject to policies of national governments. In the European Union, the European Commission supports links between the national education systems, and facilitates thinking across traditional disciplinary boundaries. UNESCO has a similar role worldwide, with themes such as the culture of peace, and sustainable development.

Technology has long been used to control the workforce. It can now be used to facilitate participation, whether physical or remote. This could be regarded as a transformation of the business process. In the current world of work, where change is the only constant, the workplace needs to be a learning environment. In turn, the school, college or university can be seen as a knowledge workplace. In this context, neither work nor learning is unchanged. Neither is necessarily tied to fixed locations, with regular hours and direct supervision. This need not mean more individualisation. Instead there are openings for new forms of work organisation, with network links across time and space.

Globalisation can have a damaging effect on institutions and relationships, but this is not inevitable. Working with alternative structures, such as Communities of Practice, networks and NGOs, we can create new arenas for collaboration.

Rather than being slaves to Taylorist work organisation, tied to narrowly specified tasks, and under the control of others at local level, we can become world citizens. This will not arise simply from use of the internet, at one level detached from normal spatial and social relationships. New meanings need to be created from fresh encounters, and experience of dialogue. Education represents a route out of slavery, but this requires the exit routes to be disclosed, and used. If the teachers themselves are not informed, then emancipation is less likely. Access must be made global, enabling practical world citizenship.

NETWORKING

With internet technologies, available to ordinary people, physical location has apparently become less critical. Learners all over the world, as long as they have access to the enabling technology, can share the same virtual space. However, this casts doubt on status relationships in given locations. Historically, locally dominant groups have been able to discriminate against those who have been regarded as inferior. Escaping physical constraints enables new partnerships to be developed.

Slavery in the Americas could not be sustained once links were made between plantations. Networking between slave communities meant that vertical steering was no longer secure, and under the control of owners. Diaspora communities can maintain patterns of networking which dilute the power of national governments.

Revolutions in America and France in the late eighteenth century were supported by international networking, exchanging ideas across borders, and accelerating processes of change. Globalisation and education bring challenges for the twenty-first century.

THE LUNAR SOCIETY

Innovation by the Lunar Society may be seen as constituting the core of the British Industrial Revolution. They were a Community of Practice, a distributed set of individuals with shared concerns and practices. Dissenting practical entrepreneurs experimented with ideas from different disciplines, and put them to the test of practice. For the Lunar Society, slavery was an anathema. These were self-made, self-taught businessmen, who wanted control over their own lives. They recognised that workers welcome an element of autonomy in the way they perform their tasks, but that owners and managers need to organise work appropriately. Their companies were intended to be learning organisations.

The Lunar Society advanced through networking, based on trust. Having identified a key person with influence, they would find a route to secure their attention. They were engaged in empirical scientific research, with a flow of technology products and improved processes which transformed the nature of the economy and society in which they worked. They took little heed of formality, so Josiah Wedgwood felt able to submit papers to the Royal Society.

The establishment view in the eighteenth century was that the universe and society were stable and well ordered. They took the flawed example of Newtonian physics as a metaphor, offering stability in the heavens as a model for European nations, which was welcome after a protracted period of war in Europe. The monarchy and the aristocracy tried to continue as before. They derived income from slavery and the Transatlantic Slave Trade, but they were not the driving force behind economic and social change.

The Lunar Society were excluded from the establishment, by virtue of their Dissenting religious views. They did not secure a political revolution in Britain, at least on the surface, but they operated internationally. Via Wedgwood's partner Bentley, they were in communication with Rousseau. Jefferson and Franklin remained close contacts. There was a flow of practical expressions of enlightenment, crossing borders.

EMANCIPATION

The pressure for emancipation was about more than freedom for slaves. British society had many people who were seeking alternatives. Dissenters rejected the theological positions of the Church of England. As they were excluded from leading academic institutions, they needed alternative ways of learning and teaching.

The Romantic poets rejected the materialism which characterised early industrial society. They explored new ways of thinking and living, and often spent time communing with nature. Even when surrounded by nature, they could feel enslaved by opium, which insulated them from reality but at the expense of destroying their health. Thomas Clarkson took extended holidays in the company of Coleridge and Wordsworth, whose poems about abolition, and the achievements of Toussaint L'Ouverture, provide an internationalist perspective.

The potential revolution was not reflected in political structures, which remained unreformed and undemocratic. There were few links between the early working class movement and former slaves. We should take a wider perspective. Once we understand the role of poets and experimental scientists as potential revolutionaries, with novel approaches to interaction, new possibilities are opened. These include fresh insights into slavery, emancipation, globalisation and education.

How is this to be reflected in the content and process of education in a globalised world?

NATIONAL MEMORIES AND HISTORIES

In order to encourage feelings of patriotism, there is a tendency for national histories to accentuate what is seen as the positive. When politicians bemoan the lack of historical knowledge among students, what they are typically lamenting is the lack of pride in national history, as they see it. It is easy to link a call to redress this perceived imbalance with programmes of citizenship education. The idea is to emphasise unifying national values, and to socialise young people and immigrants into the dominant majority culture.

Dr Johnson observed that "patriotism is the last resort of the scoundrel". It is a dangerous move to replace ignorance with officially approved prejudice. Arguments for fair trade and free trade should be extended to support an internationalist approach to education.

Nationalism has been a dominant political force for centuries, with national borders agreed at a series of conferences since the

Treaty of Westphalia in 1648, after the Thirty Years War. The later European process of diplomacy typified by the Congress of Vienna was then applied to Africa. African territories, which were regarded as needing supervision from more "mature" European nations, were used to enhance the standing of European nations.

It is not a matter of pointing the finger of blame at any one country. Where governments are educating future citizens, they take a view on what should properly be included. This does not just mean selection of content from a menu. It can result in different accounts of the same events. The war of 1812, between the UK and USA, is shown in each country's histories as a victory for their own side. The British burnt the White House, but went home.

Citizenship is not about mastery of a mass of facts. Rather, it concerns the exercise of individual judgement. This raises questions about the nature of history, and the objectives of history teaching. One early message concerns scepticism. When we read an historical account, it is good practice to consider what we know about the author. We can apply speech act theory: what is the content of the account, and what action is performed through the publication of the utterance? The recent case of David Irving, jailed in Austria for Holocaust Denial, is a useful precedent.

THE HISTORY OF SLAVERY AND THE SLAVE TRADE

There will be many new publications on the history of slavery and the Slave Trade. Some may be intended to provoke their readers to anger, while others will apply a coat of whitewash.

In recent decades, history teachers have tried to give students experience of dealing with evidence, and using it to draw appropriate conclusions, which can then be justified. History teachers have encouraged students to develop empathy with historical characters, trying to see matters from the actor's point of view. When teaching about the history of the slave trade and of slavery, the well-intentioned but simple application of these principles can lead to distorted accounts. Much of the key evidence is not available, or is not in print.

We can take the heroic story of William Wilberforce, and his campaign to abolish the slave trade, with a series of famous speeches in the House of Commons. We can note the powerful impact of Wedgwood's medal for the campaign: "Am I not a man and a brother?". The picture is of a kneeling slave, pleading for help towards freedom. This reinforces the stereotype view that abolition was a result of British benevolence and philanthropy, excluding mention of the impact of slave rebellions. Curiously this popular vignette fails to mention that the British had dominated the Slave Trade, and that abolition of the Slave Trade in 1807 did not mean immediate emancipation of the slaves. They had to wait until 1838.

There is pressure to offer good stories of heroic figures in the different national traditions. Thus Hawkins and Drake were often depicted as great sailors, opening up the world and adding to the glory of the British crown. In the histories of other countries, Hawkins and Drake appear as pirates and slave traders.

Works of history require selective accounts to be given of complex events, for which there is a mass of available data. The accounts are written in language which carries assumptions, building on the prior views and knowledge of the reader. There could be no one complete account, acceptable to all. It is of course tempting to designate particular books as definitive or official, limiting discussion of other perspectives.

On this basis we can recognise Hugh Thomas's contribution. His history of the slave trade (1997) provides a chronological perspective, and locates British activities in a wider context of overviews of different European empires. However, the book remains British in focus. We hear little about Africa, from whence the slaves were taken, or about the various slave rebellions which took place in the West Indies. The book presents an account of what was achieved by the movement to abolish the slave trade: Wilberforce and his colleagues are the heroes of the piece.

We need to visit French historians of the same period in order to understand the problem. Even if we identify the same core sets of facts, we find markedly different stories. The French Revolution in 1789 led to the abolition of slavery in 1794, offering hope to slaves in the West Indies, who saw a future as citizens.

Further study suggests that the issues of Abolition of the Transatlantic Slave Trade and the emancipation of slaves were seen at the time as less important than ongoing rivalries and warfare between the UK and France. The timing of Abolition was determined by geopolitical considerations.

GLOBALISATION

Globalisation has meant breaking down barriers between countries. This has often been to the advantage of major corporations, with budgets larger than those of small countries, and limited accountability. Globalisation has been aided by technology and communications, which can now be used as a tool by Non Governmental Organisations and United Nations agencies, restricting the capacity for corporations to act unchecked.

The world has become small. Actions in one country have rapid consequences elsewhere. It is helpful if we can understand how our actions are regarded by others.

In the twenty-first century, it is absurd for Americans and Europeans to assume that their economic power in the last century was based on inherent superiority, or that it will continue. Newly industrialised countries such as India and China are growing in economic and political power. Having developed their industrial bases through outsourcing contracts, they are now in a position to become senior partners.

In the case of Africa, it has been argued by Walter Rodney (1982) that Europe systematically undeveloped Africa. It does not follow that the damage done by the Europeans can then simply be reversed by Europeans. This book has argued that emancipation, as in the French West Indies, was achieved by the organised actions of the slaves and former slaves, and not primarily by external philanthropy.

Education has been a tool to free the individual and communities. It is not just the descendants of slaves who need to be liberated from their past. Slavery is not simply a phenomenon from the past. Examples of slavery continue today. Slaves are the victims of steering societies, where they have no control over their own lives and work, and no opportunity to participate in decision making. Citizens live in network societies, in which they have some control over their own lives and work, and are able to participate in decision making.

The change from slavery to citizenship does not happen automatically. It may not happen at all. Indeed, the change can be in the other direction, from citizenship to slavery. Individual actions make a difference.

The movement for colonial freedom was a central feature of the twentieth century, with leaders such as Gandhi gaining experience in South Africa before leading the independence movement in India. He lived and studied in London, as did many of the future leaders of independent former colonies. The colonies succeeded in gaining their freedom from their past. Arguably the Imperial powers need to learn to follow their example. This means acknowledging uncomfortable truths about the past, and accepting that, for example, the British Empire is now part of history, and ready for re-evaluation.

KNOWLEDGE WORK

It is a mistake to talk about the future as based on knowledge work, as if there were other "lesser" forms of work, which could be left to others. It is more a matter of understanding the nature of different forms of knowledge: explicit, implicit and tacit. A successful society will bring the forms of knowledge together, by enabling people to work together, on a basis of parity of esteem.

Sustainable organisations depend on continuing improvement, which involves a capacity to change. In turn this requires processes of learning from encounters and differences. This assumes a pivotal role for individuals. With control over their own work, and the opportunity to participate in decisions about their own future, thinking workers can be part of a learning organisation.

Organisations which rely on slave labour have limited chances of long term competitiveness. They can undercut the costs of rivals with workers who are paid wages. However, to the extent that organisations are competing in changing environments, slave work forces are inflexible, and inhibit innovation.

It is not that slaves lack knowledge: they tend to have lacked formal explicit knowledge based on literacy and numeracy. Slaves could be strong on implicit and tacit knowledge, and could draw on oral tradition. However, without appropriate workplace dialogue, the organisation is unable to derive benefit.

Workplaces based on slavery reflect particular attitudes from workers and managers. Arguably the experience has had corrosive effects. Slaves wanted to gain their freedom and self-respect. Slave owners wanted to be able to retain their privileged lifestyles which had been at the expense of others.

The Slave Trade and slave plantations laid the foundations for an economic system based on social class division. The precedent was established: the profits of trade provided the basis for social standing, while retaining a distance from workers and work itself. In both the Southern states of the USA and in the UK, there has been a class which remains enslaved to the past. Continued attitudes reflect assumed superiority by one group over another.

GLOBALISED EDUCATION

UNESCO Associated Schools Project network

In the UK, the Council for Education in World Citizenship is co-ordinating the UNESCO Associated Schools Project network, building a network of 100 schools by the summer of 2007, to join 7,900 schools in 175 countries around the world. The schools work together on chosen projects in areas such as the environment, human rights, peace and institutions. Among the international "flagship projects" is "The Transatlantic Slave Trade: Breaking the Silence".

There are major implications for the curriculum in schools, where issues such as slavery and the slave trade have often been neglected, in favour of safer subjects. In the UK, for example, students may encounter Henry VIII and The Rise of Hitler several times, while never addressing the intervening period.

Through ASPnet, direct links can be established between schools around the world, for example connecting schools at different points on the Slave Routes. We can learn from differences.

Cross-Community Dialogue Group

A diverse group came together to prepare to celebrate the bicentenary. We sit around the table and listen to each other's silences. There could be no one definitive account of the past which encompasses all our needs. We bring our own experiences and presuppositions. There will be questions we would like to ask. There will be questions we feel unable to answer. It is a good start if we can find a language in which we can express our partial understanding. Soon we begin to realise that others are using the same words, but that they are given different meanings through use. Our language will never achieve completeness and precision, but it may help to illuminate differences, enabling us to learn. Uncertainties will remain.

At the level of organisations we may find it useful to start by deploying the context free language of quality. We can talk about continuous improvement, and the need to apply consistent standards. Such discussion serves to highlight how far we are from uniformity. We may come to value our diversity as a resource.

The language of stress, derived from machines, can be useful as we consider organisations and societies undergoing change. It helps us to understand the key concept of social gradient, whereby relative social status determines our health and well-being. However, neither the languages of quality nor stress, of themselves, provide routes to change along lines which we might favour. Instead they provide us with a grasp of the diverse and changing contexts in which we can intervene.

Is it important for us to discover what went on in past generations, including possible mistreatment of our ancestors? Does this help us to understand who we are, and shape how we act? Alternatively, should we accept that past injustices cannot now be reversed? Can we draw a line, move on from the past, and focus on the future? Who has the right to make such a decision? What is the alternative?

Given that the Slave Trade, slavery and empire were products of nationalism and the nation state, should we now be looking to international dialogues and institutional solutions? Should this picture of the past focus constructive attention on current injustice, and the case for fair treatment of poor nations and disadvantaged groups at the WTO and through fair trade?

Can words about the past be accompanied by actions in the present, which pave the way for a sustainable future? How could such actions be facilitated and supported?

BREAKING THE SILENCES IN 2007

Research for this book has cast new light on the silences that are to be broken. More facts have been emerging regarding the trade in human beings, which transported 6 million Africans across the Atlantic to the New World as slaves in the century before abolition. Although the British transported the most slaves, some 2.5 million, there were many other countries involved in the lucrative business, including France, Portugal, Spain, the USA, Holland, Germany, Italy, Denmark, Sweden, Norway and Lithuania. There is consensus on the basic narrative, from authoritative writers such as Williams, Blackburn and Thomas. Interpretations and emphases vary.

The depths of the silences are also being plumbed. The Slave Trade was not simply an operation by criminals, like the current international trade in drugs. It formed the basis for national monopoly companies. It constituted the core business activity of the ill-fated South Sea Company in Britain in the early eighteenth century, attracting investors including the royal family, members of the House of Commons and House of Lords, philosophers and writers. The trade in human beings was regarded as acceptable business, not just in Britain, but across Africa, given that the internal slave trade provided the stocks of slaves for export. Interestingly, Adam Smith was a determined opponent of the Slave Trade, slavery and mercantilism. Churches had not been prominent in opposing slavery, but abolition was at the heart of John Wesley's Methodist preaching, and the Unitarian Josiah Wedgwood produced the campaign plaque "Am I not a man and a brother?".

It is becoming clearer what was meant by slavery, in terms of man's inhumane treatment of his fellow man. We should not assume that slavery is simply a matter of history: we must address continuing problems of child labour and oppression of women. There are now agreed international conventions, based on accepted principles of human rights. There is an international legal basis on which to proceed. More generally, we can address issues of control and participation at work, and in society.

CITIZENSHIP

Slavery had ancient roots in Europe, and around the world, and co-existed with the development of ideas of citizenship and democracy. The Transatlantic Slave Trade meant that black African residents of one country were sold into slavery, and transported to another country where they were regarded as property, rather than accorded human rights. Thomas Jefferson struggled with such legal issues as an author of the American Declaration of Independence, and later President. Two centuries later, the descendants of slaves constitute the African Diaspora, spread across the world, in numerous countries, often as part of multicultural societies. How can we address the issue of citizenship?

The slave trade was conducted in the era of nation states, and was often justified at the time in terms of patriotism and foreign policy objectives, usefully masking the trade in human beings. Slavery helped finance industrialisation of developed countries. It laid the foundations for the age of empire, and the scramble for control of portions of Africa by competing European powers. This scramble produced the current map of Africa. National boundaries are still the consequence of colonial decisions. National citizenship has been an artificial construct.

The publication of "From Slavery to Citizenship" constitutes an action, an intervention in the debate on "Breaking the Silence", which is intended to have a high profile in 2007. There will be those who will be demanding major economic reparations for a crime against humanity. Others will wish to argue that the events which are to be commemorated are long in the past, and that we must move on.

Undoubtedly there will be a complication that two of the major powers concerned in the Transatlantic Slave Trade, the UK and the USA, who abolished the trade in 1807, continue to play high profile roles in international politics in 2007. Initiatives taken by those countries to address perceived problems elsewhere in the world do not always command support.

INTERNATIONAL CITIZENSHIP

What then is to be the purpose of our action in publishing the book, and contributing to "breaking of silences" in 2007? The citizenship which we are discussing is international citizenship. There is an opportunity to give new strength to the international perspective. The legacy of slavery and the Slave Trade will not be tackled at national level, where governments tend to be defensive and secretive. Members of the African Diaspora are international citizens, and need to experience support and respect in the international community. The appropriate arena is the United Nations, and the work of specialist agencies such as UNESCO, which supports the "Breaking the Silence" project, in association with NGOs representing Diaspora community groups.

There is another positive dimension. Slaves taken from Africa for the Transatlantic Slave Trade enriched slave traders. However, the trade removed healthy adult workers from local economies, and hampered political development. Vital skills and experience were taken overseas.

Africa today remains in urgent need of development. Initiatives by the former colonial powers, such as the recent Commission for Africa, established by Tony Blair, have had a limited impact, and partly by-passed the African Union. Raising of funds and awareness, with the objective of "making poverty history", have been benign, but fine words at the G8 have not been matched by action. The members of the African Diaspora are not in a position to direct support for Africa: individual connections can be remote. However, 2007 represents a golden opportunity for the commemoration of a crime against humanity to be transmuted into a practical expression of common humanity.

THE SOUND OF MUSIC

"I have a dream", that the silences that have been the legacy of the slave trade could be broken by the sound of music, world music, which could lead a movement to help Africa, mother of humanity, to grow and prosper. We start with "the sound of silence", but can add a rhythm, a narrative, collective backing, and we have the basis of the Blues, of Jazz, and of Rock and Roll. We need an accompanying process of dialogue.

On 23 November 2005, I presided at a Model United Nations General Assembly in the Town Hall of the former slave trading city of Liverpool. We remembered William Roscoe MP, Abolitionist MP for Liverpool, who challenged local business interests, in the cause of humanity. The "Mersey Sound" synthesised contributions from the many cultures sharing the city in the 1960s, and was exported all over the world. Half a century later, the new Mersey Sound is of international citizenship. It will spread through practice: dialogue, and engagement in active citizenship.

The silence is increasingly audible. Around the world the evidence of the long term impact of slavery is all too visible. Skin colour provides initial clues. After the passage of time, these clues are not always misleading. Silence has continued, because it was not clear what should be said. Saying the wrong things could make matters worse. Silence has served to bury the problems deeper.

There has been a trend for modern leaders to say sorry, to apologise for past wrongs, for which they as individuals bear no personal responsibility. This has been the approach to Apartheid, to the Irish Potato Famine, to tobacco and asbestos. The leaders can feel better, but nothing substantive has changed. The attitudes which made slavery possible continue.

Freedom is not divisible, and it is still the goal for many people who consider themselves to be oppressed. Slavery continues, in many forms, including among children. Negro spirituals still resonate.

Although the Transatlantic Slave Trade was abolished in 1807, it is clear that attitudes persist. The civil rights campaign in the USA, with lynchings of activists, has left bitter memories. Across Europe, right wing nationalist groups are again using visible racial differences as prompts.

In the UK, we can teach A level history students about non-contentious topics, such as the Tudors and Hitler, where the material is available. What could we say about slavery and Empire? What are we going to say, when the silence breaks in 2007? How will we explain the absence of serious opposition to the Slave Trade until it became economically unviable? Will we discuss the genocide which accompanied the Slave Trade?

Are we going to describe "the great civilising mission of the British Empire, on which the sun never set"? Will there be revisionist accounts of the British in Kenya, South Africa and Zimbabwe? How was the Empire governed? These are not easy questions. The silence is deafening.

THE ORCHESTRATION OF REFLECTION

"From Slavery to Citizenship" is an international project, and much more than just a book. This experience feels more like writing a play with an international company of actors. Rather than it just being a matter of "one character after another", a new dialogue is taking shape, composed by people who are speaking a common language, although ostensibly they come from many disciplines and many countries.

The challenge of discussing slavery has often been avoided, because of the deep problems surrounding the historical phenomenon. However, the 2007 commemorations of the bicentenary of the abolition of the Transatlantic Slave Trade, and of the foundation of Wiley, publishers, mean that the subject must be addressed.

The skeleton of key facts about the Transatlantic Slave Trade is not in question, but around the skeleton we find numerous profound silences. Each country has had separate limited discussions of the history from a national perspective. It is instructive to listen for the silences: what is not discussed about one's own history, and what is left out in accounts of the histories of others (for example British histories tend to downplay the significance of events in the French West Indies). The Slave Trade was a truly international phenomenon, with African, Arab, European and American traders conducting a trade in human beings. It has not ended.

We can improve our knowledge of history, but we cannot change what happened. Many excellent academic studies of specialist aspects of the Slave Trade have gone into economic, technical and political details. The school curriculum has tended to avoid the subject. As a result, there is limited knowledge of the historical past among ordinary citizens. However, we must live in the present. Our thoughts and actions are affected by our partial knowledge and different beliefs.

It has been conventional for economists to dominate discussions of work, and of work organisation. The framework of balance sheets, discussion of profit and loss, and the supposedly neutral language of accountancy provided a way in which the complexities of business could be presented and discussed. The nature of trading activities could be hidden behind global figures, in which individual transactions escaped scrutiny. Those who wished to embark on careers in business needed to learn the language of strategy and human resource management, concentrating on what could be measured, and relegating other matters to the category of "soft" data.

Economists require one to believe several impossible things before breakfast, such as that all decisions are made on the basis of full information, that access to information is equally shared and that the natural condition of the economy is equilibrium (Stiglitz, 2003). This is virtual reality. It gave us Enron and PFI, where difficult figures have simply been removed from the balance sheet.

REPLACING FINANCE BY HEALTH AND LEARNING

Instead of considering the outcomes of work, and work organisation, in financial terms, we can concentrate on outcomes in health and learning. This means giving centre stage to what had been dismissed as "soft" factors. In the knowledge society, the assertion that "the key asset of an organisation is the workforce" is more than a cliché. Just because the conventional virtual reality model is not acceptable, it does not follow that another can be slotted in overnight (Grojier & Johansen, 1999). We have the language in which to discuss outcomes in health and learning. We can recognise what would count as progress. This enables us to make interventions and create actionable knowledge.

Slaves lack control over their own lives and work, in a society which is hierarchical, steering and directing. Citizens are able to participate in decision making about their lives and work, in a society which is more based on networking and horizontal communication. This is not a new contrast. Prospero and Caliban, in Shakespeare's "Tempest", provide a literary backdrop.

Perceptions make a great difference: in apparently similar circumstances, some people feel enslaved, while others find ways of participating in decisions. People are not simply cogs in machines. Discussion of stress, based on the analogy with machines (Cooper & Dewe, 2004), may not be helpful, despite the wealth of epidemiological data which it appears to make available.

Slavery is not just part of history, but is a feature of the modern workplace. Discussions in terms of stress may serve to extend its span of life, as actionable knowledge to lead to change is unlikely to be created. The machine may continue to exercise control over individuals. Analysis of inequalities and status differences, leading to a social gradient (Marmot, 2004), are authoritative but fail to make the link with action.

Action is needed. Practitioners with experience can describe particular cases. Suddenly there has been a flow of offers of impulse texts, using the language of work and health, and with a shared motivation to produce change. The geographical spread is global (UK, USA, France, Sweden, Norway, Lithuania, Hungary, India, Tibet, Japan, Brazil, Nicaragua, Nigeria, Kenya, Ethiopia, Korea, China, Australia), covering contexts which are now in direct contact but which historically were remote. We are not going to emerge with a single comprehensible time line, but it seems likely that many lessons will be learned from differences. We are international citizens, sharing a fragile small planet. The challenge is now to provide structure and orchestration. The resulting composition is to be heard in 2007, as a contribution to the debate on slavery and Citizenship.

EMPOWERMENT: THE COLONIAL LEGACY

The British have mastered the art of gentle empowering, or so they believe. Rather than taking the risk of giving independence to people who might lack the necessary maturity, they have developed ways of incremental facilitation of change. This is then presented as practical evolution, as opposed to revolution, which can be more uncomfortable for all. On this basis, from a starting point of impotence, with no representation of civil society, it can be possible to build up trust and mutual confidence, so that an interim group takes on a quasi representative role. Does this mean that the representatives have been co-opted, transformed into part of the establishment? How can they involve wider participation from the community? How can experience be gained, providing the necessary confidence?

There is an educational parallel with the situations of teachers and students. Teachers tend to have dominated the learning process, and have had to learn how to share power with students. On their side, students need to gain experience of what it is to take control of their own learning. Defenders of slavery used the language of education and immaturity to justify their strategy of retaining power and declining to regard slaves as capable of taking on responsible roles.

There is a long-standing tension between the approaches of evolution and revolution. Given the historical associations with the UK and France, and their ongoing competing post-colonial legacies, there is a global chessboard, where the slaves have been pawns. The movement from slavery to citizenship is global in scale. As with cookery, details of the process tend to be important.

CONFRONTING THE TRUTH

After 200 years, the general population in the UK has been allowed to develop and maintain mistaken assumptions regarding the past. It has been the line of least resistance to remain silent while stereotypes have continued.

The Church of England has made a start in confronting the truth. Whereas their publication on Abolition set the scene in terms of the conduct of businesses, their conference began to discuss the extent to which the church itself was embroiled in slavery. There is a formidable challenge for theologians. It is clear that Biblical justification was cited for the institution of slavery. It reflected the traditional order of things, of which the church was part, linked to hierarchy. This was one of the bases for the attack by Wesley.

Establishment spokesmen, including the British Prime Minister, have a moral obligation to update themselves on the truth of the past. Ignorance is not an acceptable excuse.

WHAT HAS CHANGED?

If we consider contexts which were affected by the slave trade and slavery, we find cases where little has changed. Workers feel more like slaves than citizens.

The Haitian economy is still based on sugar plantations. The Congo relies on rubber. Ghana has been trying to develop fair trade in cocoa. In Brazil, patterns of working in rural agriculture have been slow to change. In New Orleans and Louisiana, the continued divisions along racial lines were revealed in the aftermath of Hurricane Katrina. In California, illegal Hispanic immigrants continue to pick the grapes of wrath. Meanwhile, in Kano, in Northern Nigeria, trans-Saharan trade continues, after thousands of years.

In the past, the contexts were kept apart, and insulated by distance. Each knew little about the others. We now share the same small world.

Millions of men, women and children around the world are still forced to lead lives as slaves. Although this exploitation is often not called slavery, the conditions are the same. People are sold like objects, forced to work for little or no pay, and are at the mercy of their "employers".

Slavery exists today despite the fact that it is banned in most of the countries where it is practised. It is also prohibited by the 1948 Universal Declaration of Human Rights and the 1956 UN Supplementary Convention on the Abolition of slavery, the Slave Trade and Institutions and Practices Similar to Slavery.

WORLD CITIZENSHIP

Concepts of world citizenship remain weak and poorly defined. We are accustomed to thinking of citizenship in national terms, by reference to national systems of politics. No man, or country, is an island, even the United Kingdom.

UNESCO

UNESCO has long tried to encourage an approach to history which goes beyond national perspectives. This does not mean that a single agreed general history will be produced which is acceptable to all.

In certain cases where the subject matter is inherently international, such as the transatlantic slave trade, UNESCO provides a context where the different views can be considered, and links can be made between schools in the respective countries, enabling them to engage in joint projects.

Slavery, and memories of the Transatlantic Slave Trade, present continuing challenges. The impacts of slavery have affected the lives of millions of people across numerous countries. Descendants of slave owners and of slaves need to be able to rediscover their common humanity. This has been the purpose of the UNESCO "Slave Routes" project, and of "The Transatlantic Slave Trade: Breaking the Silence".

There has been nervousness from some official figures as 2007 approaches. There had been similar worries in the Netherlands in

2004, where involvement of citizens of the former colonies was restricted.

Diaspora

The Diaspora took people across national borders, and across oceans, against their will. This means that assumptions of consent by citizens, which underpin much political philosophy, do not necessarily apply. However, to be stateless is not a secure status.

National systems of citizenship are not capable of dealing with the legacy of slavery. This is a case for the United Nations, and for world citizenship. Members of the African Diaspora are citizens of the world, but may have no instinctive allegiance to current nations or governments.

Dialogue

It is important to have informed dialogue. This means that institutions have to move from rhetoric to reality. Comfortable orthodoxies face the need to grapple with uncomfortable facts. Slavery did not end with the British abolition of the Transatlantic Slave Trade in 1807, or with emancipation in 1833, a process supposedly completed in 1838. Slavery continued around the world during the nineteenth century, eventually abolished in Brazil in 1888. However, a new form of slavery was introduced in the Congo in the late nineteenth century, and in the twentieth century Apartheid in South Africa exhibited many of the same characteristics. Control was kept in the hands of the few, while the many were denied the right to participate in decision making.

Exercise

International organisations are only as strong as their members. Such organisations grow, and acquire strength, through exercise. The legacy of slavery should now exercise the United Nations, recognising the past, dealing with the present, and laying down agreements for the future. Citizens have to exercise their rights, and build new institutions. This means new relationships, new collaboration, and a recognition that diversity is a vital resource. This approach means challenging the status quo, changing current power structures and developing active citizenship.

There is only one human race. Phenomena such as the Transatlantic Slave Trade arise when one group systematically denies another group control over their own lives and work, and denies opportunities for participation in decision making. The Transatlantic Slave Trade has had an enduring legacy over 200 years. We need to be able to break the silences, reflect and intervene in the political process, confronting our past and present.

After abolition in 1807, the British Navy sought to patrol the high seas, enforcing compliance by other nations. During the centenary celebrations in 2007, the role of the United Nations must be recognised, informing the minds of men.

INTERNATIONAL LABOUR ORGANISATION

ILO conventions prohibit various modern forms of slavery. The problem is to move from ratification to implementation.

Slave labour in one country can help produce products which undercut the prices of goods from other countries where ILO conventions are observed and fair wages are paid. Slavery is thus at the expense of workers, locally, nationally and internationally.

It is thus a central concern for trade unions, who play a leading role in ILO, together with employers and governments.

Employers face hard choices. They do not like to be undercut by illegal practices, but they also want to remain competitive. One option is outsourcing, which can mean offshoring.

WORLD HEALTH ORGANISATION

WHO is concerned with the contribution of work related factors to the overall burden of disease. However, among overall policy priorities for WHO, work is given relatively low explicit priority. Analysis of the leading priorities, including stress and mental health, and MSD, suggests that work can be an underlying explanatory factor.

WHO deals primarily with medical experts and governments, rather than with companies or the social partners. It therefore has limited capacity to affect workplace practice. Furthermore, limited funds mean that WHO tends to rely largely on WHO collaborating centres, rather than providing supporting resources.

INTERNATIONAL CITIZENSHIP TO END SLAVERY

Power

If decisions are simply left to individual countries, the exercise of power by strong vested interests is likely to prevent the eradication of slavery. Instead, the current call is for deregulation, and the reduction of influence by external bodies. This inhibits the enforcement of international directives, regulations and conventions which have been the result of lengthy and intricate negotiations leading to legally binding treaties.

We encounter fundamental political paradoxes, involving sovereignty, self-determination, competitiveness, justice, equity and discrimination. In each case, the exercise of the particular principle by one group has implications for the others. Often there is a case for dialogue in order to prevent a Dutch auction, a race to the lowest possible standards. Successful international citizenship involves the deferment of gratification. In turn, this requires the exercise of mature political judgement. Nothing is gained from offering a deal whose terms cannot be delivered in practice.

In the past, international negotiations were largely a matter for diplomats, representing governments. Often they would work closely with representatives of major companies who in effect flew the flag overseas. With the globalisation of business and communications, it becomes routine to work across borders, entering into agreements, contracts and relationships. This is not just a matter for governments and big business, but also applies to smaller enterprises, public authorities, NGOs and educational institutions. Under pressure to meet short term financial targets, there is a tendency for organisations to seek deals which offer them clear financial advantages. Universities seek to maximise fee income, while externalising activities and costs which are less strategically attractive. The model of customer and supplier has been emphasised, while the more mature relationship of partnership, based on parity of esteem, has been less explored.

True parity of esteem is the result of the incremental development of trust. It involves an extended process of social capital formation over time. Social capital is now an international concept, not merely concerned with local regional development. Regions of meaning develop across borders.

At the point of change, when those who have been enslaved are emancipated, there is a price to be paid. In the past, the compensation went to the former owners of the slaves, who were being deprived of their property. Today, the descendants of former slaves recognise their case for compensation. There is a price to be paid to free those who have been slaves. This requires an element of sacrifice, or of philanthropy. Arguing a deal on market terms, when the previous market was predicated on injustice and the denial of human rights, is problematic. It is a matter of political judgement whether the loss of property rights should be compensated. The argument parallels those over renationalisation of formerly privatised industries. To what extent is the public purse required to meet private expectations?

Successful international diplomacy and negotiations depend on foundations of knowledge. This should not just be theoretical, but should include knowledge based on experience. This means that education and career development should be increasingly international, offering the necessary opportunities for insight.

A culture change is required, from the steering society, where we are expected to know our place in organisational hierarchies, to the network society, where we can communicate with others at the same level. This is not easy or comfortable, as promotion and preferment tend to have been driven by the rules of steering society, while success in the new international arena requires new skills in networking.

There is a basic question. Are the rich countries prepared to contribute to redressing past injustices, or will they continue to seek to apply their market muscle to force advantageous terms? Is this the equivalent of writing off unpayable third world debts? Will this be better organised internationally?

From the perspectives of most of the countries of the world, there is s strong case for establishing a world government and a world parliament, based on a strengthened version of the United Nations. The status quo is not sustainable. It involves the rich countries, epitomised by the G8, who have been able to set the terms. They are reluctant to lose this advantageous position. Through globalisation of international economic development, the balance is changing. In particular, India and China are moving towards a dominant position in the world economy, competing on quality as well as cost. Their concern for quality should also include a concern for peace.

Virtual Reality

Conventional approaches to business are based on self-serving virtual reality, with the consequence that important areas of human activity are not considered in public. Instead, these areas are left off the balance sheet, and there is silence. Such silence has given rise to atrocities, which some have termed genocides and holocausts. Property rights, which lend themselves to financial quantification, have dominated, at the expense of human rights.

The argument builds on the recent Nobel Prize winning work of Joseph Stiglitz on information economics, and his 2001 critique of the International Monetary Fund and modern aspects of globalisation. It seeks to apply a similar critique to the period since the start of the British industrial revolution. It looks in particular at transitions between successive stages of economic activity and work organisation, where there has been a paradigm shift, and activities have been judged by new criteria. Today such transitions arise as businesses operate in new markets, while their performance is typically judged by home shareholders.

For example, one of the devices used to aid the transition from European to colonial activity in the Americas was the engagement of African slaves. The economic contribution of slaves became less effective with the development of new production technologies and factories, where workers needed to learn new ways of working. Slave plantations were not learning organisations, and North American slaves had no prospects of promotion or freedom. When the Slave Trade ended, slave owners were compensated for the loss of their property. There was little concern for the emancipation of slaves.

Immigrants, Outsourcing and Offshoring

More recently, as the long established industrialised countries face increasing challenges from emerging economies, who are competing for international markets, there has been a search for fresh solutions. These can take the form of cheap immigrant labour, or outsourcing chosen functions to lower cost locations, known as offshoring.

Dialogue with Adam Smith

We need to reassess the work of the Enlightenment philosopher Adam Smith, who has been traduced by those who neglect the moral underpinnings of "The Wealth of Nations". "A Theory of Moral Sentiment" set out a framework for interpersonal and social relationships, which was then exemplified in Smith's account of the measures needed to improve the quality of life for workers if their occupations became more repetitive and tedious through the division of labour. Once Smith's account of the basis of capitalism is reunited with the moral and cultural context, and we recall his opposition to the slave trade, slavery, mercantilism and lotteries, we could be dealing with an enlightened contemporary. The intervening period of blinkered virtual reality has been a mistake.

Implications

If the argument is accepted, there are radical implications for the way that we regard "off balance sheet" activities such as the slave trade and the private finance initiative. In the case of the slave trade, it becomes inadequate to regard it merely as a marginal aberration, an activity of a few mercenary traders. It was rather, throughout the eighteenth century, a central contributor to the development of the British economy and the British Empire, despite the fact that few slaves landed in the UK. Although it has often been reported that the Church of England had been active in the campaign for Abolition, it was only in February 2006 that the Church gave public acknowledgement of the extent to which it had benefited financially from the slave trade. There are similar silences to be addressed across Europe, but the UK dominated the slave trade.

Furthermore, we might conclude that the racial attitudes which were created and strengthened through the Slave Trade, and applied globally through the spread of European empires, were systemically linked to the approach which was taken, and, arguably, is still being taken, to business. This provides insights into the activities of the British in India, as well as across Africa.

Accountability and Accounts

The world of business is dominated by the need for accountability, at least in the form of accounts. Whole professions devote their time to drawing up balance sheets, and to recording profits and losses. This applies in both the public and the private sectors. Whatever the moral or ethical issues involved, there is a requirement to meet targets in terms of "bottom line" performance.

In order to arrive at appropriate "headline figures" for the financial bottom line, it is necessary to make assumptions regarding what figures should properly appear in the accounts. In a complex world, there may be a number of ways in which particular transactions might be recorded, with technical arguments for and against, and different consequences for the overall accounts.

In a stable world, where most factors remained equal, it could be relatively straightforward to produce accounts year after year, showing changes on a comparable basis. In practice, the world is not stable. Change is the only constant. We only have partial information at any given time, on which to base our decisions. Only certain factors are under our control: in other cases our strategy will be affected by events. It is assumed that, in properly presented accounts, the figures will balance.

Accounts are a complex formal means of representing diverse and disparate information concerning real phenomena about which we can only have partial knowledge. The complexity of the technical issues concerned means that access to the core underlying questions is denied to those who lack the specialist knowledge to ask the right questions, and the possibility of asking the right people. There is therefore a tendency to leave accounts to the accountants and finance specialists, and for practitioners to devote their attentions to the matters where their input can make a material difference. Practitioners will ask questions on matters which concern them, but assume that other matters are under the control of those with specialist knowledge and responsibilities.

Managers will identify their priorities and requirements. Given data and accounting information, they will drill down, seeking definitive answers to their precise questions. In doing so, they tend to forget that their analysis is being applied only to explicit knowledge, which will itself be partial. Procedural knowledge may remain implicit, though it is amenable to being made explicit. Tacit knowledge of how things are, and how things are done, will not be considered. In essence, managers who depend solely on their accounts are driving while relying on their rear view mirrors, with a selected virtual reality accounting representation of the past. Much depends on what has been included in that virtual reality, and to whom the accounts are presented.

This suggests limits to the capacity of managers to account for the past and present, in a context of relative continuity. There are further complications when we consider issues of major change and transition. Moving to a new situation may present challenges, which go beyond previous experience. New business opportunities require increased supplies of labour, or increased expenditure, beyond what has been available. Sometimes it is possible to appear to solve the problem by adopting an appropriate means of presenting the information concerned.

African slavery represented an apparently indefinite flow of human beings who could be controlled by owners, with a trade which was profitable within the triangular system, and which need not cause concern among shareholders or home markets. There was silence regarding the conditions of transport, sale and working, none of which lent themselves to quantification in financial terms. There was no discussion regarding future potential for emancipation. Similar circumstances apply today regarding child labour, continuing forced labour and forms of female slavery.

In the case of outsourcing and offshoring, functions performed at new locations could bring increased returns to shareholders, with prospects for further expansion of the practice. There has been relative silence regarding working conditions and forms of work organisation. There has been little discussion of future changes, whereby outsourcing companies could become competitors.

CONCLUSION

If these arguments are accepted, there is a need both to acknowledge gross injustices in the past, and to change the way in which we account for our behaviour today.

The book considers the transformation in what has been termed the modern world. A recurrent theme is that little is what it seems. There is a tendency to take the Whig view of history, or to see a process of progression to the present day. Considered globally, that does not seem adequate.

For a British writer, there is the challenge of confronting the reality of what it has been to be British. The history of slavery and the Slave Trade poses challenges. How are we to deal with the apparent ignorance of what was going on? What can we say about the social class system which was curiously reinforced by slavery? Are we in fact so different today?

In preparations for 2007, the voice of Africa seems to have been missing. The African Diaspora continues to be scattered, hard to organise. On the other hand, much that is officially organised appears to be open to doubt. The establishment seems not to understand its own history. Decolonisation was a complex and traumatic process, but the government can look back, not in anger but in apparent ignorance, and accentuate what is perceived to have been positive.

The myth of the modern world is that we are citizens, with autonomy and free will. Perhaps there are other myths, concerning slavery, and the feeling of guilt. Perhaps we have to create ourselves through our own actions. In that case, we have much to learn from the history of NGOs, where individual actions, with focus, over time, can be seen to have effected change.

In the new global context, there are remarkable opportunities to address these issues of slavery and citizenship. These are now real time challenges. We can talk to descendants of all of those who were the successive stages in the slave trade and slavery supply chain, on the same day, at international congresses. In the scientific community, it has not been seen as necessary to relate to the policy agenda. Chattel slavery is now seen as an old agenda. The questions are now being asked about child labour, cutting across the scientific and political sectors. Thirty-five ICOH Scientific Committees have robust agendas, but they have not handled child labour.

There is an emerging new agenda. Knowledge has to be redefined in the context of accumulated experience.

As we experience automation and outsourcing, we can revisit the experience of slavery. Here there were skilled workers, taken from their home environment, relocated to a context where they were treated as sub-human, parts of machines. Western capitalism has built on this base.

There are policy choices today, with implications for the nature of business and management. The key resource is human. Managers who do not understand the past are in danger of reliving the worst complications.

This is an unfinished process. We need to restate some principles, and enable a new generation of projects to proceed. The principles of networking are not new, this does not detract from their power. They are learned in practice. One approach to reparations for the slavery of the past is preparation for the eradication of the slavery of the present, saving future generations from hazardous child labour, and laying the foundations for an international knowledge society.

CHAPTER 10
....

WORLD CITIZENSHIP

Slavery was the first violation of human rights to be fought at the international level; today we must remain vigilant so that it disappears completely. No human being is the property of another.

Kofi Annan, Secretary-General of the United Nations.

FROM SLAVERY: SUMMARY OF CHAPTERS 1–9

Slavery is a story as old as humanity itself, with examples around the world. Large number of Britons had been slaves, with tens of thousands captured by Barbary pirates, operating from what is now Morocco.

Slavery continues in many countries today, as defined by the International Labour Organisation, and as outlined in earlier chapters. It is not necessarily based on different races, but involves a dominant group and a subservient group. One example of a subservient group is children and young people, engaged in harmful child labour.

The Transatlantic Slave Trade involved moving tens of millions of Africans to the Americas, and European slave traders depended on supplies of slaves from African slave traders. It was based on racial difference, and the forced African Diaspora has caused lasting traumas. These need to be addressed. Different perspectives need to be expressed in order for dialogue and reconciliation to be possible.

Slavery was part of wider and more complex international trading systems, affecting areas where no slaves were seen. In Britain, the Slave Trade was a crucial element of the Triangular Trade, which acted as a motor for manufacturing and trade, and also financed civic buildings and public services. The British, French, Spanish and Portuguese empires in the Americas also required slaves, who played a formative role in the new economies and societies.

Abolition has to be understood in terms of economic and political realities. The campaign for abolition in Britain reflected shame felt by the British middle classes, in the late eighteenth century, as they came to realise the barbarity of the slave trade, which had been conducted out of sight. The abolitionists did not start by campaigning for full emancipation of slaves. That would have been politically impossible in light of the property interests of plantation owners in Parliament.

A vital and understated part of the history of Abolition was the achievement of Africans in rebelling against their enslavement, running their own affairs and overcoming attempts by European armies to suppress them. There can be no doubt that the slave rebellions, particularly in the French West Indies, were crucial in ending the Slave Trade. Slave owners could no longer assume that slaves would remain compliant.

Once Britain had abolished the Transatlantic Slave Trade in 1807, it was keen to ensure that other countries observed the ban, and the Royal Navy was deployed. Britain has continued to play a leading role in the campaign against slavery around the world, linked to global involvement in colonies, mandated territories and protectorates.

The history is confused and inconsistent in places, and there are a number of gaps in both the narratives and the arguments. Abolitionist campaigners were not necessarily tolerant of cultural differences: Wilberforce was an evangelical Christian who campaigned against Hinduism. He gave this equivalent priority to his efforts to abolish the slave trade. Slavery was indeed a major problem in India, as it was in so many parts of the world. In India, slavery was indigenous and did not primarily involve European owners and Indian slaves. To complicate matters further, once the import of African slaves to the West Indies halted, it was replaced by demand for Indian indentured labourers.

It might have been imagined that different groups who felt oppressed could have made common cause against injustice. There is little evidence to support such a view in eighteenth century Britain. The early industrial working class did not generally campaign on behalf of the slaves. To the extent that they were aware of the situation of slaves, they often felt similarly abused, in terms of limited control over their own lives and work, and participation in decision making. They did not combine forces against a common enemy, although there were some African members of British radical groups, and many British campaigners for the abolition of the slave trade. Members of the Aboltion Movement, and signatories to petitions, were typically members of the middle classes, who lacked the right to vote, but felt increasing guilt about slavery and the slave trade, and the involvement of Britain. History has concentrated on the achievements of the abolitionists. Accounts tend to have been written by the strong. African history has been little known in Europe.

We need to try to come to terms with the history, if we are to work together in the present, and build a sustainable world in the future. We need a process of Truth and Reconciliation. Separate national histories are not adequate for dealing with a global phenomenon. In multicultural classrooms and communities it must be possible for understanding to develop, regarding different points of view. Here we have to move beyond a single linear narrative, and provide a context in which we can learn from differences. This has been the perspective adopted by UNESCO. It is vital to be prepared to enter into dialogue.

As key motivating examples, we can learn from both the Lunar Society and Toussaint L'Ouverture, discussed earlier in the book. Both developed dialogue, operated through networking across borders of countries and disciplines, and built communities of practice. They offered models of an alternative future, in contrast to hierarchies and nation states. Their achievement was revolutionary, and not sufficiently recognised.

ENGAGEMENT

World citizenship is not just something to talk about in theoretical terms; it requires active engagement in practice. It provides a challenging educational agenda.

"From Slavery to Citizenship" addresses decision makers and citizens in today's world. The profits of the Transatlantic Slave Trade, and the rest of the Triangular Trade Route, contributed to British economic growth, and thus to current prosperity, in a manner which is rarely acknowledged. This needs to be acknowledged if closure is to be achieved. The long journey from Slavery to Citizenship can only be completed once the Truth has been recognised, and Reconciliation is achieved, based on parity of esteem between dialogue partners.

We now seek to introduce new associated educational opportunities, helping to break silences and increase mutual understanding. This is part of a process of Cross Community Dialogue, outside the conventional curriculum.

As 2007 approached, with events to commemorate the bicentenary of the Abolition of the Transatlantic Slave Trade, there was increased demand for teaching and learning materials on issues around the Slave Trade and slavery. There will be co-ordination of the celebrations in the UK. Just as NGOs played a vital role in Abolition, NGOs will play a vital role in commemoration, and in taking forward the next stages of the process of emancipation.

NEW DEBATES

The complex subject of slavery needs to be considered from many perspectives. Too often there has simply been one dominant point of view expressed, excluding others. The literature has until recently been relatively restricted. Suddenly there is a flow of new publications, challenging old orthodoxies and opening up new debate.

In the UK we see fresh accounts of the Abolition campaign, and in particular controversy over the role of William Wilberforce MP, who has traditionally been presented as an heroic figure. The Church of England has been prepared to open up debate on its own involvement in the Transatlantic Slave Trade and in slavery. In the USA, there are new revelations about Presidents George Washington and Thomas Jefferson, concerning their views on slavery and their relationships with slaves. There have been new publications concerning the French West Indies, including accounts of the successful slave rebellions in the wake of the French Revolution, and on Brazil.

In UK schools, following the recent report by the Qualifications and Curriculum Authority, it is apparent that there is a serious gap in what is taught, particularly in the period between the sixteenth and twentieth centuries, between "Henry" and "Hitler". Apart from undue focus on well-worn topics, there has been uncertainty as to how to address topics such as the Slave Trade and the British Empire. Teachers, as well as students, need to be equipped to address potentially thorny issues, taking into account the diverse backgrounds of students in multicultural classes.

There are renewed debates on current problems of slavery, using International Labour Organisation definitions, with media coverage of child labour, sex slaves, trafficking, exploitation of immigrant workers, and fresh insights into the treatment of women and of older workers. This is leading to new discussions of business ethics and corporate social responsibility. There is growing awareness that all may not be well with processes of decision-making in business, and that companies and communities may need to ask questions about their own pasts. There are many silences.

BREAKING THE SILENCE

The extent of the silence about the truth of British and European involvement in the Transatlantic Slave Trade has been such that it is not simply a matter of educating the younger generation. The UK withdrew from UNESCO in 1985, leaving a generation of current adult opinion formers who have lacked the international dimension. Although the UK returned to membership in 1997, there has still been limited re-engagement in the international agenda. The UNESCO project on "Slave Routes" has been conducted with minimal UK involvement. New facts are now being published, during the bicentenary period, which conflict with commonly accepted British historical accounts. It is not a matter of minor adjustments, but of wholesale reappraisals of the past, and of national self-image.

For example, it has long been proclaimed with pride that Britain led the campaign to abolish the Transatlantic Slave Trade in 1807. Less attention has been given to the awkward fact that Britain had dominated that trade for the previous century, with impacts across British society. However, we should not neglect the longstanding and ongoing British role in working with Anti Slavery International to tackle slavery around the world. We need to understand that adherence to the objective of abolition of slavery and emancipation of the slaves had to be accompanied by a practical approach to government in colonies, protectorates and mandated territories, with limited resources.

In the modern globalised society it is important to learn from encounters, and to have the opportunity of forming one's own views. It is important to be able to see the world from the perspective of others, including other countries. In the Appendix we provide initial briefing information, but the participants are required to go further, framing their own responses to particular situations, in the context of a Model United Nations General Assembly.

Companies and Chambers of Commerce could usefully host events, highlighting local connections with slavery, in order to enable their members to reassess their attitudes. There is a case for a new generation of projects to re-write the histories of companies and cities, in light of new evidence that some revered civic benefactors disguised the fact that their generosity derived from profits from the slave trade. Across Europe, there needs to be a recognition of the extent to which Europeans collectively exploited Africa. This is not simply a British problem.

DIALOGUE

Different concepts of citizenship underpin the formal constitutional arrangements in France, the USA and the UK. Drawing on alternative informal approaches in African societies, and recent developments in Europe, we emphasise the role of dialogue. Societies and states are constituted by processes of dialogue; given the dynamic and changing nature of dialogues where new participants are involved, it is not sufficient to refer to legal documents and formal institutional structures. Our model UN General Assembly illustrates this in practice.

As we move from Slavery towards Citizenship, we encounter issues of social capital formation, innovation and regional development. In a world of individuals and small enterprises, we need to find ways of working together, recognising that often together we can achieve what we cannot achieve in isolation. Following major political change, such as the collapse of the colonial empires or the Soviet Union, this can mean radical re-thinking of relationships in society. In order for such changes to become sustainable, there needs to be a context of trust, which is developed incrementally, through experience, over time.

These arguments provide a context for the work of the Council for Education in World Citizenship and Rendezvous of Victory in "Cross-Community Dialogue". The ground rules for that dialogue mirror those as set out for democratic dialogue (Gustavsen, 1992):

1. The dialogue is a process of exchange: ideas and arguments move to and fro between the participants.
2. It must be possible for all concerned to participate.
3. This possibility for participation is, however, not enough. Everybody should also be active. Consequently each participant has an obligation not only to put forth his or her own ideas, but also to help others to contribute their ideas.
4. All participants are equal.
5. Work experience is the basis for participation. This is the only type of experience which, by definition, all participants have.
6. At least some of the experience which each participant has when entering the dialogue must be considered legitimate.

7. It must be possible for everybody to develop an understanding of the issues at stake.

8. All arguments which pertain to the issues under discussion are legitimate. No argument should be rejected on the ground that it emerges from an illegitimate source.

9. The points, arguments etc which are to enter the dialogue must be made by a participating actor. Nobody can participate "on paper" only.

10. Each participant must accept that other participants can have better arguments.

11. The work role, authority etc of all the participants can be made subject to discussion – no participant is exempt in this respect.

12. The participants should be able to tolerate an increasing degree of difference of opinion.

13. The dialogue must continuously produce agreements which can provide platforms for practical action. Note that there is no contradiction between this criterion and the previous one. The major strength of a democratic system compared to all other ones is that it has the benefit of drawing upon a broad range of opinions and ideas which inform practice, while at the same time being able to make decisions which can gain the support of all participants. (p. 4)

The shift from Slavery redefines the nature of Citizenship for all citizens, and not simply for former slaves. Europeans have to acknowledge the extent to which their ancestors continued with the Transatlantic Slave Trade, at the same time as preaching Christianity, Enlightenment and good government. Some humility from the former Empires would be helpful.

There are differences in constitutional histories around the world, making comparisons difficult. Citizenship is constituted, on a daily basis, by dialogue. Our focus is on the facilitation of dialogue, and finding ways in which it can be sustainable. We can distinguish active citizenship from inactive citizenship, where individuals may wait for the state, or some other group, to solve their problems for them.

WHAT IS CITIZENSHIP?

Citizenship is not simply a matter of legal status. Citizens feel part of the wider community, and this is demonstrated in their actions. Citizens participate in a common form of life, in which they follow the same rules, and use a common language, in the sense that they can understand each other, sharing meanings.

Typically citizens make reference to some shared concepts of the past. The past is not over, but is very much part of the continuing reality of the present. The practicalities of citizenship may also be affected by chronological age, and attitudes to experience and wisdom.

OUT OF AFRICA

As a result of the African Diaspora consequent on the Transatlantic Slave Trade, the descendants of slaves from the same African villages can now be subject to widely varying régimes. In the modern world, they find themselves as part of organised states, across the world, which do not necessarily offer advantages over less formal arrangements, which were more typical in Africa.

Ali A. Mazrui, in "The Africans", argues that:

> the state is a less egalitarian construct than a stateless society, and often more brutal (1986, p. 68)

and

> the role of the Somali language has been particularly striking. No society has been as deeply wedded to poetry and verse as the Somali, and no society has evolved as elaborate a culture of verbal composition and eloquence, a ritual use of the Muse, as these nomads have done. Their greatest hero was Muhammad Abdilleh Hassan, whom the British designated as the 'Mad Mullah'. He fought the British and the Italians with great cunning and dexterity; but he was also

a great user of the Somali language. The so-called 'Mad Mullah' was in fact an inspired Muse. In a land where every third person is a poet, Muhammad Abdilleh Hassan stands out as one of the greatest Somali poets of all time. In him patriotism and poetry were married to each other, resounding among the hills and sand-dunes of the Horn of Africa. The career of Muhammad Abdilleh Hassan was probably the most dramatic illustration of how the Somali as a stateless society managed to achieve substantial social cohesion partly through the role of language among the clans. In the place of structures of control the Somali evolved a culture of co-operation. (p. 70)

What has often been neglected is what this informal but long-established tradition of co-operation has to offer in the new contexts in which we are now working. The capacity of Africans to survive, despite oppression, has much to teach the rest of the world. Members of the African Diaspora can take their places as world citizens.

INTO EUROPE AND THE MODERN WORLD

In French history "citizens", and citizenship, were an enduring consequence of the French Revolution. That history provides a common set of rhetorical reference points, and the French Constitution, which is written and explicit, derives from those events. The Code Napoleon provided the basis for legal systems across Europe, but not in Britain. The Consulate under Napoleon re-imposed slavery with spectacular brutality in 1802, before final abolition in 1848.

There is a similar story for the United States, where the Declaration of Independence has the status of a sacred document, but radical protesters may risk arrest if they invite people to sign it today. The resulting Constitution provides a backbone for American life, with a structure of courts from district to Supreme Court, able to overthrow legislation and define the rights of the citizen. This is part of the system of "checks and balances", intended to ensure that no one part of the system, legislature, executive or judiciary, gains excessive power. Despite the constitutional amendment outlawing slavery, interpretations based on property law delayed the process of extending civil rights.

In Britain the tradition has been different. The official terminology was in terms of British "subjects", subjects of the monarch. Both the government and the official Parliamentary opposition were regarded as "loyal" to the monarch. The constitutional monarchy then involves concepts such as "the Queen in Parliament", meaning that references to the crown can be translated into references to the elected government, typically formed by the party which wins the most seats in the House of Commons.

In recent years there have been efforts to clarify the position on citizenship, to take account of the current multicultural society in Britain. An introductory guide for new citizens was produced for the Home Office, by Professor Sir Bernard Crick and an expert committee. Unfortunately the guide gave little attention to international citizenship. The need for international citizenship remains to be met, as the number of new British citizens continues to rise. It is not simply a matter of definition, but of engagement.

ONLY CONNECT

The novelist E.M. Forster took as the central theme of many of his novels "Only Connect". He illustrated how perceived barriers, based on race, social class, or sexual orientation, could inhibit dialogue, and prevent the smooth working of democratic society.

In our Cross Community Dialogues, we are seeking to "connect". As Forster narrates, such efforts do not always meet with immediate success. We recall that the work of Thomas Clarkson, and the Society for the Abolition of the Slave Trade, founded in 1787, did not achieve the end of slavery in Britain until 1838. Emancipation from modern forms of slavery continues to be a challenge.

In our account of Slavery and Citizenship, we recognise the involvement of both Europeans and Africans in the slave trade. We now need to recognise the potential contributions of Europeans and Africans to citizenship, including world citizenship.

MODEL UNITED NATIONS

Anti Slavery International, founded in 1839, after the emancipation of slaves in Britain, is committed to eliminating all forms of slavery throughout the world. Slavery, servitude and child labour are violations of individual freedoms, which deny millions of people their basic dignity and fundamental human rights. Anti Slavery International works to end these abuses by campaigning for slavery's eradication, exposing current cases, supporting the initiatives of local organisations to release people and pressing for more effective implementation of international laws against slavery.

PARTICIPATIVE EDUCATION

One excellent way of dealing with complex international issues, where there are different contexts and perspectives, is through a Model United Nations General Assembly (MUNGA).

There can be preparatory experience centred exercises, and smaller scale activities, taking the form of Forum Theatre. Here participants take on the roles of particular characters, exploring how it could be possible to work through particular problems, as set out in the earlier chapters of the book.

Slavery, and the Transatlantic Slave Trade, crossed national borders with numerous simultaneous developments, and cannot now be dealt with simply on a country by country basis. Separate national histories and debates are not sufficient, and merely serve to strengthen stereotypical and mistaken views. We need international debate.

Pilot work has shown that this can be conducted at many levels, from primary and secondary schools through to further education, universities and workshops for senior managers and community groups.

There are two problems, both of which we seek to address with practical innovations.

1. It would be anomalous to stage a model United Nations to address issues in a period before 1945, when the United Nations was established. Our model UN addresses current issues, using briefing which provides background information for the participants.
2. The transition from taking an individual perspective to engaging in informed debate can be complex. One route is through role-based simulation exercises, accompanying the earlier chapters, where briefing is provided on individual participants and the scenarios with which they are confronted. This can be enhanced with "Forum Theatre", when actors take on the roles, and continue in character when engaging the audience in developing the situation.

CONDUCTING PARTICIPATIVE SESSIONS

Facilitation

The events need to be facilitated, with careful advance preparation, to avoid excessive anomalies. The interventions should be consistent with contemporary power relationships.

Participants

Participants work in character, with initial briefing. They may respond to impulse texts, working initially from the information given. The impulses may take various forms, such as historical events, quotations, scenarios and legal judgements. Participants need to interact in character, then offer their own overall reflections.

Preparing for Debate

Whereas it would be possible to proceed directly to a debate on the abolition of slavery, preparation is required if there are to be insights into the historical background, and the different perspectives, both over history and among member countries of the United Nations today. For example, although it would be hard to find someone to make a public defence of slavery today, that would certainly not have been the case before slavery was finally abolished in Britain in 1838, and in France in 1848.

It is useful therefore to consider a second modern case, which is currently contentious, and deals with related issues, regarding child labour. Participants can contribute from their own real life experience, and make comparisons with the position of the organisation or country which they are representing.

EXPERIENCE CENTRED EXERCISES

We do not start with either conventional analytical approaches, or by going directly into roles. Three particular experience centred exercises, developed with UNESCO (Wolsk, 1975) can contribute to setting the scene, and encouraging interactions between participants.

Level of Aspiration: Plantation Work

This simple exercise involves a group of participants, working in pairs. They are set a common task, which is new to all of them, and requires no particular prior skill. Typically the task is to take a paper clip, and drop it, from the height of the participant's nose, into a plastic or paper cup held between the participant's feet. It is unlikely that the participants will have done this before! Each pair of participants is allocated ten paper clips and a cup. They undertake the task in turn, monitoring the performance of the other.

After an initial demonstration, each individual is required to estimate their likely success level, out of ten attempts. Following a first round of trials, the results are collected and discussed. In light of their experience, the participants are asked to predict their success rates in a second trial. Again the results are collected.

- How have the performances changed?
- What evidence was there of learning, and of participants copying successful techniques used by others?
- Who emerged as leaders and opinion formers, and how?
- What determined the original estimates by participants, given their prior lack of experience?
- Did performance necessarily improve?
- Were particular groups consistently more effective?
- To what extent did participants abide by the rules?

- Did participants exploit the fact that only brief instructions were given?
- What parallels come to mind in real life?
- How could better results be achieved in a further round?

Individuals start with their own choice of posture and strategy. Typically particular approaches will appear to offer higher success rates, and the innovation will be diffused among the group. There can be considerable tensions, jealousies, insecurities and sometimes a reluctance to share what is seen as valuable information. Some individuals will emerge as trend setters and leaders.

Peaceful Negotiations: Scramble for Africa

This exercise requires the group to be divided into four sub-groups, each of which is to represent a different country. Each country is required to select a Prime Minister, then a Foreign Secretary, then a Road Builder. The task is to develop the road infrastructure for their country, bearing in mind that the four countries are adjoining. There is a map on the floor, made of large sheets of paper. Road Builders are given paint brushes, and paint of different colours. All road construction in the home country has to be approved by the Prime Minister. Any construction across borders and in other countries requires negotiations to be conducted by the Foreign Secretaries, engaging, where necessary, in shuttle diplomacy.

The event requires a facilitator, who indicates when construction work can begin, after due consideration. Pauses are declared when reflection is needed, or when negotiations are required.

At a certain point, order will break down, and the facilitator calls a halt. There is a discussion.

- What was the strategy being followed in each of the countries?

- How were the Prime Ministers, Foreign Secretaries and Road Builders selected or elected? To what extent was the process democratic and transparent?
- What were relations like between the office holders?
- How were the other members of the populations consulted by the leaders?
- To what extent was there collaboration across borders?
- Was negotiation conducted between equals?
- Were all the agreements public?
- What went wrong, requiring construction work to be suspended?
- Who won?
- Is there a single account of events? How do the accounts differ?
- How could matters have been handled better?

Star Power: Fair Trade?

Participants are divided into different groups, each wearing distinctive badges: <u>Squares</u>, <u>Circles</u>, <u>Diamonds</u> and <u>Triangles</u>. Packs for trading have been prepared, comprising tokens in different coloured cardboard: black, red, blue and yellow. Packs are issued according to groups.

The rules are introduced. The objective of the game is to exchange tokens, building up stocks of particular colours: black, red, blue and yellow. Bonus points will be awarded for multiple tokens of the same colour.

In a first trading round, exchanges are made. Those pairs of people engaging in trade have to shake hands. At the end of the first round, the outcomes are assessed. It is then revealed that the coloured tokens have different values (black: 1; red: 2; blue 3; yellow 5). An additional bonus is awarded for multiples of the same colour (5 for 5; 6 for 6; 7 for 7, etc.).

Scores are calculated. It is realised that not all participants had been given tokens of the same overall value. In general, their starting positions were, in ascending value, <u>Squares</u>, <u>Circles</u>, <u>Diamonds</u> and <u>Triangles</u>. Some social mobility is possible as a result of the first round of trading, as new dividing lines appear between the groups. New badges are awarded, following promotions and demotions. The first sets of tokens are collected.

In a second trading round, new sets of tokens are issued according to group, and exchange of tokens proceeds. Because of their success in the first round, the <u>Triangles</u> are rewarded with the right to determine their trading partners. Members of other groups have no choice but to comply.

Scores are calculated, and the dividing lines are re-drawn. The second set of tokens are collected. Members of the <u>Circle</u> group are now all designated <u>Squares</u>. <u>Diamonds</u> are unchanged, <u>Triangles</u>, because of their continued excellence, are invited to make a single change in the rules, of their own choice.

In the final trading round, the final sets of tokens are issued. Trading proceeds according to the rules set by the <u>Triangles</u>. Scores are calculated.

- Who won?
- Was the trade fair?
- What were the rules?
- How do the accounts from each of the groups compare?
- How could the trading system be improved?
- Are there parallels in real life?

CLASSROOM STRATEGY

The Bicentenary in 2007 sets the overall scene for us, with a flow of new materials now being published to add to the debate. Based on previous experience of writing and conducting role-based simulations in the history classroom, and development workshops, there can be several phases in classroom work and organised events. Schools and Chambers of Commerce will not always be able to organise MUNGAs, but may wish to address particular topics.

There have been international conferences on the issue of slavery since the early nineteenth century, where the abolitionist case was made by Wilberforce and Clarkson. In the early twentieth century the League of Nations tackled issues concerning the aftermath of empires. Only in the period since 1945 has there been a United Nations Organisation, where such matters could be discussed. This will be the set piece event for the MUNGA debates, which will concern what can now be done, and how decisions can then be implemented and enforced.

PERIODS

In principle, one could have approaches tailored for research and discussion on particular periods which are anyway taught in a conventional history curriculum, at whatever level. For example:

- European voyages of discovery
- West Africa before the Europeans
- Eighteenth century triangular slave trade
- Adam Smith and Enlightenment
- American War of Independence
- French Revolution and Napoleonic Wars
- The campaign for abolition
- Enforcement of abolition
- Emancipation
- America and Civil War
- Scramble for Africa
- First World War and League of Nations

- From Empire to Independence
- United Nations
- The African Diaspora: legacy of slavery and empire
- Modern Globalisation
- Modern slavery and child labour

EXAMPLE ARGUMENTS, BY BOOK CHAPTERS

Each chapter of "From Slavery to Citizenship" sets out arguments, linking separate discourses, inviting debate, with participants in roles.

1. NATIONS AND EMPIRES

- Slavery used to be common in Europe, until the Middle Ages: Britons have been slaves! Serfs were only freed in Russia in the nineteenth century. The feudal system, based on a hierarchical society, continued for many centuries.
- The slave trade was long established in Africa, and operated across borders.
- Islamic science and culture had a coherent world view, including religion.
- The Transatlantic Slave Trade transported black slaves from Africa.
- Slavery was associated with European empires.
- How were prisoners treated?
- The Tibetan people are still regarded as subject to Chinese rule.
- What are the continuing legacies of empire?

2. THE TRADE IN PEOPLE AND IDEAS

- Arab traders had long experience in Asia, Africa and Europe.
- Was Francis Drake an adventurer, a pirate or a slave trader?
- How were Britons enslaved by the Barbary pirates?
- Wrecks of transatlantic slave ships have been found. We can see the conditions in which slaves were transported.
- Death rates of sailors on the Triangular Trade were high. Why did they agree to sail?
- Slaves could be thrown overboard, in order to claim insurance payments.
- Thousands of Native Americans died through exposure to European diseases.
- The Pope prohibited enslavement of Native Americans, but not of Africans.
- How did the slave trade affect Africa?
- Why were few slaves brought to Britain?
- The American Founding Fathers saw the solution to the problem of slavery as the deportation of any slaves who achieved freedom.
- There have been new revelations about George Washington and Thomas Jefferson.

3. ECONOMIC DEVELOPMENT

- Why did it make economic sense to use slaves?
- Why did it make economic sense to stop using slaves?
- How important was the Slave Trade and the Triangular Trade in the British Industrial Revolution?
- How could slaves compete with paid workers, using technology?
- How did slavery vary, between the USA, West Indies and Brazil?

- Bristol schools recognise the role of the slave trade in their foundation. What was the impact on London, Liverpool, Birmingham and Glasgow?
- How did the slave trade affect other parts of Britain?
- How do companies account for human resources?
- How did the early entrepreneurs in the British Industrial Revolution work together?
- How did innovators build networks across borders?
- What was the role of banks in the slave trade?
- Do companies have responsibilities other than to make a profit?

4. EMANCIPATION

- The Church of England owned slaves.
- How was abolition of the Transatlantic Slave Trade achieved?
- A plantation hears news of a rebellion on a neighbouring plantation. News of slave rebellions was often suppressed, in the cause of maintaining public order.
- When the slave trade was abolished, compensation was paid to the former owners, not the former slaves.
- Slaves were used as pawns in wars between Britain, France and the USA.
- Slaves welcomed the status of French citizens, only to be suppressed and re-enslaved.
- Following abolition in 1807, former slaves were not freed for 31 years. This only followed emancipation in 1833 and a period of apprenticeship.
- What was the role of slavery in the American Civil War?
- How were former slaves prepared for leading roles in American society?
- How was emancipation addressed in the different European empires?

5. DIASPORA

- Why was there pressure to resettle slaves?
- How successful were efforts to resettle slaves?
- Slave communities maintained aspects of African culture through oral tradition, including the use of music and stories.
- How could Africa move from empires to independence?
- How could black and white co-exist after slavery?
- How did North and South America develop?
- Cesar Picton, a slave from Senegal, became a leading resident of Kingston.
- African Diaspora groups are demanding reparations. What does this mean?

6. CONTROL AND PARTICIPATION

- What changes were made in ways of organising work?
- How much autonomy did the individual worker have?
- Can we compare the conditions of American slaves and British factory workers?
- Can we compare the treatment of slaves and indentured labourers?
- To what extent did success in the industrial period increasingly require a motivated workforce, able to learn and to adapt to changing circumstances?
- What has been the impact of technology?
- What have been the outcomes of individual and collective approaches?

7. HUMAN RIGHTS

- Who cared about the human rights of slaves?
- How could human rights be reconciled with property rights?

- How could the Church justify its position on slavery?
- What were the arguments in favour of European empires?
- How did the truth about King Leopold II's activities in the Belgian Congo emerge?
- What was the record of the British Empire regarding human rights?
- Why does forced child labour continue?
- Who is concerned for the human rights of immigrant workers?
- How are human rights to be reconciled with the needs of the state?
- Where are the silences?

8. UNITING NATIONS

- What are the alternatives to war?
- How can peace be made and kept?
- Which are the modern empires?
- What benefits are provided by regional groupings?
- Does history have to be repeated?
- How have proxy wars been fought?
- How can international agreements be enforced?

9. GLOBALISATION AND EDUCATION

- In what sense could we regard the slave trade as an early form of globalisation?
- How could former slaves achieve citizenship of adopted countries?
- How do national histories differ in their treatment of slavery?
- Could there be a single international history?
- How has education responded to globalisation?

- Is it harder to maintain silences in an information-rich world?
- Can there be global answers to the problem of slavery?
- How can this be addressed by the United Nations?
- What can be done, 200 years after abolition of the Transatlantic Slave Trade?
- Can there be united responses to challenges such as HIV/ AIDS?
- Can poverty be made history?
- What can the individual do?
- What is the role of NGOs?

10. WORLD CITIZENSHIP

- How can Europeans come to terms with their past roles in the slave trade?
- How can past practice be reconciled with Christianity, Enlightenment and good government?
- How can the African Diaspora take a leading role in building world citizenship?
- How can active citizenship today make reparation for the past?

COUNTRIES

We can identify countries with a role at each stage in our story. Participants in the Model United Nations will speak in role, and take account of their country's history. The following briefing provides a starting point.

UK

Britain had a long seafaring history, and a geographical location which was ideal for the Triangular Trade. The Civil War in the seventeenth century removed the monarchy and after Restoration there was a constitutional monarchy from the eighteenth century. The Slave Trade brought major economic benefits to Britain, and was abolished as it became less profitable.

Having abolished the Transatlantic Slave Trade, Britain tried to enforce the ban on other nations, while developing the British Empire. Work continued with the Temporary Slavery Commission, the International Labour Organisation and the League of Nations.

The British population is now multicultural, with citizens referring to many different histories. There are now British-born terrorists, including suicide bombers.

The government emphasises the importance of education being work related, including providing work experience for school children. Britain joined the European Union in 1973. Britain is a permanent member of the UN Security Council, and retains a nuclear deterrent provided by the USA.

France

France had traditional rivalry with Britain, and an absolute monarchy until the French Revolution, during which slavery was first abolished. Anglo-French wars were fought all over the world, including the West Indies and India, in which slaves were used as political pawns. The French Empire was particularly strong in North Africa.

France and Britain were leading powers in the League of Nations, and took on a number of mandates and protectorates, for example in the Middle East.

The French population is now multicultural, and tensions have become public. France was a founding member of the European Union. France is a permanent member of the UN Security Council, and maintains its own nuclear deterrent.

USA

The Americans won their freedom from Britain, but retained trading links. The USA is a country of immigrants, who came to the land of the free, in order to escape slavery, and joining a melting pot to become integrated as Americans. However, many Southern states continued to depend on slavery, until abolition in 1865, at the end of the Civil War. Race relations have continued to be difficult.

The USA has had a tradition of alternating between international isolation and exercising the role of leading world power. Today the USA is the only superpower, with the largest defence budget, and the leading economy, with a strong new technology sector. American foreign policy had led it to be regarded as an Empire. The USA is a permanent member of the UN Security Council.

Russia

The system of serfdom continued in Imperial Russia until the late nineteenth century. During the twentieth century, following the Russian Revolution, Russia developed the Soviet Union, incorporating many neighbouring satellite states. In 1989, the fall of the Berlin Wall was followed by the collapse of the Soviet Union. The Baltic States (Lithuania, Latvia and Estonia) were quick to regain their independence, and then to join the European Union.

Russia is a permanent member of the Security Council, and is increasingly powerful as an energy supplier.

Spain

The Spanish led the early exploration and conquest of the New World. The Spanish Empire in the West Indies and Latin America was dependent on slaves, typically provided by foreign traders.

Spanish power in Europe declined. There is a growing Hispanic population in the United States, many coming from Mexico. Spain has benefited from membership of the European Union.

Portugal

The Pope ruled that Portuguese conquests in Latin America had to be to the East of a defined line, with the Spanish to the West. The Portuguese Empire in Brazil, Angola and Mozambique was based on slave labour.

Slavery continued in Brazil until 1888, and the Portuguese colonies were late in achieving independence. After years of dictatorship, Portugal was late in achieving democracy. Portugal is a member of the European Union.

Santo Domingo

The island was first discovered by Columbus, and became a base for rich sugar plantations, fought over by the Spanish, French and British. Toussaint L'Ouverture led the slave rebellion from 1791, which led to an independent Haiti in 1804.

Today Haiti is one of the poorest countries in the world, and shares the island with the Dominican Republic.

Cuba

Cuba was a major producer of sugar, based on slave labour, often imported from elsewhere in the Americas.

Fidel Castro led the revolution in 1959, and continues as President. Cuba remains proudly independent, only miles from the USA, which has maintained trade embargoes.

Jamaica

Jamaica, in the British West Indies, continued to import slaves in the late eighteenth century, when Barbados had become self-sufficient in slaves. The majority of the population were slaves, with European plantation owners, many of whom were also British Members of Parliament.

Jamaica is an active member of the Commonwealth.

Canada

Canada provided a destination for runaway American slaves, and for some resettlement projects. Having been a venue for Anglo-French wars, it maintained links with both countries.

Canada is an active member of the Commonwealth, and proud of its separate identity from the USA.

Brazil

The majority of the Brazilian population were slaves, mainly from Angola, and the different racial groups intermarried. slavery continued until 1888, within the Portuguese Empire.

The social and economic effects of slavery have been long lasting, with examples of modern slavery, especially in remote rural areas of the Amazon basin. Child labour is a current major issue. Brazil is now a major developing nation, with a commitment to social justice.

Germany

Germany played a relatively minor role in the Transatlantic Slave Trade, and in the Scramble for Africa. However, it was keen to acquire African colonies, in order to demonstrate that it was a great power.

In the twentieth century Germany was on the losing side in two World Wars. Germany was a founding member of the European Union.

Denmark

Denmark had a long maritime tradition, and was active in the slave trade, but abolished the trade before the British. Denmark ruled Norway, and Ibsen's hero Peer Gynt was portrayed as engaged in the slave trade.

Denmark is now rated the most innovative Nordic country, and is increasingly multicultural. Denmark is a member of the European Union.

Netherlands

The Netherlands had a strong navy, and were active in the slave trade to the Americas, before switching their attention to the East Indies, where they developed colonies.

The Netherlands was a founding member of the European Union.

Nigeria

Nigeria was a major trading area across the Sahara, and a source of millions of slaves sent to the Americas. The present national boundaries were a result of the British Empire, and include a number of previously separate states. There was a tradition of tribal warfare, in which the losers could be enslaved.

Nigeria is an active member of the Commonwealth and of the African Union. It now enjoys considerable oil wealth.

Ghana

Ghana was a major source of gold, and the coast had harbours which enabled the loading of slaves. There was a rich history, for example that of the Ashanti Kingdom, before the coming of European traders. Kwame Nkrumah was an early leader of an independent former British colony.

Ghana is an active member of the Commonwealth and of the African Union.

Congo

The Congo was the prized possession of King Leopold II of Belgium. Under the pretext of attacking the African slave trade, he enslaved the local population and was responsible for genocide, in the cause of commercial gain from rubber.

Congo is a member of the African Union. The Democratic Republic of Congo today has continued a tradition of civil war and atrocities.

Morocco

Morocco is a French-speaking Islamic country in North West Africa, with a tradition of trading, including slave trading, both in the Mediterranean and across the Sahara.

Development has been relatively rapid in recent years, with modernisation, and close links with France.

Australia

The immigrant population of Australia originally included British convicts, sent as indentured workers. Once they had served their time, they could become free men and citizens.

Australia now sees itself as part of the Asia Pacific region, and is an active member of the Commonwealth.

Egypt

This ancient civilisation, on the Mediterranean, close to Italy, Greece and Turkey, was part of Africa's engagement in the world when countries such as Britain were backward and isolated. There was rivalry between the British and French, who wished to add Egypt to their empires, providing reflected glory.

There have been ongoing tensions with neighbours Israel, whose people were slaves of Egypt in Old Testament times.

India

With the independence of the United States, the attention of British and French explorers and merchants turned to India. There were long traditions of slavery, often linked to caste. The ancient civilisation was raided by European collectors, who installed a limited régime of colonial administrators. Indian administrators managed much of the British Empire.

India has a fast growing economy, with increasing technological strength, and experience gained from international outsourcing. However, poverty and the caste system continue. India is an active member of the Commonwealth.

Saudi Arabia

Arab traders took Islam and intellectual development across Africa and Asia, with relatively little interaction with Europe. Islamic science and philosophy flourished during the European "dark ages" which preceded the Renaissance. On the other hand, patterns of slavery and slave trading continued until the twentieth century.

Today Saudi Arabia has strong alliances with the USA and UK, involving oil and defence deals.

China

The People's Republic of China had a long imperial past, and regards Tibet as part of its territory. A new railway is under construction, linking Tibet to Beijing. China has reincorporated Hong Kong, and has a rapid rate of economic development.

In 2008 China will host the Olympic Games. China is a permanent member of the Security Council.

UNITED NATIONS AGENCIES

International Labour Organisation (ILO)

The ILO is concerned with employment and labour issues, and works on a tripartite basis, involving governments, employers organisations and trade unions. Governments are asked to ratify a series of conventions, agreeing employment standards.

World Health Organisation (WHO)

Priorities for WHO are set by national governments, and the work deals with issues which cross national borders.

United Nations International Childrens Emergency Fund (UNICEF)

UNICEF provides relief assistance for children around the world.

United Nations Educational, Scientific and Cultural Organisation (UNESCO)

UNESCO involves civil society in an active role, and has specialist sectors concerned with education, culture, communication, natural sciences, and social and human sciences.

United Nations High Commissioner for Human Rights

There is a specialist focus on human rights concerns, for example minorities.

United Nations High Commissioner for Refugees (UNHCR)

UNHCR seeks to address the problems of displaced people following wars, whether civil or international.

United Nations Development Programme (UNDP)

UNDP assists in economic development programmes in developing and transitional economies.

UNAIDS

This specialist agency deals with HIV/AIDS, and links with other agencies such as ILO, WHO and UNICEF.

World Bank

The World Bank addresses issues of development and human capital.

International Monetary Fund

The IMF works with governments on the finances of development.

Peacekeeping Forces

The Security Council establishes peacekeeping forces to deal with the consequences of individual conflicts, and usually assigns a major role to other countries in the region.

NGOs

There are numerous officially recognised NGOs, including:

- Anti slavery International
- Amnesty International
- Save the Children Fund
- Tearfund
- International Commission on Occupational Health

MEDIA ORGANISATIONS

- BBC World
- CNN

METHOD

Participants start in single country-based roles, with their own allocated briefing, which gives them initial access to part of a given problem, but with conspicuous silences. They have to identify what they need to know, and work out how they might find out, who they might talk to.

We introduce NGOs and UN agencies, which have their own specialist starting points, and the ability to make connections. Again, initial briefing is provided.

Anti Slavery International, with a variety of names since 1787, has been incremental in its approach to the removal of slavery around the world. It involves identifying practical next steps, who has to make the decisions, what arguments would have an impact, and the best ways of getting the message across. Other NGOs, such as Amnesty International, have taken a similar approach, working behind the scenes. On this basis, the public debate, which is a standard part of a MUNGA, is always accompanied by the pressure group work of NGOs and campaigners.

Importantly, it is not until one is able to operate at the international level, linking the parts of the jigsaw, that real progress on slavery and the Slave Trade can be made. This motivates the introduction of the UN, and the MUNGA.

THE MODEL UNITED NATIONS

The present Secretary–General, Kofi Annan, is from Ghana. His successor, Ban Ki-Moon, is from South Korea.

The Security Council has 5 Permanent Members (UK, France, USA, China, Russia) and 10 other Members elected by rotation.

All United Nations Member Countries have a vote in the General Assembly.

United Nations Specialised Agencies deliver humanitarian roles, and peacekeeping forces involve the United Nations and regional bodies such as the African Union. In particular, the International Labour Organisation has developed a range of conventions, which have then been ratified by member countries. The Framework Convention means that member countries are bound to comply with internationally agreed standards.

THE RESOLUTIONS

The resolutions will involve the participants as representatives of Member Countries, specialised agencies and regional bodies. Progress in the eradication of slavery has been slow, and has required detailed work. This has involved international conferences and organisations.

There should be two resolutions:

Reparations following the Abolition of the Transatlantic Slave Trade

This debate is retrospective and historic in content, but reflects strongly held current views.

Some African countries and African Diaspora groups may call for financial reparations to be paid, in recognition of the harm done to Africa through slavery and the Transatlantic Slave Trade.

Other countries may argue that it is more appropriate to assign top priority to the needs of Africa today, rather than arguing about allocation of blame for the past.

The UNESCO position has been to try to enhance international understanding of what took place. Having addressed the truth, there can be movement towards reconciliation, and engagement in joint activities as world citizens.

Different countries will present their perspectives. The international community may be able to move on, having learned from the differences, and acknowledged painful truths. The debate will determine whether there is to be reconciliation.

Eradication of Harmful Child Labour

This debate concerns current practice.

ILO Conventions have established that harmful child labour is not acceptable. This represents a tipping point in terms of attitudes. How can we proceed? There may be lessons learned from the two hundred years since abolition.

Child labour is closely linked to poverty, and may be seen as vital if family incomes are to be maintained. However, children at work are not at school, and so are missing the chance of education, and participation in the knowledge society.

THE WAY FORWARD

The two suggested debates both deal with practical issues of human rights, which have framed the development of the United Nations.

The best way of achieving reparations for the past is by jointly preparing for the future. Child labour is closely linked to poverty, and is a problem in many countries with legacies from the past of the Transatlantic Slave Trade. The linked debates could provide fresh momentum to address child labour, fuelled by experience of the problems of eradicating other forms of slavery.

Our children are the next generation of world citizens.

BIBLIOGRAPHY

Alexander, T. (1996) *Unravelling Global Apartheid.* Cambridge, Polity.

Amnesty International and The Prince of Wales Business Leaders Forum (2000) *Human rights: is it any of your business?* London, Amnesty International.

Annan, K. Secretary-General of the United Nations (2004) UNESCO.

Archer, L. (ed.) (1988) *Slavery and Other Forms of Unfree Labour.* London, Routledge.

Augsberger, D. (1981) *Caring Enough to Forgive.* Ventura, CA, Regal.

Avery, C.L. (2000) *Business and Human Rights in a time of change.* London, Amnesty International.

Bales, K. (1999) *Disposable People: New Slavery in the Global Economy.* Berkeley, University of California Press.

Banham, M. and Plastow, J. (eds) (1999) *Contemporary African Plays.* London, Methuen.

Beckles, H. McD. and Shepherd, V. (2002) *Slave Voyages: The Sounds of Freedom.* Paris, UNESCO.

Beloff, M. (1972) *Thomas Jefferson and American Democracy.* London, Penguin.

Black, D., Morris, J.N., Smith, C., Townsend, P. and Whitehead, M. (1992) *Inequalities in Health: The Black Report. Health Divide.* London, Penguin.

Black, M. and Blagbrough, J. (1999) *Child Domestic Work,* Innocenti Digest No. 5, UNICEF ICDC.

Blackburn, R. (1988) *The Overthrow of Colonial Slavery 1776–1848.* London, Verso.

Blackburn, R. (1988b). In L. Archer, (ed.), *Slavery and Other Forms of Unfree Labour.* London, Routledge.

Blackburn, R. (1997) *The Making of New World Slavery: from the Baroque to the Modern 1492–1800.* London, Verso.

Bobak, M. and Marmot, M. (1996) East-West mortality divide: Proposed research agenda. *British Medical Journal.* **312**, 421–5.

Bobak, M., Pikhart, H., Rose, R., Hertzman, C. and Marmot, M. (2000) Socioeconomic factors, material inequalities and perceived control in self-rated health: cross sectional data from seven post-communist countries. *Social Science and Medicine.* **51**, 1343–50.

Box, R.C. (1998) *Citizen Governance: leading American communities into the 21st century.* Thousand Oaks, CA, Sage.

Brandt, W. (1980) *North-South: a programme for survival.* London, Pan.

Brockway, F. (1973) *The Colonial Revolution.* London, Hart-Davis.

Brougham, H. (1803) *Inquiry into the Colonial Policy of the European Powers.* Edinburgh.

Bryant, C. (1996) *Possible Dreams: a personal history of the British Christian Socialists.* London, Hodder and Stoughton.

Bwibo, N.O. and Onyango, P. (1987) *Final report of the child labour and health research.* Nairobi, University of Nairobi.

Camacho, A.Z.V., Flores-Oebanda, C., Montano, V., Pacis, R.R. and Robidillo, R. (1997) The Phenomenon of Child Domestic Work: Issues, Responses and Research Findings. Unpublished paper presented by Visayan Forum Foundation at the ILO-IPEC supported Asian Regional Consultation on Child Domestic Workers, Manila, 19–23 November.

Clark, D. and Williamson, R. (eds) (1996) Self-determination: international perspectives. London, Macmillan.

Clarke, P.B. (1994) *Citizenship.* London, Pluto.

Clarke, R. (1985) *Science and Technology in World Development.* Oxford, Oxford University Press.

Clayre, A. (ed.) (1977) *Nature and Industrialization*. Oxford, Oxford University Press.

Clegg, S.R. and Palmer, G. (eds) (1996) *The Politics of Management Knowledge*. London, Sage.

Colley, L. (2002) *Captives: Britain, Empire and the World 1600–1850*. London, Jonathan Cape.

Coomarasamy, R. (1997) UN Economic and Social Council, Commission on Human Rights. "Report of the Special Rapporteur on violence against women, its causes and consequences, Ms Radhika Coomaraswamy", E/CN.4/1997/47, 12 February.

Cooper, C.L. (ed.) (2005) *Handbook of Stress Medicine and Health*. Boca Raton, CRC Press.

Cooper, C.L. (2006) The changing nature of work: workplace stress and strategies to deal with it. *Medicina del Lavoro* **97(2)**, 132–6.

Cooper, C.L. and Dewe, P. (2004) *Stress: a brief history*. Oxford, Blackwell.

Cornia, G.A. and Panicia, R. (eds) (2000) *The Mortality Crisis in Transitional Economies*. Oxford, Oxford University Press.

Costa, G. (2006) Flexibility of working hours in the 24-hour society. *Medicina del Lavoro* **97(3)**, 280–7.

Cugoano, O. (1787) *Thoughts and Sentiments on the Evil and Wicked Traffic of Slavery and the Commerce of the Human Species*. London.

Curto, J.C. and Lovejoy, P.E. (eds) (1999) *Enslaving Connections: changing cultures of Africa and Brazil during the era of slavery*. New York, Humanity Books.

Daniel, W.W. (1968) *Racial Discrimination in England*. London, Penguin.

Davidson, B. (1961) *Black Mother: a study of the precolonial connection between Africa and Europe*. London, Longman.

Davidson, B. (1965) *A Guide to African History*. New York, Zenith.

Davidson, B. (1974) *Africa in History*. London, Paladin.

De Blank, J. (1967) *Human Rights*. London, Heinemann.

Degler, C.N. (1971) *Neither Black nor White: slavery and race relations in Brazil and the United States*. Madison, University of Wisconsin Press.

Diamond, J. (1998) *Guns, Germs and Steel*. London, Vintage.

Dolan, B. (2004) *Josiah Wedgwood: Entrepreneur to the Enlightenment*. London, Harper Collins.

Dubois, L. (2004) *A Colony of Citizens: revolution and slave emancipation in the French Caribbean 1787–1804*. Chapel Hill, University of North Carolina Press.

Dummett, A. (1973) *A Portrait of English Racism*. London, Penguin.

Dunn, J. (1972) *Modern Revolutions*. Cambridge, Cambridge University Press.

Dunn, J. (2000) *The Cunning of Unreason*. London, Harper Collins.

Edwards, P. (ed.) (1988) *The Life of Oloudah Equiano, of Gustavus Vassa the African: written by himself*. London, Longmans.

Eltis, D. (2000) *The Rise of African Slavery in the Americas*. Cambridge, Cambridge University Press.

Ennals, R. (ed.) (1999) *Work Life 2000. Yearbook 1*. London, Springer Verlag.

Ennals, R. (ed.) (2000) *Work Life 2000. Yearbook 2*. London, Springer Verlag.

Ennals, R. (ed.) (2001) *Work Life 2000. Yearbook 3*. London, Springer Verlag.

Ennals, R. (2002) Partnership for Sustainable Workplaces. *The Annals of Occupational Hygiene* **46(6)**, 423–8.

Ennals, R. (ed.) (2005) Mobility, Technology and Development. *Special Issue of AI & Society,* **19(4)**, 331–333.

Ennals, R. and Gustavsen, B. (1999) *Work Organisation and Europe as a Development Coalition*. Amsterdam, John Benjamins.

European Commission (2002) DIRECTIVE 2002/14/EC OF THE EUROPEAN PARLIAMENT AND OF THE COUNCIL of 11 March 2002 establishing a general framework for informing and consulting employees in the European Community, Official Journal of the European Communities, 23/12/2002, L80/29–33.

Ferguson, N. (2003) *Empire*. London, Penguin.

Fick, C. (1990) *The Making of Haiti: the Saint Domingue Revolution from Below*. Knoxville, University of Tennessee Press.

Fingerhut, M., Nelson, D.I., Driscoll, T., Concha-Barrientos, M., Steenland, K., Punnett, L., Pruss-Ustun, A., Leigh, J., Corralan, C., Eijkemans, G. and Takala, J. (2006) The contribution of occupational risks to the global burden of disease: summary and next steps. *Medicina del Lavoro* **97(2)**, 313–21.

First, R. (1970) *The Barrel of a Gun*. London, Penguin.

Foot, P. (1965) *Immigration and Race in British Politics*. London, Penguin.

Foray, D. and Freeman, C. (eds) (1993) *Technology and the Wealth of Nations: the dynamics of constructed advantage*. London, Pinter.

Forstater, M., MacDonald, J. and Ranard, P. (2002) *Business and Poverty: bridging the gap*. London, Prince of Wales International Business Leaders Forum.

Foucault, M. (1970) *The Order of Things*. London, Tavistock.

Foucault, M. (1972) *The Archaeology of Knowledge*. London, Tavistock.

Foucault, M. (1977) *Discipline and Punish: the birth of the prison*. London, Allen Lane.

Foucault, M. (1989) *The Birth of the Clinic*. London, Routledge.

Foucault, M. (2001) *Madness and Civilisation*. London, Routledge.

Foucault, M. (2003) *Society must be Defended*. London, Allen Lane.

Frick, K., Jensen, P.L., Quinlan, M. and Wilthagen, T. (eds) (2000) *Systematic Occupational Health and Safety Management*. Amsterdam, Pergamon.

Fricke, W. and Totterdill, P. (2004) *Action Research in Workplace Innovation and Regional Development*. Amsterdam, John Benjamins.

Friedman, T.L. (2005) *The World is Flat*. New York, Farrar, Straus and Giroux.

Fryer, P. (1984) *Staying Power: the history of black people in Britain*. London, Pluto.

Fukuyama, F. (1995) *Trust: the social virtues and the creation of prosperity*. New York, Free Press.

Gaine, C. (1987) *No Problem here: A practical approach to education and race in white schools*. London, Hutchinson.

Gandhi, M. (1971) *Selected Writings of Mahatma Gandhi*. London, Fontana.

Gibbons, M., Limoges, C., Nowotny, H., Schwartzman, S., Scott, P. and Trow, M. (1994) *The New Production of Knowledge: the dynamics of science and research in contemporary societies*. London, Sage.

Gladwell, M. (2000) *The Tipping Point: how little things can make a big difference*. London, Abacus.

Gold, M. (ed.) (2003) *New Frontiers of Democratic Participation at Work*. London, Ashgate.

Goldsmith, O. (1764) *The Traveller or A Prospect of Society*.

Göranzon, B. (1992) The metaphor of Caliban in our technological culture. In B. Göranzon and M. Florin, (eds), *Skill and Education: Reflection and Experience*. London, Springer Verlag.

Göranzon, B. (ed.) (1995) *Skill, Technology and Enlightenment: on practical philosophy*. London, Springer Verlag.

Göranzon, B. and Florin, M. (eds) (1992) *Skill and Education: Reflection and Experience*. London, Springer Verlag.

Göranzon, B., Hammarén, M. and Ennals, R. (eds) (2005) *Dialogue, Skill and Tacit Knowledge*. Chichester, John Wiley & Sons, Ltd.

Gore, L.L. (2001) *Memories of the Old Plantation Home.* Vacharie LA, Zoe.

Grant, D., Keenoy, T. and Oswick, C. (eds) (1998) *Discourse & Organization.* London, Sage.

Grojier, J.-E. and Johansen, U. (1999) Managing and Accounting for Human Capital. Workshop in Brussels September 1998. In R. Ennals, (ed.), *Work Life 2000. Yearbook 1.* London, Springer Verlag.

Gustafsson, R.A. and Lundberg, I. (eds) (2004) *Worklife and Health in Sweden 2004.* National Institute for Working Life, Stockholm.

Gustavsen, B. (1992) *Dialogue and Development.* Maastricht, Van Gorcum.

Gustavsen, B., Ennals, R. and Nyhan, B. (eds.) (2007) *Learning together for local innovation: promoting learning regions.* Thessaloniki, Cedefop.

Habermas, J. (1971) *Towards a Rational Society.* London, Heinemann.

Habermas, J. (1990) *Moral Consciousness and Communicative Action.* Cambridge, Polity.

Hague, W. (2004) *William Pitt the Younger.* London, Harper Collins.

Haley, A. (1977) *Roots.* London, Hutchinson.

Hämäläinen, R.-M., Husman, K., Räsänen, K., Westerholm, P. and Rantanen, J. (2001) Survey of the Quality and Effectiveness of Occupational Health Services in the European Union and Norway and Switzerland. People and Work Research Reports 45, Finnish Institute for Occupational Health, Helsinki.

Hampson, N. (1968) *The Enlightenment.* London, Penguin.

Handy, C. (1989) *The Age of Unreason.* London, Business Books.

Handy, C. (1994) *The Empty Raincoat: Making sense of the future.* London, Hutchinson.

Handy, C. (1995) *Beyond Certainty: The changing worlds of organisations.* London, Hutchinson.

Handy, C. (1998) *The Hungry Spirit: Beyond capitalism, a quest for purpose in the modern world.* London, Arrow.

Handy, C. (2002) *The Elephant and the Flea: New thinking for a new world.* London, Arrow.

Harrison, P. (1979) *Inside the Third World.* London, Penguin.

Herman, A. (2005) *To Rule the Waves: How the British Navy Shaped the Modern World.* London, Hodder.

Hobsbawm, E. (1975) *The Age of Revolution.* London, Weidenfeld and Nicolson.

Hochschild, A. (1999) *Leopold's Ghost: A story of greed, terror and heroism in Colonial Africa*. London, Macmillan.

Hochschild, A. (2005) *Bury the Chains: the British struggle to abolish slavery*. London, Macmillan.

Hughes, L. (1971) *The Ways of White Folks*. New York, Vintage.

Hunt, T. (2004) *Building Jerusalem: The rise and fall of the Victorian City*. London, Weidenfeld and Nicolson.

Husband, C. (ed.) (1975) *White Media and Black Britain*. London, Arrow.

Hutton, W. (1995) *The State We're In*. London, Cape.

Hutton, W. (2002) *The World We're In*. London, Little, Brown.

Hutton, W. and Giddens, A. (eds) (2000) *On the Edge: living with global capitalism*. London, Cape.

Ilmarinen, J. and Lehtinen, S. (eds) (2004) Past, present and future of work ability. People and Work research report 65. Finnish Institute for Occupational Health, Helsinki.

Ilmarinen, J. (2006) Towards a longer and better working life: a challenge of work force ageing. *Medicina del Lavoro* **97(2)**, 143–7.

International Work Group for Indigenous Affairs (1997) *Enslaved Peoples in the 1990s*. Copenhagen, Anti Slavery International.

International Labour Organisation (1999) *Key Indicators of the Labour Market*. Geneva, ILO.

International Labour Organisation (2004) *Helping hands or shackled lives? Understanding child domestic labour and responses to it*. Geneva, ILO.

International Labour Organisation (2006) *The End of Child Labour: within reach*. Global Report under the Follow-up to the ILO Declaration on Fundamental Principles and Rights at Work 2000. Geneva.

Jakobsson, S. (1972) *Am I not a Man and a Brother? British missions and the abolition of the slave trade and slavery in West Africa and the West Indies 1786–1838*. Uppsala, Almqvist and Wiksells.

James, C.L.R. (1963) *The Black Jacobins: Toussaint L'Ouverture and the San Domingo Revolution*. New York, Vintage.

James, L. (1995) *The Rise and Fall of the British Empire*. London, Abacus.

James, L. Raj (1997) *The making and unmaking of British India*. London, Little, Brown.

Janik, A. (1992) Caliban's Revenge. In B. Göranzon and M. Florin, (eds), *Skill and Education: Reflection and Experience*. London, Springer Verlag.

Jasanoff, M. (2005) *Edge of Empire: Conquest and Collecting in the East 1750–1850*. London, 4th Estate.

Jefferson, T. (1944) *Life and Selected Writings*. New York, Random House.

Jeyeratnam, J. and Chia, K.S. (1994) *Occupational Health in National Development*. Singapore, World Scientific.

Jones, R. Merfyn (1981) *The North Wales Quarrymen 1874–1922* Cardiff, University of Wales Press.

Jordan, M. (2005) *The Great Abolition Sham: The true story of the end of the British Slave Trade*. Slough, Sutton.

Karasek, R. (2006) The stress-disequilibrium theory: chronic disease development, low social control, and physiological de-regulation. *Medicine da Lavoro* **97(2)**, 258–71.

Karasek, R. and Theorell, T. (1990) *Healthy Work: stress, productivity and the reconstruction of working life*. New York, Basic Books.

Kelly, P.K. (2002) Micro-Finance Interventions: tools to combat the worst forms of child labour, including trafficking. ILO-IPEC, Geneva.

King, R., Sandhu, S., Walvin, J. and Girdham, J. (eds) (1997) *Ignatius Sancho: An African Man of Letters*. London, National Portrait Gallery.

Klein, H.S. (1999) *The Atlantic Slave Trade*. Cambridge, Cambridge University Press.

Kopp, M.S. and Skrabski, Á. (1996) *Behavioural Sciences Applied to a Changing Society*. Budapest, Bibl Septem Artium Liberalium.

Kopp, M.S., Szedmák, S. and Skrabski, Á. (1998) Socioeconomic differences and psychosocial aspects of stress in a changing society. In P. Csermely, (ed.), *Stress of Life from Molecules to Man*. Ann. New York Acad. Sci., **85**, 538–43.

Kopp, M.S., Skrabski, Á., Lőke, J. and Szedmák, S. (1999) The Hungarian state of Mind in a Transforming society. In Zs. Spéder, (ed.), *Hungary in Flux, Society, Politics and Transformation*. Hamburg, Verlag Dr. Reinhold Kramer, 117–34.

Kopp, M.S. (interview) (2000) Stress: The invisible Hand in Eastern Europe's Death Rates. *Science*, **288**, 1732–3.

Kopp, M.S. (2000) Cultural transition. In E.G. Fink, (ed.), *Encyclopedia of Stress*, vol. 1. San Diego, Academic Press, 611–15.

Kopp, M.S., Skrabski, Á. and Szedmák, S. (2000) Psychosocial risk factors, inequality and self-rated morbidity in a changing society. *Social Sciences and Medicine*, **51**, 1350–61.

Kopp, M.S., Skrabski, Á. and Szedmák, S. (2001) The influence of societal structure on depressive symptomatology and morbidity in the Hungarian population. In W. Wosinska, R.B. Cialdini, J. Reykowski and D.W. Barrett, (eds), *The Practice of Social Influence in Multiple Cultures.* New York, Lawrence Erlbaum, 207–21.

Kopp, M.S., Skrabski, Á., Kawachi, I. and Adler, N.E. (2005) Low socioeconomic status of the opposite gender is a risk factor for middle aged mortality. *J. Epidemiology and Community Health*, **59**, 675–8.

Kopp, M.S. and Réthelyi, J. (2004) Where psychology meets physiology: chronic stress and premature mortality – the Central-Eastern European health paradox, *Brain Research Bulletin*, **62**, 351–67.

Layard, R. (2005) *Happiness: lessons from a new science.* London, Allen Lane.

Le Breton, B. (2003) *Trapped: Modern Day Slavery in the Brazilian Amazon.* Bloomfield, Kumarian.

Levi, L. (ed.) (1981) *Society, Stress and Disease. Vol 4. Working Life.* New York, Oxford University Press.

Levi, L. and Levi, I. (2000) *Guidance on Work-Related Stress: Spice of Life or Kiss of Death?* Luxembourg, European Commission DG Health and Consumer Protection.

Levi, L. (2002) The European Commission's Guidance on work-related stress: from words to action. *TUTB Newsletter*, No. 19-20, September, pp. 12–17.

Lindhult, E. (2005) *Management by Freedom.* Stockholm, Royal Institute of Technology.

Lugard, F.D. (1965) *The Dual Mandate in British Tropical Africa.* Hamden, CT, Archon Books.

Lukes, S. (2004) *Power: A Radical View*, 2nd edn. London, Palgrave Macmillan.

Mackenbach, J.P., Kunst, A.E., Groenhof, F., Borgan, J.K., Costa, G., Faggiano, F., Józan, P., Leinsalu, M., Martikainen, P., Rychtarikova, J. and Valkonen, T. (1999) Socioeconomic inequalities in Mortality among Women and among Men: an International study. *Am. J. Public Health*, **89(12)**, 1800–6.

Mair, L. (1974) *African Societies.* Cambridge, Cambridge University Press.

Manning, P. (1990) *Slavery and African Life.* Cambridge, Cambridge University Press.

Marmot, M. (2004) *Status Syndrome.* London, Bloomsbury.

Marmot, M. and Wilkinson, R. (1999) *Social Determinants of Health.* Oxford, Oxford University Press.

Martin, S.O. (1999) *Britain's Slave Trade.* London, Macmillan.

Masuda, Y. (ed.) (1992) *Human-Centred Systems in the Global Economy.* London, Springer Verlag.

Mathias, P. (1964) *The First Industrial Nation.* London, Methuen.

Mazrui, A.A. (1986) *The Africans: A Triple Heritage.* London, BBC.

Mbeki, T. (2004) President of the Republic of South Africa, 1 January.

Meillassoux, C. (1991) *The Anthropology of Slavery: the womb of iron and gold.* London, Athlone.

Middleton, D. and Totterdill, P. (1992) Competitiveness, Working Life and Public Intervention: Teamworking in the Clothing Industry. In A. Kasvio, (ed.), *Industry without Blue Collar Workers*, Tampere: Work Research Centre, Tampere.

Miers, S. (1975) *Britain and the ending of the slave trade.* London, Longman.

Miers, S. (2003) *Slavery in the Twentieth Century: the evolution of a global problem.* Walnut Creek, Altamira.

Mooney, C. (2005) *The Republican War on Science.* New York, Basic Books.

Nohria, N. and Eccles, R.G. (eds) (1992) *Networks and Organisations: structure, form and action.* Cambridge, Harvard Business School Press.

Nowotny, H., Scott, P. and Gibbons, M. (2001) *Re-Thinking Science: knowledge and the public in an age of uncertainty.* Cambridge, Polity.

Oldfield, J.R. (1998) *Popular Politics and British Anti-Slavery: The Mobilisation of Public Opinion against the Slave Trade 1787–1807.* London, Frank Cass.

Oliver, R. and Fage, J.D. (1962) *A Short History of Africa.* London, Penguin.

Olivier, L. (1929) *White Capital and Coloured Labour.* London, Hogarth Press.

Omolewa, M. (2004) Permanent Delegate of Nigeria to UNESCO. UNESCO.

Paine, T. (1969) *Rights of Man.* London, Penguin.

Pålshausen, Ö. (2004) How to do things with words: Towards a linguistic turn in action research. *Concepts and Transformation* **9(2)**, 181–204.

Paoli, P. and Merllié, D. (2000) *Third European Survey on Working Conditions*. Dublin, European Foundation for the Improvement of Living and Working Conditions.

Patten, C. (2005) *Not Quite the Diplomat*. London, Allen Lane.

Pilger, J. (2006) *Freedom Next Time*. London, Bantam.

Pocock, N.D. (2000) "Slavery series" documents, vol. 2 *The Effects of European Slavery on Africa*. London, Vision Training and Research.

Pocock, N.D. (2001) "Slavery series" documents, vol. 5 *The Liverpool Boom. People and Places Connected with Slavery in Liverpool and Lancaster*. London, Vision Training and Research.

Pocock, N.D. (2003) "Slavery series" documents, vol. 4 *Where the Money Went. People and Places Connected with Slavery in Bath and Bristol*. London, Vision Training and Research.

Porter, R. (2000) *Enlightenment: Britain and the creation of the modern world*. London, Penguin.

Putnam, R. (1993) *Making democracy work: civic traditions in modern Italy*. Princeton, Princeton University Press.

Putnam, R. (2000) *Bowling alone: the collapse and revival of American community*. New York, Simon and Schuster.

Rahman, H. (1995) *Child domestic workers: Is servitude the only option?* Dhaka, Shoishab Bangladesh.

Rantanen, J., Kauppinen, T., Toikkanen, J., Kurppa, K., Lehtinen, S. and Leino, T. (2001) Work and Health Country Profiles: country profiles and national surveillance indicators in occupational health and safety. People and Work Research Reports 44, Finnish Institute for Occupational Health, Helsinki.

Regional Working Group on Child Labour. (2001) *Child Labour: getting the message across*. Bangkok, Keen.

Reich, R. (1992) *The Work of Nations*. London, Vintage.

Rodney, W. (1982) *How Europe underdeveloped Africa*. Washington, Howard University Press.

Rossi, A.M. (2004) Estresse Masculino – Um guia para identificar o estresse nos homens. Artes e Ofícios Ed. Ltda. (4ª ed.), Porto Alegre, Brazil.

Rossi, A.M. (2005) Estressores ocupacionais e diferenças de gênero. In A.M. Rossi, P.L. Perrewé and S.L. Sauter, (eds), *Stress e Qualidade de Vida no Trabalho – perspectivas atuais da saúde ocupacional* (pp. 9–18). São Paulo, Brazil, Editora Atlas, S.A.

Sachs, J. (2005) *The End of Poverty*. New York, Penguin.

Said, E. (1993) *Culture and Imperialism*. London, Chatto and Windus.

Salazar, M.C. (1998) Child Work and Education in Latin America. In M.C. Salazar and W.A. Glasinovich, (eds) *Child Work and Education: Five Case Studies from Latin America*. Aldershot, Ashgate Publishing Ltd and UNICEF ICDC.

Sapolsky, R.M., Romero, L.M. and Munck, A.U. (2000) How do glucocorticoids influence stress responses? Integrating permissive, suppressive, stimulatory and preparative actions. *Endocrine Reviews*, **21**, 55–89.

Sartorius, N. (2002) *Fighting for Mental Health*. Cambridge, Cambridge University Press.

Schama, S. (2005) *Rough Crossings: Britain, the slaves and the American Revolution*. London, BBC.

Schnall, P. (2006) Work and cardiovascular disease. *Medicine del Lavoro*, **97(2)**, 278–9.

Selye, H. (1956) *The Stress of Life*. New York, McGraw Hill.

Sen, A. (1975) *Employment, Technology and Development*. Oxford, Oxford University Press.

Sen, A. (1997) *On Economic Inequality*. Oxford, Clarendon Press.

Sen, A. (1999) *Development as Freedom*. Oxford, Oxford University Press.

Sherrard, O.A. (1959) *Freedom from Fear: the slave and his emancipation*. London, Bodley Head.

Shyllon, F.O. (1974) *Black Slaves in Britain*. Oxford, Institute for Race Relations and Oxford University Press.

Skiöld, L. (ed.) (2000) *A Look into Modern Working Life*. Stockholm, National Institute for Working Life.

Skrabski, Á., Kopp, M.S. and Kawachi, I. (2003) Social capital in a changing society: cross sectional associations with middle aged female and male mortality. *J. Epidemiology and Community Health*, **57**, 114–19.

Skrabski, Á., Kopp, M.S. and Kawachi, I. (2004) Social capital and collective efficacy in Hungary: cross-sectional associations with middle-aged female and male mortality rates. *J. Epidemiology and Community Health*, **58**, 340–5.

Skrabski Á., Kopp, M.S., Rózsa, S., Réthelyi, J. and Rahe, R. (2005) Life meaning: an important correlate of health in the Hungarian population, *Int, J. Behavioral Medicine*, **12(2)**, 78–85.

Smith, D.J. (1977) *Racial Disadvantage in Britain*. London, Penguin.

Somavia, J. (2003) *Working out of Poverty*. Geneva, ILO.

Somavia, J. (2003) *Time for Equality at Work*. Geneva, ILO.

Soros, G. (2004) *The Bubble of American Supremacy*. London, Weidenfeld and Nicolson.

Southam, B. (2005) *Jane Austen and the Navy*. London, National Maritime Museum.

Stiglitz, J. (2001) *Lecture at Global Employment Forum*. Geneva, International Labour Organisation, October.

Stiglitz, J. (2002) *Globalisation and its discontents*. London, Cape.

Stiglitz, J. (2003) *The Roaring Nineties*. New York, W.W. Norton.

Stuckey, S. (1987) *Culture: Nationalist Theory and the Foundations of Black America*. Oxford, Oxford University Press, pp. 224.

Sutton, A. (1994) *Slavery in Brazil: a link in the chain of modernisation*. London, Anti Slavery International.

Taylor, F.W. (1911) *The Principles of Scientific Management*. New York, Harper (1947 edition).

Thomas, H. (1997) *The Slave Trade: the story of the Atlantic Slave Trade 1440–1870*. New York, Simon and Schuster.

Thompson, P. (1978) *The Voice of the Past: oral history*. Oxford, Oxford University Press.

Thornton, J. (1998) *Africa and Africans in the Making of the Atlantic World 1400–1800*. 2nd edn. Cambridge, Cambridge University Press.

Totterdill, P. and Hague, J. (2004) "Workplace innovation as regional development" in W. Fricke and P. Totterdill, *Action Research in Workplace Innovation and Regional Development*. Amsterdam, John Benjamins.

Toulmin, S. (1995) Imaginary Confessions. In B. Göranzon, (ed.), *Skill, Technology and Enlightenment: On Practical Philosophy*. London, Springer Verlag, pp. 37–56.

Toulmin, S. (2001) *Return to Reason*. Cambridge, Mass., Harvard University Press.

Townsend, P. and Davidson, N. (1980) *Inequalities in Health: the Black Report*. London, Penguin.

Trouillot, M.-R. (1995) *Silencing the Past: power and the production of history*. Boston, Beacon.

Tyson, G. Jr. (ed.) (1973) *Toussaint L'Ouverture*, New York, Prentice Hall, pp. 27–45.

Uglow, J. (1993) *Elizabeth Gaskell*. London, Faber.

Uglow, J. (2002) *The Lunar Men: the friends who made the future*. London, Faber.

USA State Department (2005) *Trafficking in Persons Report*. Washington DC.

Verteuil, A. de. (1992) *Seven Slaves and Slavery: Trinidad 1777–1838*. Port of Spain, NP, pp. 266–9.

Von Wright, G.H. (1974) *Explanation and Understanding*. London, Routledge.

Wallace, E.K. (2006) *The British Slave Trade and Public Memory*. New York, Columbia University Press.

Walters, D. (2001) *Health and Safety in Small Enterprises: European strategies for managing improvement*. Brussels, P.I.E.–Peter Lang.

Walters, D. (ed.) (2002) *Regulating Health and Safety Management in the European Union: a study of the dynamics of change*. Brussels, P.I.E.–Peter Lang.

Walvin, J. (1992) *Black Ivory: A History of British Slavery*. London, Harper Collins.

Washington, Booker T. (1895) The Atlanta Exposition Address, 18 September.

Wiencek, H. (2004) *An Imperfect God: George Washington, His Slaves and the Creation of America*. London, Macmillan.

Wilkinson, R. (1996) *Unhealthy Societies: the afflictions of inequality*. London, Routledge.

Williams, E. (1944) *Capitalism and Slavery*. London, Andre Deutsch.

Williams, G.A. (1991) *When was Wales?* London, Penguin.

Wilson, E.G. (1989) *Thomas Clarkson: A Biography*. London, Macmillan.

Wittgenstein, L. (1954) *Philosophical Investigations*. Oxford, Blackwell.

Wolsk, D. (ed.) (1975) *An Experience-Centred Curriculum*. Copenhagen, UNESCO.

Woodhead, M. (2004) Psychosocial impacts of child work: a framework for research, monitoring and intervention, for Understanding Children's Work. World Bank, ILO, UNICEF, New York.

World Health Organisation (1999) Health for all (HFA) Data Base. WHO Regional Office for Europe. Copenhagen.

World Health Organisation (2001) World Health Report 2001. WHO, Geneva.

INDEX